BRING ME LAUGHTER

BRING ME LAUGHTER

Four decades of TV comedy

**BRUCE CROWTHER
AND
MIKE PINFOLD**

COLUMBUS BOOKS
LONDON

Copyright © 1987 Bruce Crowther and Mike Pinfold

First published in Great Britain in 1987 by
Columbus Books Limited
19-23 Ludgate Hill, London EC4M 7PD

Designed by Rupert Kirby

British Library Cataloguing in Publication Data
Crowther, Bruce
    Bring me laughter: four decades of TV comedy.
    1. Comedy programmes —— History
    2. Television programmes —— History
    I. Title   II. Pinfold, Mike
    791.45'5 PN1992.8.C66

    ISBN 0-86287-318-5

Typeset by Facet Film Composing Limited, Leigh-on-Sea, Essex
Printed and bound by R. J. Acford, Chichester, Sussex.

CONTENTS

INTRODUCTION 7

1 The 'fifties surveyed 9

2 Gee, Sarge, it's Lucy 21

3 The 'sixties surveyed 35

4 Whatever became of the stand-up comic? 49

5 Just an average family 59

6 The 'seventies surveyed 71

7 Women and the sexual revolution 85

8 War is hell…on the ratings 108

9 Alternative to what? 123

10 Black, beautiful, and now box-office 134

11 Us and them 143

12 Class 153

13 The 'eighties surveyed 164

APPENDIX 179

BIBLIOGRAPHY 181

ACKNOWLEDGEMENTS 183

INDEX 185

INTRODUCTION

Whatever became of television comedy?

This question has been asked at regular intervals over recent years. Sometimes it may be a querulous reaction to change or a nostalgic view that the past was always better than the present.

However, looking objectively at comedy on television it is easy to understand the worries of those who pose such questions.

Where, among today's shows, is comedy of the quality of *Porridge, The Likely Lads, Rising Damp* or *Dad's Army*?

Where is the modern equivalent of Tony Hancock or Morecambe and Wise? Where are shows like *Steptoe and Son, Till Death Us Do Part* and *The Good Life*? When can we expect to see a new *That Was the Week That Was, Monty Python's Flying Circus* or *Fawlty Towers*?

And there is no need to stop with British shows. Where are the modern American equivalents of *Sergeant Bilko, All in the Family, The Dick Van Dyke Show, The Mary Tyler Moore Show* or *M*A*S*H*? Who do we have today taking the place of Burns and Allen, Jack Benny and Lucille Ball?

Of course there are good American shows today: *The Golden Girls, Cheers* and *The Cosby Show*, for example. But they are few, representing tiny oases of laughter and professionalism in a desert of gloom, rank amateurism and shows about, for and, to judge from their childishness, possibly written by children.

As for British TV, what is there to laugh about as endless 'new' shows are paraded across our screens at peak viewing hours? Most of them seem to be about kids leaving home, or kids returning home, or are about parents arguing between themselves about their kids. Is there no original thought? How many more permutations can be wrung out of middle-aged, middle-class moping women dreaming of romance?

But when opportunities arise to allow new and supposedly original comedians on to television, what happens? On comes a parade of aggressively manic individuals whose technique and sense of humour bear all the hallmarks of a cornered rat. Unappetizing young men use the language of Lenny Bruce without for one moment pausing to consider what lay behind his humour and what made it work.

Given the choice between unpleasant aggression and stupefying blandness is it any wonder that for most viewers in Britain the best comedy is found in re-runs of old favourites, many of them American?

But is TV comedy important enough to worry over?

It must be, because in any average week in Britain more than 30 hours are allocated to comedy. Audience figures for an episode of a run-of-the-mill show on British TV can often exceed 12 million viewers. But these figures are overwhelmed by American statistics. In the New York area alone an average week offers on all available channels a staggering 500 comedy shows.

In this book the story of forty years of TV comedy is told, recalling old shows and stars, favourite episodes and scenes. There is no attempt within it to discover the secret of why people laugh, but by looking at what people have laughed at in the past, and laugh at still, some measure can be gained of the importance of comedy on TV and, perhaps, why today we depend so much on yesterday's shows.

Ever since television's earliest days situation comedy has been the main outlet for humour, except perhaps in the 1950s. Today, something like 95 per cent of TV comedy comes in the form of the sitcom, which therefore features heavily in these pages; however, stand-up comics, sketch- and revue-type formats are also considered along the way.

Not simply a chronological survey, *Bring Me Laughter* examines comedy shows mainly in terms of category – some in detail, others only briefly. Inevitably, many shows and artists are omitted entirely, simply for reasons of space, and it has to admitted that the final selection reflects nothing more significant than the authors' personal taste.

CHAPTER ONE

THE 'FIFTIES SURVEYED

'Vaudeville is dead – and television is the box they buried it in.'
Fred Allen

It should surprise no one that the 1950s were cautious days for TV comedy. Indeed, they were not very sure or certain days for television programmes of any kind. Television sets were none too reliable either. They were curious things: tiny, almost round, 10- or 12-inch screens were mounted in elaborate glossy cabinets with bakelite knobs and buttons, some of which had functions no one fully understood. Then there were those giant pieces of furniture designed to look like something else – *anything* else – with folding or shuttered doors behind which lurked the television receiver, the One-Eyed Monster, the Goggle-box, the Telly, the End of Conversation As We Know It.

In Britain for most of the 1950s ownership of a set was almost a mark of status – almost but not quite, because there was a curious shift along the line. If you were poor you didn't have one because the damn things cost more than a month's wages; if you were very rich or intellectually superior it was beneath your dignity to own one or at least to *admit* to ownership. In a contemporary newspaper interview one titled lady conceded that she occasionally saw television but only because her maid had a set.

Set owners in those days had no problems over what programmes to watch. Choice was easy: the BBC's single channel or nothing. Viewing was restricted to a few hours in the mid-evening and, just so viewers didn't get eyestrain, the longer programmes had a convenient interval to allow for conversation, tea-making and a quick trip to the loo (which was also called something else at that time). Due partly to the novelty of the medium and partly to the limited hours it was available, viewers tended to watch everything. Adults were as familiar with Muffin the Mule and Bill and Ben the Flowerpot Men as their children were; at the other end of the evening, in countless homes, the National Anthem echoed until the white dot faded from reluctantly darkened screens. There may be less excuse for them today, but the indiscriminate viewing habits originated in those days linger on.

Oh yes, and it was all in black and white, too.

By the end of the decade everything had changed. Screens were bigger, a better shape, cabinet design was less self-conscious, viewing hours were longer and, most significant of all in terms of the spread of viewing habits, there was now a commercial channel. Whole generations of children grew up singing advertising jingles before they could hold an intelligent conversation. Many of those early commercials are still remembered while the programmes they interrupted have long since faded from memory: 'You'll wonder where the yellow went when you brush your teeth with Pepsodent.' One ad failed miserably to sell the product but everyone remembers the slogan 'You're never alone with a Strand.'

As for the feared loss of conversation –

there was still plenty of it around even if then, as now, most early-morning encounters began with a review of last night's telly: 'Did you see…?'

If the advent of television was surrounded by learned discussions on its educational and artistic possibilities, the arrival of the commercial channel was accompanied by gloomy forecasts that it meant the end of any hopes of TV becoming an Art Form. For neither the first nor last time, the intellectual approach missed the point. Television, like the movies before it, was first and foremost a medium for entertainment.

The commercial stations occupying the new alternative channel had no illusions. Aware that their survival depended upon high viewing figures they homed in on those programmes which offered entertainment for the masses. ATV's *Sunday Night at the London Palladium* emptied the pubs and after veteran comic Tommy Trinder, the show's first compère, had bowed out, his successors, Bruce Forsyth, Don Errol, Dickie Henderson, Robert Morley, Jim Dale, Jimmy Tarbuck and Norman Vaughan, were hoisted to national prominence.

Competition between the channels gave an enormous boost to light entertainment. The BBC already had variety shows which gave opportunities to comedians old and new. ITV quickly matched them.

A veteran from the variety stage and radio, Arthur Askey already enjoyed considerable success in the theatre. He had adapted to radio much better than most and his career now entered a third and equally successful phase with such shows as *Before Your Very Eyes*. Askey refused to be intimidated by the restrictions of the medium. He would happily walk off camera, inviting the cameraman to follow him to reveal the end of the set and the bare studio beyond.

Although Norman Wisdom had enjoyed some success on the boards, he had none of the professional status of Askey even if he matched the older man's lack of inches. Thanks to television Wisdom zoomed to national fame and his gormless, gump-suited character became a firm favourite, soon to progress to film stardom.

Richard Hearne (Mr Pastry) also enjoyed an enormous boost from television and such slapstick routines as 'The Lancers', in which he cavorted through a ballroom filled with imaginary sober-suited dancers, were hugely popular.

Fred Emney lumbered on to screens too small for his barrage-balloon bulk, exuding cynicism on- and off-stage. Asked why he wrote his own material for such shows as *Emney Enterprises*, he observed: 'If I've got to memorize crap, it might as well be my own crap.'

Norman Evans, with *Over the Garden Wall*, and Jimmy Clitheroe's Kid had ready-made acts which were just as effective on TV as they had been on radio and on the halls.

The setting for most of these comics was the variety show, such as the BBC's *Music Hall*, a kind of televised stage show with acrobats and singers, jugglers and magicians but usually with the addition of a compère. Although initially of a good overall standard, such shows eventually became vehicles for promoting the limited talents of a host whose guests became simply appendages to his ego as they eagerly plugged their latest record or film or their own TV show. These shows reflected the programme-makers' striking inability to separate good from bad, the funny from the merely good-natured. Worse, all too quickly blandness set in.

Nevertheless, even allowing for the fact that nostalgia is the art of consigning all the rubbish to memory's graveyard while permitting the rest to live on uncritically, there was much to be proud of. Particularly impressive in those years was drama, then of course live in both Britain and America. In Britain *Armchair Theatre* and *Sunday Night Theatre* found new talents among writers, directors and actors: Alun Owen, Philip Mackie, Philip Saville, Billie Whitelaw, Ian Hendry, Tony Britton. In America *Playhouse 90, Studio One* and other drama slots had Rod Serling, Paddy Chayefsky, John Frankenheimer, Charlton Heston, Jack Palance and Robert Redford.

If the 1950s were golden years for drama then similarly golden, thanks to nostalgia's accommodating effect, was American TV comedy of the decade. In fact, it wasn't quite as good as it might now seem, but after 30 years the same could be said about most of life's early pleasures. British TV comedy of the period has stood up less well in the memory, mainly because it was followed in the 1960s by an extraordinary wealth of comedy shows, many of them outstanding. But for all its shortcomings, 1950s TV comedy in Britain boasts several shows and stars that are still remembered with affection.

Both Britain and America drew much of their early inspiration for comedy from radio. As radio had drawn and was still drawing its talent from the music halls, variety and vaudeville, not much was new. But the TV camera was quick to decide which performers it would let live and which would die before its intimately probing lens, and talent was not necessarily the sole criterion for its decisions.

An enormous number of the great visual clowns from the theatre and cinema and many of the verbal comics from radio failed to make a successful transition to TV, if they made it at all. Some visual comics from the halls and especially pantomime failed to grasp the need for intimacy; some verbal comedians worked to the microphone, not the camera. Therefore, however successful they were in their own milieu, the art of people like Clarkson Rose and Al Read did not meet the demands of the new medium.

Britain in the 1950s was still struggling with the vestiges of wartime shortages. Austerity was the order of the day and the generation that had gone to war was bitterly discovering that the hard times of the pre-war years were far from over. Officialdom was, as ever, confusing its task with officiousness and overall there was not very much to smile at, let alone laugh about. Indeed, it was easier to be angry than happy. In literature and on the legitimate stage Joe Lampton, Lucky Jim and Jimmy Porter looked about them in anger.

Into this unpromising arena wandered Tony Hancock, a sad-faced clown with a devastating line in ultimately ineffectual attempts to prick pomposity in others while invariably failing to note such failings in himself. Aided and abetted by the talents of two scriptwriters who fitted him better than his own skin, Hancock faced the world with a kind of fearful aggression and became the comic giant of the 1950s.

First on radio, later on TV, Anthony Aloysius Hancock dolefully viewed life from the vantage point of his seedy dwelling at 23 Railway Cuttings, East Cheam, and delivered the verdict of writers Ray Galton and Alan Simpson. One way or another, he didn't think much of what he saw. When Hancock sighed lugubriously before declaring, 'Stone me, what a life!' audiences numbered in millions broke up in delighted laughter. They felt the same way.

It is difficult to demonstrate verbal and visual humour in written words. Even a Hancock script is not necessarily filled to overflowing with gags. What emerged in the radio and TV broadcasts of 'the Lad Himself' was an almost miraculous blending of writing, performance and audience identification. When Tony Hancock began a radio show entitled 'A Sunday Afternoon at Home' with two lines of essentially meaningless dialogue filled with several sighs and 'dear me's and made this tiny scrap of script last over a minute, he mirrored the frustration so familiar to most of his listeners.

Hancock: Ahh, oh dear. Mmm, oh dear, oh dear. Ahh, dear me. Ahhh. Stone me, what a life! What's the time?
Bill Kerr: Two o'clock.
Hancock: Is that all? Ahh, dear, oh dear. Ah, dear me. I dunno. Ah. Ohhh. Oh, I'm fed up!

Blessed with a face which seemed never to have set properly after being lifted from its mould and which perfectly reflected his mournful radio persona, Hancock had no problems in transferring to television. Galton and Simpson similarly took to the new medium with enormous skill and deceptive ease.

It is not entirely accurate to label the BBC's *Hancock's Half Hour* a situation comedy as it relied far more heavily upon the comic persona of the star than, say, *Steptoe and Son*, which Galton and Simpson wrote in the following decade. True, *Hancock's Half Hour* was a comedy and it did have situations, but unlike most later TV sitcoms, which were written with no specific actor in mind and almost never cast with a comic, *Hancock's Half Hour* was a vehicle for a comedian. Even more important, it was designed for one comic in particular and so completely caught his personality that Tony Hancock would never

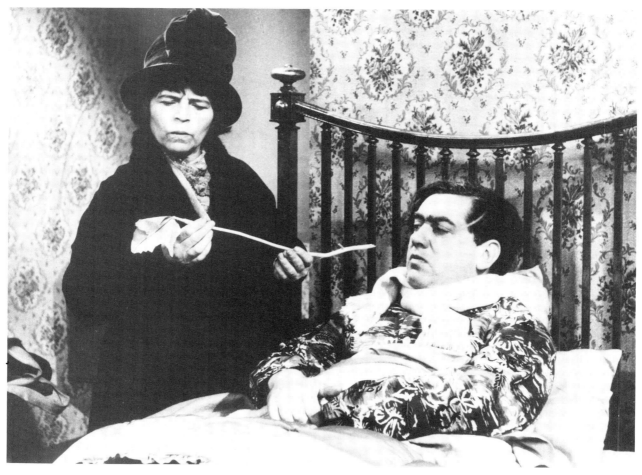

The Lad Himself receives little comfort from Mrs Cravat (Tony Hancock, Patricia Hayes).

afterwards fully emerge from the shadow of the rôle.

Beginning on TV in 1956 Tony Hancock had five glorious years — and after that some pretty good ones. The show was eventually shortened to 25 minutes (and correspondingly retitled *Hancock*) in an abortive attempt to infiltrate the American market, which needed space for commercials.

Whether trying desperately to emigrate, to give blood or to discover what happened on the last page of a vandalized library book, Hancock managed to stay closer to Everyman than most other British comics either before or afterwards. As so many would like to have done, Hancock took on bureaucracy. The fact that he failed to change anything endeared him to his audience, who had no more success in real life than he did. In his study of several famous British comedians, Eric Midwinter interestingly likens Hancock to Don Quixote.

Like the noble Don, Tony tilted hopelessly but defiantly at the windmills of a world he knew to be cock-eyed, even if it was often all too unalterably real.

In 1950s Britain Tony Hancock became the most loved comedian of his day, but it was a different kind of love to that which surrounded Laurel and Hardy and which would envelop Morecambe and Wise a few years later. Hancock was lovable, but he did not attract the same kind of warmth. He was always a bit too pompous, a bit too arrogant, a bit too argumentative, a bit too much the common man ... a bit too much like all of us, in fact.

Like us, Hancock also recognized the importance of television and, unusually for the time, comments upon it in a show in which his set breaks down.

One whole night with no telly. This could break the strongest man. What am I going to do? I'll go mad, I know I will.

'Very nearly an armful.' Tony Hancock prepares to give blood while Frank Thornton waits his turn.

In Galton and Simpson, Hancock had the perfect writers; in Sid James he had an impeccable comic foil. Whenever Hancock rose to the bait of society's injustices, Sid was always there to puncture the romantic nonsense — but not before he had made a few bob out of the latest unlikely situation.

In 'Twelve Angry Men', while Hancock scolds his fellow jurors — 'Does Magna Carta mean nothing to you? Did she die in vain?' — Sid is figuring out ways to keep the trial going so they can continue to draw expenses. Planning, in 'The Emigrant', to depart Albion's shores forever, Tony declares, 'There have been Hancocks in this country since 1066. We came over on the *Mayflower*,' but then finds himself led by Sid on to a seedy tramp steamer bound for God-knows-where.

In 1960 Hancock went on without Sid and often with considerable success. In the 'Blood Donor' sketch he exclaims: 'A pint? A pint?

That's very nearly an armful.' In 'The Radio Ham' his success on contacting a mariner in distress is countered by his inability to find a pencil to write down the man's bearings, to say nothing of interfering neighbours and a fellow 'ham' from Tokyo whose transmissions are limited entirely to local weather reports.

In 'The Lift' he infuriates his fellow passengers when they are trapped between floors by pontificating on the diminishing supply of oxygen and the increase in the world's population.

I mean, the rate we're multiplying, we're going to use it all up. There'll be a thousand million Chinamen by 1980 and they've all got noses, you know. I reckon in a couple of hundred years' time you won't be able to move. We'll all be standing shoulder to shoulder all over the world, heads up fighting for breath. The tallest bloke with the biggest hooter survives. That's the way it's going to be. Natural selection. We'll be a race of giants with big hooters.

Hancock marshals an army of cold cures but Sid James is typically sceptical.

'The Bedsitter' was an entirely solo effort, during which he struggles vainly to understand the first line of Bertrand Russell's latest book. He had referred to the great philosopher in an earlier show with Sid James.

Sid: Bertrand Russell, didn't he write *Kiss the Blood Off My Hands*?
Tony: Of course he didn't. You're thinking of Aldous Huxley.

For the most part the shows without Sid James maintained the previous high standard. Perhaps there was something missing but the risk Hancock took in deliberately shedding Sid almost came off. His later decision, to discard Galton and Simpson, was a disastrous error of judgement that signalled the disintegration of his world.

Although the seriousness of the decline which began as the 1960s opened was not at first evident, Hancock had run his course. Like the rest of the world, Britain was changing. The 1950s in Britain were a peculiar time. Still emerging from the shadows of war and deprivation, unable to believe that the nation's former glory and global importance were a thing of the past, the public responded to the deluded grandeur of Tony Hancock with affection and understanding. He was, for a few marvellous years, a kind of *vox populi* — when he wasn't playing the fool and pricking the pomposity of those who would still be kings. In the inappropriately named 'Swinging 'Sixties' the public wanted a different kind of comic, to reflect prevailing attitudes.

Perhaps Hancock sensed the change in the times and his actions in separating himself from his friends and colleagues were part of an instinctive struggle for survival. In the event, the result of these changes was catastrophic. When he committed suicide in Australia in 1968 his career had been going downhill for as many years as it had been at its peak, yet his death brought an enormous sense of loss.

Among the comedies which dotted British TV screens in the 1950s were several which have faded from all but the reference books. *After Hours* starred Michael Bentine in the kind of show which he would later do so much better as *It's a Square World*, in which he was supported by Dick Emery. Bentine had left radio's Goons before they really took off and pursued his own line of inventive and slowly developed visual comedy. This included routines featuring a flea circus and a Chinese junk attack on the Houses of Parliament.

Alfred Marks Time featured Marks and his wife, Paddy O'Neill, and the somewhat dubious talents of former-Regimental Sergeant Major Brittain. *Idiot Weekly, Price 2d* was written by Spike Milligan and starred Peter Sellers and Kenneth Connor. This somewhat anarchic comedy emitted small warning signals of the more outrageous form Milligan's comedy would take and which in time was picked up and developed by the *Monty Python* team.

Of the four original Goons Spike Milligan's career has been the least conspicuously successful. The majority of that radio show's innovative scripts were written by him alone, the rest in collaboration. Curiously, those solo efforts suffered from the untidiness which permeates much of his later TV work, perhaps because there is something in his personality which leads him to start things, then to lose interest once the innovatory becomes familiar. Nevertheless, it was thanks to Milligan's writing that some of his friends became stars. At the outset Peter Sellers was a good impressionist, Harry Secombe an adequate stand-up comic, but once given characters to perform in Milligan's wildly improbable radio sagas, Sellers and Secombe expanded to superstar status. Milligan never seems to have sought fame of this kind and very probably was too rebellious to conform to the demands of being a showbiz establishment figure. Nevertheless, he continues to work extensively in TV comedy shows, mostly of his own creation. As indicated, Bentine, perhaps the most original mind in the group, left early.

Until their personalities and styles clashed Milligan co-wrote some of *The Goon Shows* with Eric Sykes. Like Milligan, Sykes was also a performer and wrote and starred in several highly successful TV sitcoms. In such shows as *Sykes and a ...* he was ably supported by Hattie Jacques (who had worked in Tony Hancock's radio shows), Richard Wattis and Deryck Guyler. At his best Eric Sykes filled a part of the gap left by Hancock. Like the lad from East Cheam, Sykes faces up to authority with similarly cautious aggression, even if he is often sublimely unaware of the realities of life outside his cosy suburban semi. It was an effective persona which reflected one of Sykes's views of his work: 'I never write jokes. I write attitudes.'

There are some 1950s shows which live on more in a kind of mistily recalled folklore than in real memory. ATV's *The Larkins* was a vehicle for the contrasting talents of David Kossoff and Peggy Mount. The interplay between Kossoff, indignantly ineffectual, and Mount, the overbearing mistress of the crushing put-down, was highly effective but strongly reminiscent of the comic traditions of past times.

The links between earlier forms of show business and TV remain today but were very strong 30 years ago. This has led some observers, including Sir Denis Forman, Chairman of Granada Television, to suggest that situation comedy is little more than a music-hall sketch stretched out to twice or three times its optimum length. Rarely was this true, and when it was the strain of the extension quickly forced out those performers who could not make the adjustment to the new, more confidential medium.

Contemporary with *The Larkins*, created for television by Fred Robinson, were many shows which were relatively direct transfers of artists, characters and formats from successful radio shows. These included north countryman Dave Morris's *Club Night* and *Life with the Lyons*, which starred Bebe Daniels and Ben Lyon. The Lyons were American movie stars who had gained a devoted and grateful following through staying in London during the war.

Some TV shows brought to wide attention several soon-to-be famous comedians, actors and writers. Thanks to repeats, revivals and spin-offs, the shows live on in (fairly accurate) memory. The BBC's *The Rag Trade*, written by Ronald Wolfe and Ronald Chesney, starred

Peter Jones, Reg Varney, Sheila Hancock and Miriam Karlin, whose clarion-cry of 'Everybody out!' became as famous as the more cynical 'I'm all right, Jack' of the same period. Set exclusively in the workplace (an uncommon situation in sitcom) and rarely giving any indication that the characters had any private lives, the series used every possible variation on the central conflict between hapless employer Mr Fenner (Jones) and his workers, led by Paddy (Karlin). The workers, aware of their boss's unscrupulous dodges, do everything they can to wangle a few extra pounds in their pay packets, covering their activities with a shield of faked militancy. An ill-judged revival in the 1970s retained Jones and Karlin but the rest of the scatty cast was inferior to the original. Christopher Beeny lacked Reg Varney's masterly comic timing as the unfortunate foreman caught between shop-floor and management and Sheila Hancock was also greatly missed.

American TV boomed in the years between 1948, when fewer than 200,000 sets were owned, and 1951 when the number exceeded 22 million. As was the case in Britain, American TV drew its early comedy shows and stars from radio, the stage and the movies. One genre which would however quickly fall into disfavour was that of ethnic comedy, some examples of which provided the smash-hit sitcoms of the 1949-50 season.

The Goldbergs had started out in vaudeville in 1925 before moving to radio in the early 1930s. Molly and Jake Goldberg helped bring to the wider American audience the cadences of Jewish humour that form such a significant part of American comedy. Played by Gertrude Berg, who wrote all the vaudeville, radio and TV shows, Molly Goldberg was the archetypal Jewish mother, facing crises with an inexhaustible fund of wisdom and chicken soup.

In 1948 RKO made a highly successful movie based on Kathryn Forbes' book *Mama's Bank Account*, which had already been adapted for the stage by John Van Druten. Directed by George Stevens, *I Remember Mama* starred Irene Dunne and Barbara Bel Geddes (later the matriarch of TV's *Dallas*) and caused millions to weep copiously into handkerchieves not only across the USA but around the world. Regular repeats on Sunday-afternoon TV continued to bring to sentimental life this saga of a family of Norwegian immigrants facing life in San Francisco at the turn of the century. It was a natural for TV, combining warm humour with affectionate family life as it was lived by warm and affectionate human beings. Categorizing *Mama* as a sitcom is not too accurate, any more than it would be correct to apply the term to *The Waltons* twenty years later. But it certainly did not qualify for the implied seriousness of the term 'drama'. The central core of sentimentality which afflicts so much American comedy, especially sitcoms, was in full and awful flower when the series *Mama* appeared in 1949 and was showing no signs of drooping when the show closed seven years later.

The fact that ethnicity was not yet a dirty word on TV suggests that an air of innocence pervaded American TV in the 1950s, and to some extent this is true. Sponsors and the advertising agencies had not learned of the problems their products might encounter if associated too closely in the public mind with certain races. The prejudice against some minority groups, especially Jews and blacks, was slow to make itself apparent but when it did the axe came down with a vengeance. After *The Goldbergs, Mama* and *Amos 'n' Andy* (which is discussed in Chapter 10) it was a very long time before the sitcom was to feature anything other than clean-cut all-American types.

Closely linked to the vaudeville tradition was *The George Burns and Gracie Allen Show*, which began in the 1950-1 season and was initially an extension of a stage partnership that had started almost 30 years earlier. The show was part sitcom and part George and Gracie performing one of their vaudeville routines. The audience's favourites were those chronicling the saga of Gracie's strange family, of which her Uncle Harry was perhaps the oddest.

Gracie: Did you know my Uncle Harry was a hold-up man?
George: Oh?
Gracie: Yeah, but his gang was just getting started and couldn't afford a getaway car so my uncle used to meet them outside the bank with bus fare.

Two vaudevilleans who made the shift to television with consummate ease: Gracie Allen and George Burns.

There were others:

Gracie: I can still see little baby Oscar sitting in his high chair chewing on lobster.
George: The baby had lobster?
Gracie: Oscar was too young to hold on to his food so they gave him food that could hold on to him.

Another former vaudevillean who succeeded on TV was Milton Berle. From 1948 until 1953 he hosted *Texaco Star Theatre* for NBC. Berle's wisecracking routines, allegedly stolen from every other comic, many of whom claimed to have seen him attending their shows, notebook in hand, proved staggeringly popular with the public. The huge viewing audiences his brashly arrogant style attracted eventually led NBC to overlook the legendary fickleness of the public and he was offered an unprecedented lifetime contract. Unfortunately for the network, the 'King of Comedy' failed to match up to the rising TV star of another former vaudevillean, Phil Silvers. Berle, who had a habit of loudly informing his audience, 'I'll tell ya what I'm gonna do,' was now being told. When he eventually and permanently toppled from his seemingly impregnable top-slot, not surprisingly lifetime contracts went with him.

Sid Caesar was another major comedy star whose talent far exceeded the sometimes limiting confines of the TV studio and screen. Supported by some of the brightest and best upcoming writing talents in America – Mel Brooks, Neil Simon, Larry Gelbart, Carl Reiner and Woody Allen – Sid's *Your Show of Shows* ran for four seasons from 1950 and was followed by the much less successful *Caesar's Hour* and *Sid Caesar Invites You.*

Unusually, *Your Show of Shows* occupied a 90-minute slot and introduced a wide range of characters portrayed by Caesar and his partner Imogene Coca.

One of Caesar's characters was a jungle denizen visiting New York. Clad only in an animal skin, he was interviewed for TV.

Interviewer: Sir, how do you survive in New York City? What do you eat?
Caesar: Pigeon.
Interviewer: Don't the pigeons object?
Caesar: Only for a minute.

Caesar achieved fame and popularity comparable to that of Milton Berle. The intensity of live TV comedy was enough to burn out many men in a season or two. Caesar withstood the pressure for ten years.

Jack Benny, Bob Hope, Danny Kaye and Red Skelton were four entertainers who brought echoes of their previous successes on radio and in vaudeville and films to television. All proved extremely popular for many years, although neither Benny nor Hope ever substantially changed or improved upon their previous radio styles; Hope in fact settled for occasional high-paying TV specials. Both Kaye and Skelton were in the old tradition of the clown but only Skelton wholly succeeded in adapting to the small screen. Kaye was not notably well-treated by TV, being obliged to narrow his act to suit the real and supposed limitations of the medium.

Jack Benny was, of course, Jack Benny. He continued adding to his reputation and his bank balance with a series of shows which, like *Burns and Allen*, blended styles from his radio and vaudeville days.

A lesser but equally loved comic was Jimmy Durante, who became hugely popular as he swaggered and smashed his way through many years of often-destructive comedy.

Ernie Kovacs became the first performer to make full use of the technical resources of television and was to prove an inspiration to people not even born during his years on the screen. His enormous potential remained unfulfilled when he was killed in 1962 in a car crash.

Among popular American TV sitcoms of the 1950s were *Mr Peepers* and *The Adventures of Hiram Holliday*, both of which starred skinny, bespectacled Wally Cox. Mr Peepers was a mild-mannered science teacher who dreamed of adventures but never had any. Hiram was a mild-mannered, lowly newspaper employee who had similar dreams. Unlike Mr Peepers', Hiram's dreams came true. Sent on a world tour by the newspaper as a reward for spotting a potentially libellous misprint, Hiram regularly pulled off remarkable feats thanks to previously untapped resources which allowed him to become a pilot, a surgeon, or anything else the script demanded. Early in his career Cox had shared a room with another struggling young actor, Marlon Brando – whom no one had the nerve to suggest should appear in a sitcom like the meek and mild Cox.

George and Gracie.

There was also *Make Room for Daddy*, starring Danny Thomas as a nightclub comic who managed to display considerably more intelligence than the average TV dad of the time. *The Real McCoys* starred Walter Brennan as an irascible old hick from Ma and Pa Kettle country. The first TV fantasy comedy, *Topper*, starring Leo G. Carroll, was based upon the highly successful series of movies. Very nearly as popular in Britain as in its home country was *Dennis the Menace* (known in Britain as *Just Dennis*), with young Jay North as Dennis Mitchell and Joseph Kearns as much-put-upon George Wilson (later replaced by Gale Gordon as John Wilson). *Life with Elizabeth* and *A Date with the Angels* both provided early starring rôles for Betty White, who would later come to prominence in *The Mary Tyler Moore Show* and make her real breakthrough in the mid-1980s with *The Golden Girls*.

The 1950s saw early rôles for Natalie Wood, who in 1956 made *Pride of the Family* (with *King Kong* star Fay Wray). Jack Lemmon and his wife Cynthia Stone made *That Wonderful Guy* in 1950-1 and *Heaven for Betsy* in 1952-3. The distinguished British-born star Ronald Colman made *Halls of Ivy* with his wife, Benita Hume, in 1954.

Other major American shows of the decade which are featured elsewhere in this book include *The Honeymooners*, *The Adventures of Ozzie and Harriet*, *I Married Joan*, *The Life of Riley*, *Our Miss Brooks*, *December Bride*, *Father Knows Best*, *Leave It to Beaver* and *The Many Loves of Dobie Gillis*.

The caution displayed as TV comedy programme-makers felt their way through the 1950s is apparent from the extensive use of performers who had previously succeeded in other media. In part this was due to most shows being live; no one wanted to run the risk of an artist drying up or freezing before an audience of millions. One result of this caution was that in both Britain and America new performers were slow in coming through. It was no wonder, therefore, that the major comedy stars of the decade were people like Tony Hancock, Lucille Ball and Phil Silvers.

Just as Hancock had starred in the British smash-hit of the 1950s so these last-named artists were the stars of America's biggest hits: *I Love Lucy* and *Sergeant Bilko*.

CHAPTER TWO

GEE, SARGE, IT'S LUCY

'Stay in the theatre.'
Jack Benny

Before their success in, respectively, *I Love Lucy* in 1951 and *The Phil Silvers Show: You'll Never Get Rich* in 1955, the careers of Lucille Ball and Phil Silvers bore several similarities. Afterwards, their careers could not have been more different.

Lucille Ball and Phil Silvers were both born in 1911, she in Celoron, a suburb of Jamestown in upstate New York, he in Brownsville, New York City. It is a showbiz cliché to say of a famous artist that he or she never wanted anything else but to be a star of the movies or TV or the theatre. In the case of these two, the cliché is true.

Between the ages of 15 and 22 Lucille tried, failed, returned home, and later tried again to enter showbiz in New York. In the summer of 1933, after a period as a model, the early struggles were quickly forgotten when she was booked to appear in a Sam Goldwyn movie, although in later years she was quick to acknowledge that times had not been as hard as her publicity suggested. 'I was making good money as a model,' she observed. 'Then I went to Hollywood and Sam Goldwyn immediately placed me under contract. Some struggle!'

Lucille's first real break came in 1942 with *The Big Street*, a movie in which she played the lead opposite Henry Fonda. The attractive if skinny glamorous blonde bit-part player finally had a rôle with substance, even if it was as a decidedly unsympathetic character. Despite good notices her career still did not take off and soon she moved to MGM, where

her blonde hair was dyed red, but this studio had no more idea than any other how best to use her.

In her idle moments, and they were many, Lucille hung around with director Eddie Sedgwick and Buster Keaton. Between them this unlikely trio worked up a number of slapstick routines. But glamorous actresses did not 'lower' themselves to play slapstick, and if anyone in authority noticed her skills, nothing was done about it.

In the late 1940s, in between making several more movies which hovered uneasily between glamour-girl parts and light comedy, Lucille worked for CBS radio on the series *My Favourite Husband*, in which she co-starred with Richard Denning. The rôle, that of a scatterbrained wife endlessly involving her husband in one dire emergency after another, was a huge hit but the motion picture studios did not capitalize upon Lucille's clearly revealed talent. Although the show ran for four years, the movie rôles followed the same old pattern. There were exceptions, however, and Lucille made strong comedic impact in *Sorrowful Jones* (1949) and *Fancy Pants* (1950), both with Bob Hope.

Her TV show was evolved by Lucille and her husband Desi Arnaz, whom she had met in 1940 on the set of the movie *Dance, Girl, Dance*. They risked everything on making the pilot show, blundering in where experienced TV producers would never have dared to tread. Desi decided to make the TV show as if it were a movie. Because he knew no better he

Lucy was forever scheming her way into husband Desi's act.

planned to shoot in sequence on three cameras and in the process learned the hard way everything there was to know about the right and wrong way to produce TV comedy. By the time they were through with the pilot they had attracted the interest of a sponsor (Philip Morris, the cigarette people) and a network (CBS).

Despite the great enthusiasm and help of two CBS vice-presidents, Harry Ackerman and Hubbell Robinson, it was an uphill fight for Lucille and Desi. They battled all the way, even over where the show would be made. New York was still the centre of the TV world but the Arnazes wanted to stay on the West Coast and work before a live audience. Eventually, thanks to a compromise deal, they won this argument and several others of what probably seemed at the time to be of even more fundamental importance.

For one thing, Lucille and Desi wanted their show to be about Real People. Not so the network. Lucille remarked on this in an interview with journalist Cecil Smith, reprinted in Judy Fireman's *TV Book*.

They wanted us to do a script about a Hollywood couple, two movie stars, I said, 'Where's the conflict?' To the rest of the world, a Hollywood couple has no problems. (We do, but they don't believe it.) Two cars and a swimming pool; what the hell kind of problems could we have? But everyone has money problems. Lucy always had to bake something, borrow something, sell something, steal something; she always had to tell those white lies because of what she did.

They settled for another compromise. This time it was that Desi would play a bandleader — still show business, but not super-showbiz.

Another argument stemmed from the fact that the outsiders were understandably nervous about Desi's ability to produce a weekly networked show. The network did not want control of the enterprise in the hands of a man with no proven talent at anything other than singing and playing the conga drum, neither of which he did particularly well. The fact that, in time and largely through seat-of-the-pants learning, he became a master of the game was as unexpected as the show's massive success.

Neither were the outsiders very keen on having Desi in front of the camera. They wanted to bring in Richard Denning, Lucille's co-star from the radio series. They certainly did not want an obviously ethnic individual; Desi's heavily accented speech became a permanent hurdle for anyone in the audience who wasn't prepared to concentrate.

One way and another Desi was being made to sound like a hopeless liability, but Lucille stuck out for his co-starring rôle. She wanted his name in the title too but eventually agreed to another compromise: *I Love Lucy* — in which, she reasoned, the placing and sense of the word 'I' meant that Desi got top billing.

But most important in the long term was that other compromise over where the show would be shot. In winning agreement for the show to be made in Los Angeles, Lucille and Desi had to accept a salary reduction. As compensation for this, they elicited a concession: 100 per cent residuals. This meant that after the first transmission of a show all rights reverted to the production company. Thus, after the first transmission, every subsequent screening of *I Love Lucy* provided income for Desilu Productions. It was a concession which cost CBS millions and made a fortune for Desilu.

From the start, *I Love Lucy* was a runaway success. Essentially, the structure of the show reflected that most ancient if occasionally dishonourable of institutions, the Battle of the Sexes. Lucille and Desi played the rôles of Lucy and Ricky Ricardo and if they were not exactly Mr and Mrs Average at least, as Lucille had insisted, their problems were the same as everyone else's. Every week Lucy wanted something husband Ricky disapproved of or disagreed with or which simply clashed with what he wanted. Lucy would begin by wheedling or whining (Lucy's 'Whaaa!' became the nearest equivalent the show had to a catchphrase) and when that failed she would connive and cheat until she got what she wanted.

In her endeavours Lucy was aided and abetted by her next-door neighbour, Ethel Mertz (played by Vivian Vance), whose husband Fred (played by William Frawley, a solitary alcoholic who was as irascible in private life as he was on-screen) stood by Ricky in a doomed male stand against the wiles of their women.

Week after week, to the delight of millions, the schemes of Lucy and Ethel succeeded — but

Business may look bad here but Desilu was making millions.

'The Ballet' included an excellent piece of ad-libbing when Lucy accidentally caught her foot in the barre while exercising.

Wangling a job on a TV commercial, Lucy's endless rehearsals deteriorate rapidly thanks to the alcohol content of a tonic she has to sip. The pitch she has to deliver went in part:

I'm your Vitameatavegamin girl. Are you tired, rundown, listless? Do you poop out at parties? Are you unpopular? The answer to all your problems is in this little bottle: Vitameatavegamin. Vitameatavegamin contains vitamins, meat, vegetables, and minerals. Yes, with Vitameatavegamin you can spoon your way to health. All you do is take a spoonful after every meal. It's so tasty, too. Just like candy. So why don't you join the thousands of happy, peppy people and get a great big bottle of Vitameatavegamin tomorrow?

Not surprisingly, when she was drunk this tongue-twisting script became even more incomprehensible than it was to start with.

The show's list of guest stars, usually people eager to plug a new movie or TV show, included William Holden, Bob Hope, Rock Hudson, Harpo Marx (in an episode in which Lucy impersonates him), Red Skelton, John Wayne and Richard Widmark.

In the show's first season it zoomed into second place in the ratings behind Red Skelton who, like Lucy, was very much in favour of sight-gags. The usually untoppable Milton Berle was down in eighth place. By January 1953 not even the inaugural address of the new president, Dwight D. 'Ike' Eisenhower, could match Lucy. Of course, it was no ordinary episode of *I Love Lucy* which was screened the evening before Ike's inauguration. Lucille Ball was pregnant and in a decision of considerable boldness for the time, her pregnancy was written into the script. Set against her 44 million audience, Ike's 29 million gave some indication of the people's priorities.

Today, when divorce, premarital sex, abortion and even rape and AIDS have become accepted in TV sitcoms, an ordinary everyday occurrence like the birth of a child to a married couple may seem decidedly uncontroversial. But 1953 was a time when even the use of the word 'pregnant' could cause corporate heads to roll. For this show several advisers of different religious persua-

not before they had been thrust into one desperate situation after another. These situations, almost invariably slapstick routines, were usually highly unlikely but had about them a certain logic which allowed the stars to carry them off with considerable aplomb. Watched again years later (and somewhere in the world all these shows are still being shown today), a certain crudity of construction is in evidence. Too often, the central joke is weak but is played with such abandon and all-stops-out volume that the audience is bulldozed into acceptance and laughter.

Among the hundreds of routines were 'Lucy's Fake Illness', which had Lucy pretending to have a nervous breakdown because Ricky won't let her join his act. She fakes three symptoms: she 'becomes' a celebrity (in this case movie star Tallulah Bankhead); she loses her memory; and she reverts to childhood. The sight of 'Tallulah' furiously pedalling her tricycle around the room convulsed the audience as did her inability to recognize herself in a mirror. Of course, Ricky saw through it and brought in a phony doctor who convinced Lucy that she really was suffering from a serious disease: the 'gobloots'.

A moment of calm in the usually frantic home life of Lucy and Desi.

sions were hired to ensure that nothing was shown or said that could offend anyone. Among the adjustments made to accommodate the viewing audience's supposed susceptibilities was the sponsor's request that Lucy would not smoke during her pregnancy. Bearing in mind that the sponsor was cigarette maker Philip Morris, this is an early if tacit admission of the possible dangers of tobacco. Another accommodation was the use of the word 'expectant' instead of 'pregnant'. Were Americans really that easily upset in 1953?

After some deliberation it was decided that the scriptwriters would settle on the sex of the baby in advance of the show and they wrote in a male child. The timing of the 'birth episode' was no serious problem because the birth was to be by caesarian section. When Lucille had her baby on the day the appropriate episode was to be screened, she obliged everyone and doubtless helped boost subsequent ratings a few more points by having a baby boy.

The show and Lucille gathered awards, including Emmies for the best sitcom of 1952 and best comedienne. CBS renewed the show's contract for a massive $8 million complete with a remarkable 'no cancellation' clause.

*

Like so many American immigrants, Phil Silvers' parents, who were Russian Jews, had settled in New York City. Phil discovered what he wanted to do with his life thanks to the Bushwick theatre in Brooklyn not far from his parents' home in Brownsville. At the Bushwick the young boy saw such artists as Sophie Tucker and George Jessell and eventually he became a member of a song-and-dance trio. Spotted by impresario Gus Edwards, the man who discovered Jessell and Eddie Cantor, Silvers was a full-time pro by the age of 12.

In 1939 he was offered a contract with MGM but after signing he hung around Hollywood for a year doing nothing until, not surprisingly, his option was not picked up and he moved to Twentieth Century-Fox.

This move didn't help much and the films he made were often highly forgettable musicals in which, he would later observe, he always played the same rôle, 'Blinky: the good-humoured, bespectacled confidant' of the movie's stars.

By 1946, Silvers was disenchanted with Hollywood and returned to New York where he starred in *High Button Shoes* on Broadway, picking up the kind of rave reviews artists dream about but seldom receive. He also headlined a TV variety show but there was no follow-up.

In the early 1950s he starred in another Broadway show, *Top Banana*, and was again a smash. This show was based loosely on the character of Milton Berle and won numerous awards. Co-starring was Rose Marie, who would later achieve national recognition in *The Dick Van Dyke Show*. A disastrous movie version of the show used 3-D for no apparent reason and with dire results.

At about this time, 1953, Silvers was talking to Jack Benny, who predicted, 'They're going to be after you for television. That's the wave of the future. But it's a drain. Stay in the theatre. It isn't the most fruitful in terms of money, but a performer has dignity on the stage. People *pay* to see you.'

The advice was largely meaningless to Silvers. No one had made any suggestion that he might be wanted for TV. Then, in 1954, he visited Washington to appear in a show for President Eisenhower. With vice-president Richard Nixon, most of the cabinet, several senators and other members of the legislature in attendance, Silvers came on stage, looked at everyone in a deepening and mildly embarrassed silence before looking straight at Ike and demanding, 'My God, who's minding the store?'

From that point on he had the president and everyone else in the palm of his hand. Most important, however, was that in the audience was Hubbell Robinson, the CBS vice-president who had been one of the collaborators at the birth of *I Love Lucy*. Three days after the Washington show, CBS was in touch with Phil Silvers and he was soon introduced to Nat Hiken, formerly a writer for Fred Allen and Milton Berle.

Hiken had an idea for a show about a glib, fast-talking con-man. One of his earliest ideas, rejected by Silvers, was to make the con-man an army sergeant. They tried numerous other settings but to no avail until

Ernie Bilko (Phil Silvers) charms the ladies, including, at left, Elizabeth Fraser as Joan Hogan.

Silvers began to see the possibilities of the army idea. A day later and Hiken had the idea roughed out; CBS gave the go-ahead and the pilot script was written. The show acquired a sponsor, Camel cigarettes, the con-man was given a name, rank and number: 15042699 Master Sergeant Ernest T. Bilko. The show was tagged *You'll Never Get Rich*, a title which was later extended to *The Phil Silvers Show: You'll Never Get Rich* and later still, fortunately, simplified to *Sergeant Bilko.*

Put into the schedules opposite Milton Berle on NBC, and timed so that it came on half way through Berle's hour-long show, the ratings were a disaster. Then it was pulled back half an hour so that it started at the same time as Berle. Almost at once it began to gain points and by December 1954 (the show had débuted in September) the impossible happened and they passed Berle in the ratings. Shortly afterwards, perhaps taking the success of the Silvers show as a portent of future doom,

Milton Berle, generally acclaimed as the greatest TV comedy success of all time, hung up his joke book and retired.

Bilko differed greatly from other sitcoms (and dramas) in the number of regular cast members. There were almost two dozen of them, all on contract. Herein lay part of the reason for the show's comparatively early demise. Many of the characters bore sporting names: Bilko was the name of minor league baseball player Steve Bilko but also had highly appropriate connotations with the word 'bilk'; Corporal Rocco Barbella (Harvey Lembeck) took the real name of former boxing champion Rocky Graziano, who was the show's casting director. This fact doubtless accounted for the number of ex-pugs who popped into episodes over the years.

Casting the main rôles was the usual mixture of intent and chance. The supporting rôle of Barbella had first been offered to Buddy Hackett, who turned it down at the last moment in order to take a stage job. Hiken later stated that this was the best thing that could have happened because in rehearsal Silvers, who greatly admired Hackett, was forever feeding him the best lines. An old vaudeville colleague of Silvers', Herbie Faye, played Private Fender, who morosely greeted yet another of Bilko's get-rich-quick schemes with: 'I knew it, he's sold us into slavery.' Paul Ford had given up a career as an insurance salesman to take a fling at acting at the age of 40. He became a writer's dream as Colonel John 'Melon Head' Hall. How many other actors could forget their lines so often and yet appear to be doing what the script demanded? Then there was Maurice Gosfield. In his autobiography Silvers recalls the actor's appearance at the audition: '...we opened the doors wide and there he was ... We had to have him – the Slob of the Century.' Gosfield became Private Duane Doberman, whose on-screen appearance of gravy-spattered sloth was surpassed only by his off-screen appearance of gravy-drenched slob. Not that Gosfield thought of himself in this way. As Silvers once remarked in a TV interview, Gosfield believed he was like 'Cary Grant *playing* the part of a slob'.

Bilko enjoyed a remarkably high standard of writing and performance throughout its run but most fans and critics are agreed on the best-ever episode – one in which Private Doberman does not appear, although Maurice Gosfield played an important off-screen rôle. On this occasion a chimpanzee is accidentally inducted into the United States army when an over-zealous officer tries to break the record for speedy induction of men. Unfortunately, one of the men is one half of a vaudeville roller-skating act of which the other half is a chimpanzee. The chimp gets into the line of men being processed. 'Hurry,' yells one official, 'Speak up,' urges another, and the chimp becomes Private Harry Speakup. By the time the error is discovered it is too late – the chimp is in the army. It is, of course, Bilko who comes up with the solution. The only way to get rid of the chimp, whose records are on their way to the Pentagon, is to court-martial it.

With Bilko as his defence attorney, the chimp is arraigned – and the way was open for the only scene in the entire series in which the cast is visibly straining to avoid laughing.

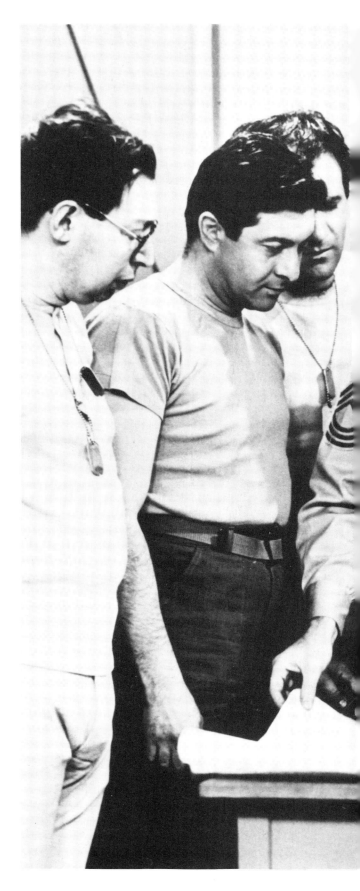

Bilko plans another get-rich-quick scheme. Front row, left to right: Gerald Hiken, Harvey Lembeck, Phil Silvers, Maurice Gosfield, Mickey Freeman.

Another raw deal for someone (Phil Silvers).

Perhaps it was no wonder that the chimp, during rehearsals, had discovered an affinity for Maurice Gosfield. Doberman was therefore written out of the script for this episode so that Gosfield could stand off-camera and act as a kind of trainer. As it turned out, the chimp, who mostly worked well with Silvers, had a mind of its own – to say nothing of having more natural acting talent than Gosfield.

In the court-martial scene, Silvers discovered that if he made an almost inaudible 'tsk tsk' sound the chimp would lean towards him as if consulting on some matter of legal significance. Silvers capitalized on this with appropriate comments: 'Don't worry, I'll bring that up.' This started the other members of the cast giggling. The highlight came when the chimp spotted a telephone in the corner of the courtroom set. The animal, fascinated by telephones, promptly leaped from its seat, ran to the 'phone and picked it up. In what must surely be the finest ad-lib ever heard on TV outside Groucho Marx's show, Silvers turned to the president of the court-martial and declared: 'I plead for an adjournment. My client is calling for a new attorney.'

In its time the show saw a number of actors at an early stage in their careers: Dick Van Dyke, George Kennedy, Dina Merrill, Dick Cavett, Fred Gwynne (patrolman Muldoon in *Car 54, Where Are You?* and, later, Herman Munster), and Joe E. Ross (patrolman Toody in *Car 54*).

For its first three years *Bilko* was made before an audience, the 25-minute episode taking some 50 minutes to shoot. By chance, following an episode that could not be made this way, it was discovered that the show went just as well without an audience. Thereafter it was always made in an empty studio and, after editing, was screened before an audience of GIs and the laugh track added.

After four years the show was still hugely successful but CBS was concerned about that large cast list, which included 22 contract regulars. More significantly, perhaps, the network wanted to capitalize upon its investment. That meant syndication. Although there have been exceptions to this rule, in those days it was customary for a show to end before it was syndicated.

So, wanting to cash in by selling *Bilko* into syndication, CBS killed the show. The show's termination and the reasons for it demonstrate vividly and unpleasantly the mercenary streak at the core of American TV.

In September 1959 the final episode was screened and ended with a beaming Colonel Hall watching his favourite TV show: a closed-circuit camera focused on Bilko who was finally behind bars in the camp prison.

At its best, and *Bilko* was rarely less than very good, the show displayed American humour at its snappiest. One-liners tumbled after one another in a dazzling display of writing and delivery. The laughs not only came faster than in any other show, they also came thicker. Many series before and since have been lucky to register in a dozen episodes the number of laughs *Bilko* clocked up in one 25-minute show.

Good as the writing, production and individual performances were, no one can seriously deny that the show's success was wholly dependent upon Phil Silvers. As he himself would observe, his entire career up to this point had been preparing him for Bilko. The unlikeliest man ever to wear a sergeant's stripes epitomized the fast-talking, wise-cracking vaudeville comics Silvers admired and alongside whom he could stand without fear. That powerful strain of humour which originated with America's Jewish immigrants in the nineteenth century reached its apogee with the lovable, tough-seeming but essentially soft-hearted Ernie Bilko.

After *Bilko*, despite odd moments of success such as *Do-Re-Mi* on Broadway, it was all downhill for Phil Silvers. He made a short-lived return to TV in 1963 with *The New Phil Silvers Show*, a sitcom which featured the exploits of a Bilko clone named Harry Grafton, a factory foreman by trade but Bilko in everything but uniform, and also appeared in several episodes of *The Beverly Hillbillies* and a TV pilot, *Bel-Air Patrol*, but his catalogue of illnesses, physical and psychological, grew.

In the 1960s he made several films: *It's a Mad, Mad, Mad, Mad World* (1963), *Carry On, Follow that Camel* (1967) and, in 1968, *Buona Sera Mrs Campbell*, but after winning a Tony award for the stage version in 1971 of his

1966 film *A Funny Thing Happened on the Way to the Forum* he suffered a stroke. This was in 1972 and he did very little thereafter until his death in 1985.

*

By contrast, Lucille Ball's career after her early 1950s success with *I Love Lucy* was a continuing catalogue of superlatives. In 1958 the format of *I Love Lucy* was changed in favour of fewer but longer (one-hour) shows. Then, in 1959, after eight years of success, *I Love Lucy* ended. The following year, the Arnaz marriage ended in divorce. With no apparent diminution of her energy, Lucille appeared on Broadway in *Wildcat* at the age of 49, married comedian Gary Morton in 1961, and then, in 1962, started work on a new TV sitcom.

The break-up of Lucille's and Desi's marriage had not led to a similar dissolving of their business interests, although in 1962 Lucille bought out Desi's share of the company. For a while she ran Desilu (which produced such successful shows as *Star Trek* and *Mission: Impossible*) before selling out to Paramount. It was this buy-out that finally separated Lucille from the format of *I Love Lucy* and pushed her into establishing a new structure for her continuing career in TV sitcom. The new show was again produced by Desi Arnaz for Desilu.

Lucille's co-star in *The Lucy Show* was once again Vivian Vance (as Vivian Bagley). Lucille played Lucy Carmichael, a scatterbrained widow with two children living in Danfield, Connecticut. The Battle of the Sexes continued in a less overt manner with Lucy involved in a perpetual conflict of will with bank president Theodore J. Mooney (Gale Gordon). If the show was not the smash-hit its predecessor had been it was still very successful, although running a fair way behind the season's top shows: *Car 54, Where Are You?* and *The Dick Van Dyke Show*. It even trailed half a length behind the talking-horse sitcom, *Mr Ed*.

In an attempt to improve its ratings *The Lucy Show* shifted format, but only marginally. Lucy moved to San Francisco, along the way mislaying her children and Vivian Vance although hanging on to Gale Gordon. In 1968,

after seven years, the show folded and was replaced that same year by *Here's Lucy*. Now Lucille was Lucy Carter, she lived in Los Angeles, she had a brother-in-law named Harry (Gale Gordon again) and two children named Kim and Craig, played by her real-life children Lucie and Desi Jr. Not much else had changed. Lucy Carter, like Lucy Carmichael and Lucy Ricardo before her, was still scatterbrained, still flinging herself into improbable situations which involved more than a touch of slapstick and a lot of noise and which, to a considerable extent, played on the audience's knee-jerk reponses.

Here's Lucy didn't have a lot of competition in its début year, or indeed for the first two seasons of its run. By 1970, however, TV sitcom was changing and it never really stood a chance against such newcomers as *All in the Family* and *The Mary Tyler Moore Show*. The show ran on, however, offering an interesting contrast with such later shows as *M*A*S*H*, *Maude* and *Happy Days*. Eventually, in 1974, *Here's Lucy* ended and Lucille Ball retired from on-screen activity.

She was far from retired altogether, however, and continued to work in administration (for NBC); but the pull of TV was still strong. In 1985 she appeared in a TV movie, *Stone Pillow*, in which she played the rôle of an aged New York bag-lady. Press comment suggested that Lucille found the new breed of director tough to get along with but her enthusiasm for TV work remained strong. Late in 1986 rumours began to emerge that Lucille Ball, by then 75 years old, was seriously considering returning to TV sitcom-land.

Today, dedicated Lucy-watchers can see her at the touch of a button, especially in the New York area. There, on Wednesday 25 February 1987 at 5 a.m., WNBC screened an episode of *Here's Lucy* followed by another at 5.30. At 9.35 a.m. *I Love Lucy* was on WTBS, at 10 a.m. on WNYW and on WTXX at 2 p.m. A midnight movie on cable was *Dance, Girl, Dance*, the one where she first met Desi; also on cable, at 2.20 a.m., she played a small rôle in the Marx Brothers' *Room Service*. At 3.30 a.m. *Here's Lucy* was on WNBC, at 4 a.m. *The Lucy Show* was on WTBS and at 5 a.m. because most of these shows are on daily, the whole thing started over again on WNBC.

Lucy and daughter Lucie in a bigger pickle than usual.

Watching re-runs of Lucille Ball's old shows today, as Lucy Ricardo-Carmichael-Carter zaps around the screen in frenetic pursuit of Ricky Ricardo or Mr Mooney, it is sometimes hard to understand their appeal. Perhaps it stems from the original concept evolved for *I Love Lucy*, that of the eternal Battle of the Sexes. This clearly struck a universal chord of understanding of a kind for which TV programme-makers would happily sell their souls. The shows' appeal certainly cannot be their sublety or sophistication.

Writing on situation comedy in *TV Genres*, a book edited by Brian G. Rose, Lawrence E. Mintz observes that 'Lucy was funny the same way that Jerry Lewis is funny — by contrasting normal appearance, normal situation, and moments of calm with bursts of insane energy, childish abandon, and unbridled enthusiasm.' The comment is valid, but so too is a related point: for many people too much insane energy and childish abandon can very quickly become tiresome. A 25-minute episode of *Lucy* is one thing; week after week the cumulative effect is much like seeing a full-length Jerry Lewis film more than once: embarrassment, quickly followed by boredom. Millions, however, were not in the least bored. Millions more, in the empty hours before dawn, are still laughing.

If, for all their popularity, the various Lucy shows have not stood the test of time too well, *Bilko* appears as good as ever. Largely this is due to its reliance upon first-class wisecrack writing and faultless delivery. Additionally, that large cast which helped sink the show was made up of well-rounded characters with distinctive individual personalities. Lucy's noisy slapstick routines and the improbable behaviour of her show's small cast has helped date her.

As for the network domination that was largely circumvented by Lucille Ball and Desi Arnaz, and which ruthlessly consigned Phil Silvers to TV's scrap-heap, that still exercises power and control. True, there are differences today. Many independent companies are making sitcoms, and some local TV stations are backing the 'indies' by taking their shows in preference to those from the networks.

But shows like *Lucy* and *Bilko* need stars, and where today can anyone be found of the calibre of Lucille Ball or Phil Silvers? These two artists brought to TV echoes of a long-lost world of entertainment and their shows, so very different from one another in structure, content and style can never be repeated because the training ground that spawned them no longer exists.

The lack of artists of this quality was beginning to make its effect as far back as the 1960s. At first the effect went either unnoticed or unmourned because the times were changing attitudes towards TV comedy.

Just as 1950s television on both sides of the Atlantic had needed the traditions, experience and reliability of stars of radio and the vaudeville and variety theatres, so the comedy-show makers of the 1960s began to look elsewhere for their stars and their writers.

CHAPTER THREE

THE 'SIXTIES SURVEYED

'...until then there had been televised radio.'
Dick Martin

The background from which new writers and performers were emerging inevitably changed TV comedy itself in the 1960s.

In Britain, the old training grounds — the variety halls — were on their last legs. Many performers who had learned their trade in such places continued, and in some cases rose to the very top of the TV tree, but the new television comedy writers and artists emerged from the legitimate theatre and the universities. As for the stand-up comics, they were soon heavily concentrated in a third environment: the working-men's clubs, located chiefly in the north of England.

Situation comedy flourished but it was changing as programme-makers began to understand their trade. Brian Armstrong of Granada TV has remarked, 'The best situation comedy isn't about situations at all; it's about vulnerable people ... comedy springs from character.'

Increasingly, writers created characters and wrote scripts for actors, not comics. It was not even necessary for the artists cast in these rôles to be 'comic actors'. What was needed was an ability to make the created characters real and believable and to deliver lines with perfect timing. Numerous actors who benefited from this shift in emphasis became enormously popular and if they sometimes grudgingly accepted the accolade of comedian, their audience might well have taken offence at any suggestion that this is precisely what they were not. Among the notable actors involved in this revolution were Arthur Lowe, John Le Mesurier, James Bolam, Rodney Bewes, Warren Mitchell, Harry H. Corbett and Wilfrid Brambell.

The second and perhaps least expected source of new comedy for television, the universities, produced a radically different style of humour. Combining the improbably compatible strands of intellectual wit and schoolboy lavatory jokes, hordes of young men (rarely women) overran the TV comedy slots and for a while threatened to prevail with their undermining and irreverent brand of insanity. The prime movers were Jonathan Miller, Alan Bennett, Peter Cook and Dudley Moore, but they were soon followed, and in some respects overtaken by, David Frost, William Rushton, Eleanor Bron, John Cleese, Eric Idle, Terry Jones, Michael Palin, Graham Chapman, Tim Brooke-Taylor, Graeme Garden and Bill Oddie.

The theatrical group almost always entered TV comedy by way of the sitcom; the university group almost never did.

The two groups were not mutually exclusive, indeed a striking example of an unknown performer materializing in one form, shifting to the other and reaching stardom is Ronnie Barker. Eric Idle wrote a monologue for Barker to use in *The Frost Report*, a show in which Barker and Ronnie Corbett were regular performers of sketches. Barker and Corbett subsequently appeared separately in numerous TV sitcoms but retained their partnership for their show *The Two Ronnies*. This vehicle for their versatility shows no signs of fading more than 20 years on.

The newcomers soon became professionals even if, for a while at least, TV comedy in Britain did appear, in Eric Midwinter's phrase, to make 'a fetish of amateurism'.

The new professionals had much less attachment to the old traditions, though these were sustained for a while by highly popular contributions from such established artists as Charlie Drake and Arthur Haynes.

Drake is one of numerous latterday comics who came up through the forcing house of entertaining at seaside holiday camps. A small, rotund and outwardly cherubic individual, he has attributed his stature to his childhood diet: 'I was raised on condensed milk.' His TV shows, transmitted live, included complicated sight gags which were often as dangerous as they looked. On several occasions he was hurt and was once knocked unconscious, which brought the show to an unexpected conclusion. It could have been worse. Commenting in advance on one 1961 episode, 'Bingo Madness', Charlie remarked: 'There's one scene which is very big, slapstickwise, and very dangerous. It has been rehearsed to the nth degree, but if it doesn't work – I'll break my neck.'

Drake's later show, The Worker, with Henry McGhee, ran for most of the last half of the 1960s.

Arthur Haynes, who had been a bit-part player on Charlie Chester's radio show, blossomed in the new medium. His gallery of characters included an aggressive tramp and an ex-army man whose resentful view of the world he had fought for ('I was up to my neck in muck and bullets') ably caught the prevailing mood.

Many of Haynes's scripts were written by Johnny Speight, whose own combative spirit blended well with the comic's. It was in Alf Garnett that Speight's work reached its apotheosis but the signs were well in evidence earlier. When Arthur Haynes visited a psychiatrist demanding treatment, the occasion allowed Speight to hold up to sharp ridicule the swiftly developing 'something for nothing' streak that was affecting the nation.

Haynes: Well, I'm entitled to it, ain' I? I pay into the National Health and I'm entitled to see a psychiatrist under that, ain' I? I'm entitled to

psychiatric treatment, so I thought I'd come along and have a bash at it.
Psychiatrist: Have a bash at it? But, really, I...
Haynes: Well I'm entitled to it, mate, ain' I? If I'm paying in for a thing I'm entitled to share the benefits. I'm a poor man, mate, I can't afford to pay into things for nothing. That's why I had me teeth out. As soon as they brought it under the National Health I went and 'ad 'em out, mate. All out. There was nothing wrong with 'em. But I thought, if I'm entitled to free dentures I'm going to have 'em. Same with me truss.
Psychiatrist: Oh, er, you have a rupture?
Haynes: No, mate, just a truss, that's all. Well, I'm entitled to it. I've paid for it.

The sitcoms of the 1960s played to massive audiences in Britain. By 1966 90 per cent of the population either owned or had regular access to a TV set. Responding to the rising demand, the TV companies resurrected some old favourites in new formats: among these were Alfie Bass and Bill Fraser in Bootsie and Snudge, a spin-off from The Army Game with several writers including Harry Driver, Jack Rosenthal and Ray Alan; and Kenneth Horne in Horne A'Plenty, written by Barry Took and co-starring Sheila Steafel, an actress of great comic talent who has been notably underused by television.

Horne A'Plenty vividly demonstrated the fact that a radio hit had no guarantee of success on TV. Kenneth Horne had taken part in three highly successful radio series. Much Binding in the Marsh was a wartime show in which he co-starred with Richard Murdoch; Beyond Our Ken, aired in the mid-1950s, was written by Eric Merriman and Barry Took and featured Kenneth Williams, Hugh Paddick and Betty Marsden; and in the mid-1960s the best of all was Round the Horne, written by Took and Marty Feldman and featuring the same cast. Despite this excellent record of radio successes, Kenneth Horne failed to click with TV audiences.

Another radio comic who transferred to television with varying degrees of success was Jimmy Edwards, one of the stars of Take It From Here. The writers of this radio show were Frank Muir and Denis Norden. Despite being the best radio comedy writers to emerge in the post-war years, they were never among the front-runners on TV – yet their influence was enormous. Their radio family, the Glums, foreshadowed the Garnetts and Steptoes. Few of their contemporaries or successors were Muir and Norden's equals in wit and sophisticated humour. They have a love for and a way with language that should have earned them a knighthood apiece, were writers recognized thus. (Norden was co-screenwriter for the movie *Buona Sera Mrs Campbell* in which Phil Silvers appeared.) For Jimmy Edwards Muir and Norden wrote the TV series *Seven Faces of Jim* and *Six More Faces of Jim*, although neither show was as successful as the earlier *Whack-O!* which featured Edwards in the blustering school-master rôle he perfected.

The 1960s saw a run of 'religious' sitcoms (or, to be more precise, sitcoms with a religious setting). These included *Our Man at St Mark's*, with Donald Sinden and Leslie Phillips, and *All Gas and Gaiters*, which starred William Mervyn, Robertson Hare and Derek Nimmo. *Oh Brother!* also had Nimmo, whose plummy-voiced cleric became very popular. He kept his collar on backwards for *Oh Father!* and, in 1986, *Hell's Bells*, which took a much more realistic view of matters spiritual in contemporary Britain than had the earlier series.

Among the sitcoms of the 1960s were several which quickly became classics and which are discussed in other chapters of this book: *The Likely Lads, Steptoe and Son, Till Death Us Do Part* and *Dad's Army*.

Much less than classic but still attracting large audiences were *Father, Dear Father* and *Never Mind the Quality, Feel the Width*. The former, which starred Patrick Cargill, Ursula Howells, Noel Dyson and Joyce Carey, centred upon a widower bringing up his daughters while attempting to fend off his ex-wife, his housekeeper and his dotty mother. The latter was a rarity on British television, an ethnic comedy; it featured Joe Lynch as Patrick Kelly and John Bluthal as Manny Cohen. As the show's title suggests Kelly and Cohen were bespoke tailors whose conflicting religious beliefs (Irish Catholic and Jewish) provided the main source of humour

There was also *Please Sir!*, which could have been an ethnic comedy but wasn't. The show was inspired by the 1967 movie *To Sir with Love* which starred Sidney Poitier, Judy Geeson and Lulu, and which also ducked most of the issues of a black teacher in a school in London's East End. The TV version played everything for laughs and avoided the central point of the movie by not having a black actor as the teacher. John Alderton as Mr Hedges, aptly nicknamed 'Privet' by his pupils, battled away against the Fenn Street gang aided and abetted by excellent performances from a strong cast of 'teachers' including Joan Sanderson, Erik Chitty, Richard Davies and Noel Howlett. *Please Sir!* had an American counterpart in the 1970s when Gabriel Kaplan wrote and starred in *Welcome Back, Kotter*, a show which gave an early acting break to John Travolta in the rôle of Vinnie Barbarino.

Appearing regularly on British TV through-out the 1960s were several exponents of a much older form of comedy which drew its inspiration from the halls. Some real old-stagers brought their original routines to TV in variety shows allowing millions to enjoy the perfected artistry of such comics as the incomparable Jimmy James.

The principals of a younger group from the same tradition were Benny Hill, Frankie Howerd and, way above all others in the genre, Morecambe and Wise.

The Benny Hill Show has been likened to an animated seaside postcard. Although neither entirely fair nor accurate, this description does serve to convey the sort of visual image that typifies Hill's on-screen antics. Hardly chang-ing either the format or the basic content of his show over the years, Hill has managed to survive waves of indignation from women and is still eager to see how far he can go without offending the mass audience. In the late 1980s he is one of the most popular of the tiny handful of British comics whose shows have proved successful on American television. Despite his enormous following, Hill restricts himself to three hours of new television each year. In this context, 'new' means additional rather than original. That Hill has the capacity to be so much better than he is was observed by Hal Roach, the veteran American film-maker who helped bring to the big screen such comic giants as Harold Lloyd and Laurel and Hardy. At his 1986 Guardian Lecture in London Roach noted that Hill's potential would seem to be limitless, if he could only

John Alderton risks turning his back on the Fenn Street Gang in Please Sir!

learn to curb his desire to exploit bare-bottom humour with such single-minded dedication. He could be 'one of the greatest — only for one thing. His comedy is all below the belt. That's no use for comedy. It won't do for children, and in the end it's children who have made all the great comedians — Chaplin, Laurel and Hardy, all of them.'

Frankie Howerd is an interesting case in that he has steadfastly refused to move with the times. Starting out on the variety stage, he took his act, which consists largely of a rambling, gossipy monologue heavily dependent upon innuendo and a knowing leer rather than on jokes as such, on to radio in the 1940s. The move to radio was aided by the fact that he had a remarkable talent for leering audibly — and for making conspiratorial asides to his audiences. From early in the next decade he was headlining TV shows and by the late

1950s he was a major attraction whether on stage or on the air. At the end of the 1950s he was suddenly and calamitously out of fashion. Galton and Simpson were eager to write for him but failed to raise any interest. If Howerd panicked it didn't show on the surface and he retained his old act until he was given the opportunity of appearing at the Establishment Club, where he followed, of all people, Lenny Bruce. His unexpected success at the club led to an appearance on *That Was the Week That Was* in 1963. This was currently the TV show with the top critical rating, and a strong viewing audience too. Howerd took his act as it had been for years, added a few topical gags (after all, *TW3* was supposed to be satire) and made everyone else on the show look like the talented amateurs they were. The years on the stage and on radio had honed his professionalism to a marvellous sharpness

Benny Hill, one of the few British comics to make real impact in America.

and from then onwards he never cast a backward glance – nor did he ever really change his act. Howerd's TV shows, such as *Up Pompeii*, in which he plays the slave Lurcio and which followed his West End appearance in *A Funny Thing Happened on the Way to the Forum*, may be loosely termed sitcoms but, as George Burns had done before him, he directed a large part of the show into the camera complete with all the innuendo, leers and *double-entendres* he could muster. Thus, when his master, Ludicrus Sextus, remarks that his daughter, Erotica, is 'so delightfully chaste', Lurcio is prompt to mutter, '... and so easily caught up with.'

Among the writers who have served Howerd are Barry Took and Marty Feldman, and in his book *Laughter in the Air* Took reveals that they were expected to put in all the 'oohs' and 'aahs' and 'listens' which they, and

presumably millions of listeners, had assumed to be part of Howerd rather than an element of the script.

The 1960s brought to the fore an eccentric magician named Tommy Cooper. From TV's earliest days magicians were popular, even if a few suffered from unfortunately placed cameras which gave away their trade trickery. Cooper's first appearances, in the early 1950s, successfully undercut the occasional pomposity of such acts. Audiences were subjected to a barrage of failed tricks, unco-operative props and a non-stop line in childlike explanatory dialogue: 'Glass, bottle, bottle, glass'; 'Not like that, like that.'

An ungainly bear of a man, Cooper contrived through great skill to maintain an air of bewildered innocence and appeared always to be thoroughly enjoying himself as his manic laughter echoed above the audience's. His jokes were always amiably infantile: 'I got home last night and found my car in the dining room. I did. I said to my wife, "How did you get there?" She said, "It was easy, I made a left turn at the kitchen."'

His success in the 1960s was maintained fairly consistently through to the 1980s and he retained his audience's affection to the end. In 1984 he collapsed and died on camera as he came to the end of his act on a live TV show.

Dick Emery crafted a line in eccentric individuals which were really comic portraits. His toothy vicar, Mandy (a lady of dubious virtue), a gentlemanly tramp, bovver boy and creaking grandfather so captured the public imagination that the format of his shows changed to become what he termed a series of 'lengthy character sketches'. Usually, these characters were interviewed in the street:

Interviewer: Excuse me, sir.
Bovver boy: Yer?
Interviewer: Is there anything in life you feel you've missed?
Bovver boy: Yer, I never learned to drive.
Interviewer: That's no handicap, not being able to drive.
Bovver boy: It is when you're a car thief.

And:

Interviewer: Excuse me.
Mandy: Yes?
Interviewer: Here's a charming young lady. Tell me, are you impressed by aristocratic titles?
Mandy: Oh, no. I speak my mind, no matter who I'm talking to.
Interviewer: I see. You mean you wouldn't let anyone take advantage of you?
Mandy: Pardon?
Interviewer: I mean, you wouldn't take things lying down, even from a duke?
Mandy: Ooh, you are awful ... But I like you.

*

Morecambe and Wise hold a special place in the hearts of British audiences. In the best sense of the term they were an old-fashioned cross-talk act of the kind with which the music-halls, variety theatres and, in America, vaudeville were studded for the best part of a hundred years. They came to television, via radio, in the early 1950s in a show entitled *Running Wild.* Not to put too fine a point on it, the show was a disaster. Had they been a

newly-formed act they might have called it a day, but being seasoned performers they knew what had to be done.

Both Eric Morecambe and Ernie Wise were born in 1926 and were on the stage while still very young boys. They first appeared together in 1941 but had to wait until after the war before they could build upon the remarkable empathy each discovered in the other. From 1947 until their breakthrough into the big time they honed and polished an act which drew inspiration, and sometimes gags too, from other noted double-acts, particularly the Americans Abbott and Costello and Wheeler and Woolsley (to which pair they bore a remarkable physical resemblance). Later, as their ability and material transcended such ordinary acts, they began paying more attention to the greatest comedy duo of them all: Laurel and Hardy. If they learned the value of quickfire cross-talk from Abbott and Costello, from Laurel and Hardy they learned the more important lesson of developing their characters and allowing the comedy to grow from this. Along the way, entirely fortuitously (indeed, it is something that cannot be deliberately sought), they achieved a similar status in the hearts of British audiences to that occupied by Stan and Ollie. Quite simply, audiences loved them.

Morecambe and Wise's TV shows were much the same as their stage presentations. More than any other TV comics they spoke directly to their audience, many of their best routines taking place in front of the curtain. The sketches in which they indulged were usually plays 'wot Ernie wrote' and made no concessions to a pretence of reality however serious Ernie might try to be. Being serious, never all that easy for this pair, was impossible when Eric's Roman soldier had suspenders holding up his socks. Eric also had the habit of turning to such inanimate props as a statue for a critical verdict on the show demanding, 'What do you think of it so far?' Aided by Eric's unconvincing ventriloquism, the statue would reply, 'Rubbish!'

Then there were the guest stars, to whom Ernie would crawl shamelessly while Eric treated them with contempt and forever managed to get their names wrong. In time, it became a kind of showbiz accolade to appear

Morecambe and Wise, best-loved of British TV comics.

Another play wot Ernie wrote is sabotaged by Eric.

as a guest on *The Morecambe and Wise Show* and be subjected to one indignity after another. André Previn, whose name Eric translated unforgettably into 'Andrew Preview', was obliged to leap into the air while conducting his symphony orchestra so that Eric, who was playing Grieg's Piano Concerto, could see him over the piano lid. Shirley Bassey had to give one of her ultra-dramatic renditions of 'Smoke Gets in Your Eyes' while Eric and Ernie, togged up as a pair of stagehands, attempted to extricate her foot from a hole in the staircase and, having lost her shoe in the process, replaced it with a huge, clumsy, man's boot. And a staircase proved the undoing of Glenda Jackson. Fresh from winning an Oscar for a somewhat more serious film rôle, she participated in a splendid pastiche of an Astaire-Rogers dance routine. Hindered only by Eric's cane, which grew longer and longer throughout, the threesome mounted the staircase for a final flourish. Unfortunately for Glenda, who was one step higher than Eric and Ernie, the staircase didn't lead anywhere and she vanished from sight. On a chat show in 1987 Glenda Jackson remarked, quite seriously, that her appearances with Eric and Ernie had been the highlights of her career.

The sight gags were carefully developed, well-rehearsed and showed a complete grasp of the fundamentals of visual comedy. Not that the duo's scripts showed any signs of weakness in verbal humour. And there was always room for an apparent ad-lib. In the Previn sketch, Eric glanced sideways at the symphony orchestra and asked the obviously scripted question, 'Is this the band?' While the 'band' was still smiling, he slid in a quick musician's joke: 'Which one's the fixer?'

The third regular feature of their shows was one which came closest to the sitcom format. This featured Eric and Ernie at home where Eric would alleviate boredom by sabotaging Ernie's attempts to dash off a couple of plays before lunch. Sometimes he played with children's toys, or spied on a neighbour, Ada Bailey, whose underwear was forever being hung on the line, or slid in a few irreverent one-liners. 'Where's the tea, Ern?' And he never failed to prick Ernie's pomposity.

Ernie: My mother has a Whistler.
Eric: Now there's a novelty.

Sometimes their domestic scenes took place in the bedroom, where Eric and Ernie shared a bed with the same unremarkable propriety displayed by Laurel and Hardy.

Morecambe and Wise stayed at the top throughout the 1960s and on into the 1980s. A change in scriptwriters from Sid Green and Dick Hills to Eddie Braben brought changes of emphasis. Although early in their careers there was a clear division into comic and straight man, this later became much less distinct and both would unselfishly feed the other lines to raise laughs. But there was no let-up in the laughs and the basics of the duo's characters remained unchanged. Ernie was always a bit too pompous for his own good, and Eric, ever ready with a flicker of an eyelid to let the audience know what he was thinking, was a regular mischief-maker. There was about them an endearing sameness that was never dull, never became stale and was always very funny.

Eric Morecambe died in 1984 but the couple's shows are still screened regularly and have become a favourite Christmas feature on both the BBC and the Independent channels, introduced by Ernie Wise. Ernie's own career continues: he played a major stage rôle in the musical version of *The Mystery of Edwin Drood*, and regularly appears on panel games. But some impression of the gap left by his partnership with Eric Morecambe may be gained from the fact that these Christmas screenings are often the best comedy there is to be seen throughout the whole year.

*

American TV comedy in the 1960s was something of a mixed bag. As usual there were scores of new shows but few of them scored a hit in the all-important ratings. For those that did hit the jackpot, however, the bells are still ringing a quarter-century on. *The Dick Van Dyke Show* and *The Beverly Hillbillies* are dealt with later in this book, but these apart there were still some shows that warrant closer examination.

The Andy Griffith Show and *My Three Sons* both began in the 1960-1 season. *Griffith* ran for eight years and when it ended was still topping the ratings; *Sons* ran even longer, clocking up a dozen years but undergoing several format shifts along the way, to say nothing of losing points in the ratings war.

Andy Griffith played the sheriff in Mayberry, a small North Carolina town where because little happened to require his professional abilities he was left free to philosophize about the way of the world. Unlike that earlier cracker-barrel philosopher Will Rogers, Sheriff Andy Taylor invariably told middle-Americans what they most wanted to hear. Life was good, people were good, God was good and so long as everyone remained true to the code by which their parents had lived all would be well.

Outside in the real world, 1960s America was filled with the crashing changes that made the decade the most painful in the nation's recent history: the tail end of the Beat Generation, hippies, flower power, the assassination of President John F. Kennedy,

desegregation of schools, Martin Luther King, the beginnings of the plunge into the Vietnam War.

For all it showed of these events, sleepy Mayberry could have been on another planet. There, like some nostalgic dream of a yesteryear that never was, life went on its typical sitcom way. No one got hurt, demonstrated, or went barefoot with flowers in their hair — hair which, incidentally, was clean and, for the men at least, never too long. No-siree-bob!

My Three Sons, which starred Fred MacMurray, was similarly all-American in style and presentation. Widower Steve Douglas (MacMurray's character) brought up his three sons with the assistance of their grandfather (played by William Frawley, formerly Fred Mertz of *I Love Lucy*) and was later helped by Uncle Charley (William Demarest).

Steve Douglas and his family lived in a town named Bryant Park, which was an urban version of Mayberry. It was quiet, easy-going and free from hassles. Maybe the big cities of real America were plagued by muggers, riots and all kinds of dissatisfaction, unrest and violence, but small-town America was still innocent and trusting and glowing with love, companionship and apple-pie innocence. At least, it was according to television.

The 1961-2 season saw the appearance of Nat Hiken's follow up to *Bilko*. A cop show like no other cop show before it (and precious few afterwards, although *Barney Miller* would come close in the 1970s), *Car 54, Where Are You?* extended the superbly scripted lunacy of Hiken's forerunner into the setting of New York's Finest. Unlike *Bilko* where, Colonel Hall apart, there were sometimes brains beneath the khaki, the protagonists of *Car 54* were decidedly lacking in grey matter beneath their blues.

Leading this anarchic romp through a New York which appeared remarkably free of serious crime were Joe E. Ross and Fred Gwynne as Gunther Toody and Francis Muldoon. Ross had been Mess Sergeant Rupert Ritzik in *Bilko*, in which Fred Gwynne had also done a couple of guest spots; Gwynne would later go on to play Herman in *The Munsters*. Toody was stupid, but lovably so, and his partner, while clearly much more

Toody and Muldoon: mutually astounded at so much stupidity in one police car, Joe E. Ross takes it easy in Car 54 while Fred Gwynne stretches his legs.

Gwynne in *The Munsters*, and there was always a sprinkling of *Bilko* faces in the cast. One was Beatrice Pons, who had played Ross's 'wife' in *Bilko* and continued to do so in *Car 54*. As before, she perpetually nagged her erring husband in the impossible hope of improving him. Toody was resigned to his rôle in their marriage:

When we got married, every morning Lucille would ask me what I want for dinner. Now, not only does she not ask me what I want for dinner, she won't even tell me what I ate.

Nat Hiken's love of boxing, which had resulted in several ex-pugs turning up in *Bilko*, made its presence felt in *Car 54* too. One episode featured former champions Rocky Graziano and Sugar Ray Robinson in acting rôles, while Jake La Motta turned up on a number of occasions.

The show ran for only two seasons, but re-runs keep it alive. In 1987 *Car 54* and its occupants could be seen all over American TV and also on Britain's Channel 4, still driving amiably around the Bronx and with Toody still greeting the unexpected arrival of an idea in his head with an excited, 'Ooh, ooh!'

Midway through the 1960s someone had the bright idea of cashing in on the fact that there was fun to be had in parodying the plethora of espionage movies being churned out in Hollywood and, especially, in Britain. Admittedly, the James Bond movies had their tongue ever so slightly in their cheek, but there was room for improvement.

The show was written by Mel Brooks, who had completed his stint on Sid Caesar's shows but had yet to find fame in Hollywood, and Buck Henry, who would later write the screenplay for the 1967 movie *The Graduate*.

Like the movies that provided its impetus, *Get Smart!* featured a hero bent on solving incredible problems and defeating arch-villains who wanted to take over the world. Unlike the movies, the hero was no superman but a well-meaning incompetent who screwed up every time the Chief sent him on a case. Smart he wasn't but his name was Maxwell Smart, Agent 86, played by Don Adams. His assistant, Agent 99, was played by Barbara Feldon and the Chief by Edward Platt.

The show's scripts bristled with snappy

intelligent, somehow always managed to end up being equally dumb. Needless to say, the country's police forces were not amused — officially, that is. Unofficially, the cops loved the show just as much as everyone else did.

Captain Martin Block (played by Paul Reed), upon whom Toody and Muldoon were inflicted, suffered more than any precinct captain had a right to expect until Captain Furillo faced a somewhat more realistic crime wave with more realistic (but still humorous) cops in *Hill Street Blues*. Toody and Muldoon's fellow patrolmen included Leo Schnauzer, played by Al Lewis, who later co-starred with one-liners and every step taken by Smart and 99 was threatened by well-executed sight gags. The entire show was conducted at a smart canter and seen again more than 20 years afterwards it stands up rather better than the movies it parodied.

As Smart prepares for a dangerous assignment in Latin America the Chief urges caution:

Chief: There's one supreme danger you've got to be on guard against every moment.
Smart: What's that, Chief?
Chief: The entire time you're there — don't drink the water.

Smart faces a villain holding a hat who declares: 'And now — a little magic trick.' To Smart's amazement the villain pulls a rabbit from the hat, then pulls a gun from the rabbit. 'The old gun-in-the-rabbit trick — and I fell for it.' The trigger is pulled and a flame pops up. Smart isn't at all fazed by this development. 'Ah — it's the old lighter-gun-in-the-rabbit trick — and I fell for it.'

Apart from simply enjoying good-natured, well-written and performed comedy the sharp-eyed latterday viewer may also spot a young Stacy Keach, who played one of Agent 86's associates in several episodes.

Perhaps as a side-effect of America's real-life adventures in space, or maybe just as a result of the national addiction to comic books and newspaper 'funnies', the idea of sitcoms set in fantasyland was awakened during the 1960s.

Martin, an early version of ET, landed on Earth in 1963 and met up with a young reporter named Tim O'Hara. Played with waspish delight by Ray Walston, Martin the Martian was a great favourite with the kids (upper age limit 75) and stayed close to the top of the ratings for three years. The actor who played Tim, Bill Bixby, went on to 'serious' fantasy TV shows including *The Magician* and *The Incredible Hulk*.

When *My Favourite Martian* folded in 1966 it left quite a hole and no one really plugged the gap until after Steven Spielberg had come along to remake Hollywood in his own childhood imagery and reawaken interest in science fiction. TV would then of course have its own reawakening with *Mork and Mindy*.

In Get Smart *Agent 86 (Don Adams) used more hardware than James Bond.*

Herman and Lily Munster risk giving themselves nightmares (Yvonne De Carlo, Fred Gwynne).

With the kind of coincidence that must induce galloping paranoia among network executives, two horror-comic fantasies appeared right on top of one another in 1964. *The Addams Family* was based upon cartoon characters created by Charles Addams while *The Munsters* amiably spoofed all the old Frankenstein and Dracula movies.

The Addamses included Gomez and Morticia (John Astin and Carolyn Jones) and one-time child star Jackie Coogan as Uncle Fester. Coogan had made his name in the title rôle of the 1921 Charlie Chaplin movie, *The Kid*, before falling on hard times as an adult. Despite Astin's hat-peg eyes and Uncle Fester's death's-head make-up and cackling voice, the Addamses were not very scary at all. Indeed, Carolyn Jones was elegant enough to pass unnoticed, except for complimentary remarks, in any New York nightclub.

Morticia's counterpart in *The Munsters* was Yvonne De Carlo as Lily and she too was not especially horrific. But then, neither was Fred Gwynne's monstrous Herman. Complete with Boris Karloff make-up and huge boots which enhanced his natural 6 feet 7 inches, he was the most easy-going monster anyone could ever hope to meet on a not-too-dark night. In place of an uncle, the Munsters had a Grandpa (played by Al Lewis, who had worked with Gwynne on *Car 54*).

In the same year that the Addamses and the Munsters materialized from the outer darkness another fantasy sitcom appeared. Unlike the other two shows this one featured a family who looked normal. In all respects save one they were. The exception was that Samantha Stevens was a witch: one twitch of her nose and anything could happen.

Playing Samantha in *Bewitched* was Elizabeth Montgomery, daughter of movie actor Robert; she was aided and abetted by her mother, Endora (Agnes Moorehead), and an array of witch and warlock relatives including the delightfully bumbling Aunt Clara (Marion Lorne), who was forever forgetting her magic spells, usually when she was halfway through one.

As one-joke sitcoms go this one wasn't bad for a short run. Unfortunately, it ran for eight years, which is a bit too long for one joke.

The 1965 fantasy *I Dream of Jeannie* starred Barbara Eden as Jeannie, who happened to be a genie, and Larry Hagman as astronaut Tony Nelson, who found the bottle inside which she was trapped when he crash-landed on a Pacific island. Another one-joke show, this one ran until 1970, after which Mr Hagman was free to prepare for his later TV rôle as JR in *Dallas*. One curiosity about *I Dream of Jeannie*, raised by Rick Mitz, still requires further investigation. Jeannie wears a costume that leaves her stomach bare. So where's her navel?

American sitcoms of the 1960s produced any number of also-rans which occasionally offered moments of enjoyment. Elaine Stritch and Jim Backus had shows and so too did the movie veteran Pat O'Brien. Male pin-up Tab Hunter tried to make the grade but failed while a show about a talking horse, *Mr Ed*, starring Alan Young, ran for six years (a success countered by a show featuring two humans bringing up three chimpanzees, and which quickly fell out of the tree). Broadway star

Shirley Booth made *Hazel* and dancer Gene Kelly followed in Bing Crosby's clerical collar with *Going My Way*, but not for long. Not to be outdone, Bing himself turned up in a sitcom about a singing electrician but failed to convince either audiences or networks that this was what he was best at.

Two British actors who tried their luck in America were Glynis Johns in *Glynis* and Stanley Holloway in *Our Man Higgins*, but neither lasted long. Much more successful was *Petticoat Junction*, a *Beverly Hillbillies* spin-off, which ran for seven years. George Burns took an unsuccessful fling with *Wendy and Me*; so too did Mickey Rooney, Red Buttons, Walter Brennan and John Forsythe (before his hair turned blue and he became *Dynasty*'s Blake Carrington). Brennan and Forsythe also tried one together, *To Rome with Love*, but with no better luck.

The Monkees were a made-to-measure pop group whose series was modelled very loosely upon Richard Lester's Beatles movie *A Hard Day's Night. He and She* starred real-life married movie actors Richard Benjamin and Paula Prentiss, but though it benefited from witty dialogue and good performances it lasted only a season. Other movie-star vehicles included *The Doris Day Show* and *The Debbie Reynolds Show*.

Then there was Sally Field. Long before she grew up to embarrass millions with her acceptance speech for her second Oscar, Ms Field was embarrassing even more millions in a succession of abysmal TV sitcoms.

First for Ms Field was *Gidget*, which started life as a movie starring Sandra Dee and was about surfers in Southern California. The trouble was that if you've seen one wave you've seen 'em all, and the show was washed out to sea after one season. Sally survived to play a supporting rôle in *Hey, Landlord!* and then rose above it all in 1967's *The Flying Nun*, which had the dubious accolade of being 'approved' by the Church. Despite fervent prayers it didn't do too well but Sally swallowed her pride, primed her dimples and tried again in 1973 with *The Girl with Something Extra*, in which, contrary to the show's title, she soon proved that she hadn't.

Shortly afterwards Sally gave up TV sitcoms for Hollywood feature films. When she

You can bet your sweet bippy that Dan Rowan and Dick Martin's Laugh-in *was anything but televised radio.*

managed to immerse herself in her rôles long enough to stop being twee she produced some superb acting performances, notably in *Sybil* (actually a TV mini-series), which won her a deserved Emmy in 1977; *Norma Rae*, for which she received a Cannes Best Actress award and an Academy Award in 1975; *Places in the Heart* brought her second Oscar, in 1984. And, of course, that dreadful speech. 'The first time I didn't feel it, but this time I feel it and I can't deny the fact you like me — right now, you *like* me.' Maybe some do; others can still remember her before she kicked her flying habit in sitcom-land.

In 1987 Sally's Sister Bertrille was still swooping across America's TV channels thanks to re-runs of *The Flying Nun* while, heaven help us all, a new show entitled *New Gidget*, starring Sydney Penny, was also available to the undiscerning viewer.

The show which tried hardest to change the pattern of TV comedy in America in the 1960s was *Rowan and Martin's Laugh-in*. Although looking terribly dated on re-runs, at the time it seemed like a ground-breaker. In fact, it had returned to the old revue format of the stage, but considerably speeded up in the manner of

Two Laugh-In *regulars, Ruth Buzzi and Arte Johnson, in one of their Gladys and Tyrone sketches.*

an animated cartoon. Dick Martin: 'Up until then there had been televised radio and televised vaudeville ... but it was never an electronic use of the material.'

With quick-fire gags, a constantly shifting and brightly lit and decorated set, the show was one of few that brought a measure of political awareness to American TV screens. By 1980s standards the political and satirical content seems minimal, but in its time it offered something more than yet another dreary sitcom manufactured in the happy-families mould. The show gave early breaks to several young people, among them Judy Carne, the 'Sock-it-to-me' girl, Lily Tomlin and Goldie Hawn, and also attracted guest personalities, including Sammy Davis Jr, John Wayne and Richard Nixon.

Laugh-in was, however, one of few exceptions to the rule that in both Britain and America TV comedy usually came in the form of situation comedy.

In sitcoms the shift away from using comics to using actors became steadily more pronounced. The use of actors proved to be very helpful to the best writers, who were consequently able to develop their creations with considerably greater depth and sublety than when catering for an established comic persona. The success of these sitcoms also depended in part upon the skill of the casting department in fitting the right face and personality to the script, and on audiences' acceptance of these actors into their homes as regular visitors.

The tentativeness of the 1950s had been replaced in the new decade by a greater confidence. The veterans of radio and vaudeville and variety stages were still around but had been outnumbered by those straight actors and television performers with no comparable track record in other fields ... outnumbered, maybe, but a long way from being overwhelmed.

CHAPTER FOUR

WHATEVER BECAME OF THE STAND-UP COMIC?

'Now there's a funny thing.'
Max Miller

With the effective death in the 1960s of the variety-theatre circuit in Britain those stand-up comics who did not make the transition to television found increasingly lucrative work in working-men's clubs. They and their successors built up good but often parochial followings. In 1971 some of them were given an opportunity to appear before a bigger audience thanks to Granada TV's *The Comedians.*

Usually fast-talking, often abrasive and irreverent, the comics played their routines before a studio audience and the cameras. The results were then edited to offer the viewer a non-stop stream of jokes, cutting back and forth between individual comics, many of whom became, though sometimes only fleetingly, nationally famous as a result.

Among them was Bernard Manning, a burly northern club-owner who steamrollers any finer sensibilities his audience might possess with a steady barrage of insults. Another was Charlie Williams, one of very few black comedians in Britain, and whose physical appearance contrasts vividly with his strong Yorkshire accent. Although dominated by northerners, probably due to Granada's northern base and the fact that the club scene itself was much stronger in the north than elsewhere in Britain, *The Comedians* also featured a good smattering of Irishmen, including Ulster comic Frank Carson. This helped ameliorate the wearisome Paddy and 'Paki' jokes abounding at the time and which threatened to unbalance the show. Mike Reid

was one of the few southerners to appear.

Sharply edited as it was for *The Comedians*, the work of many of these comics looked better than it might have done live on stage. Later exposure in shows of their own or as game-show hosts proved that for some their original milieu, the clubland setting of noisy, smoke-filled rooms and punters having a good time at all costs was the right place for them. Television was not. A different brand of comic was given his head on *Jokers Wild*. This group, of whom Ted Ray was the outstanding example, proved not only better and quicker-witted than their latterday counterparts but also displayed great enthusiasm for one another's material. Perhaps it was the result of that snappy editing, but *The Comedians* always seemed uncongenial by comparison.

Other newer names who make regular appearances on British screens as singles but who built their careers largely outside television include Jasper Carrott, Mike Harding, Max Boyce and Billy Connolly, all of whom came out of the folk-club circuit.

Birmingham comedian Bob Davies changed his name to Jasper Carrott and became famous — though not quite as easily as that, of course. Carrott's stage technique reveals a layer of engaging charm beneath a slightly brittle exterior, which serves him well on television where the camera looks a little deeper than theatre audiences may. His routine consists largely of extended anecdotes about real places peopled with recognizable if eccentric men and women. He gains his

Dave Allen, master of a casually intimate style.

laughs from making his audience recognize the manifest absurdities of everyday life. Jack Waterman, writing in *The Listener*, has referred to Carrott's ability to jab his audience in the ribs by means of such dismissive techniques: for instance, in a terse condemnation of a place which could stand for Anytown, he remarks:

If you're passing through Solihull … and most people do … well, there's not much to do there … though, of course you can always sit at the front window and watch the smoke from the crematorium…

Carrott's originally localized reputation spread rapidly after his LWT series *An Audience with Jasper Carrott*. Unlike many of the younger generation of comics, he found an ability to attract alien souls who had never ventured into his home territory, the Midlands. An early reliance on football jokes was swiftly expanded to accommodate his wider audience and by the time of his later series for the BBC he was extremely popular.

Mike Harding, from Salford, is another

anecdotal comic; in his case the anecdotes tend to become lengthy sagas which pile improbability upon absurdity until the structure of the piece creaks dangerously. Unlike those of other monologuists, Harding's tales seldom have a central point or progress to a logical conclusion. Indeed, some are so long and there are so many well-timed laughs along the way that his audience often loses track of how, where and why the tale began. Like Jasper Carrott's, Harding's television work is frequently a filmed version of a stage performance and he too gives the impression that he is more comfortable with an audience he can see.

Max Boyce's reputation outside his native Wales is largely restricted to filmed club appearances where his tales, built as they are upon the quasi-religious respect the Welsh have for rugby football, sometimes prove to have limited potential.

Glasgow's Billy Connolly burst upon unsuspecting Sassenachs with a line in scatology that confirmed for many all they had always suspected about Scotsmen in general and Glaswegians in particular. In fact Connolly's routines demonstrate an acute observer's eye and a secure grasp of the fine line which daily separates contemporary inner-city dwellers from the abyss. His more recent decision to enter motion pictures could prove a mistake. The presence of a live audience is an essential element in the success of many comics, Connolly included.

Ken Dodd, too, is essentially a man of the theatre, where his control over his audience is truly extraordinary. On television, although he always works with a studio audience, the gap between him and the millions watching at home causes some problems. To some extent he overcomes these by shifting the balance of his TV work from what he does in the theatre. Music, colour, dance, spectacle and his Diddy Men all help add up to performances which are very much in the tradition of the variety show.

Much more attuned to the intimate nature of television is Dave Allen, whose television shows have two distinct components: monologue and sketches. These sketches are in the revue format but his main target, organized religion, gives the show an edge lacking in

Ken Dodd, zany dominator of a live audience.

Les Dawson, acutely pessimistic — when he isn't being wildly lustful.

are so awful they become mesmeric. Only rarely are the proceedings illuminated with any hint of intelligence, and when that does happen it is often thanks to a comic.

Back in the 1950s in America Groucho Marx hosted the smash-hit show *You Bet Your Life.* Although essentially a quiz show, audiences tuned in not for the vicarious thrill of seeing their fellows win prizes but to hear them innocently set up Groucho's quicksilver ad libs:

'What do you do?'

'I drive a Yellow Cab.'

'The cabs in this town aren't yellow, they'll attack anybody.'

Bruce Forsythe's take-no-prisoners style of comedy.

many others which utilize the revue style.

Apart from commenting sharply on religion, Allen's monologues dig mercilessly at sexual mores. Unlike many American and British comics who take swings at similar targets, Allen is much more incisive, far more perceptive, and also contrives to make his attacks without recourse to vulgarity. As a result, his shows are watched and listened to by people who might well turn off a cruder practitioner within the first few minutes. He is a rare kind of comedian and, as his success continues into the late 1980s, it is hard to see anyone coming along who is likely to improve upon his particular style.

Many who have made their names as stand-up comics continue practising their craft in the 1980s in the ubiquitous game shows. Mostly American in origin, these tend to vary from weak to abysmal, including some which

Roy Castle, who learned his trade on the variety halls.

Quiz and game shows in Britain differ from their American counterparts only in the value and quality of the prizes. In the early years of television, possibly due partly to historical factors but more especially to the relative poverty of post-war Britain, quiz shows followed the same general premise upon which the British have long conducted their sporting encounters: that it should be enough just to take part. Things haven't changed much, as a glance at almost any game show of the late 1980s will testify.

Les Dawson hosts *Blankety Blank*, which he wisely sends up by perpetually demeaning the show, the prizes and the guest celebrities. Dawson's lugubrious manner, his soggy-dumpling appearance and his strong line in pessimistic humour make his one of the few 'different' talents among TV comics. In fact, Dawson draws heavily upon the old-time comics: Norman Evans, Frank Randle, Robb Wilton, Dave Morris and Jimmy James, amalgamating their mannerisms and style into his own gloomy personality. Over the years Dawson, a fully paid-up misogynist, has mercilessly pilloried mothers-in-law: 'I knew my mother-in-law was coming to stay when the mice started throwing themselves on the traps.' He isn't too kind about former girlfriends either: 'I once courted a girl who was so small, when she hitched her knickers up she blindfolded herself.'

Bruce Forsyth also became best known as a game-show host. Since his stint on *Sunday Night at the London Palladium* with its 'Beat the Clock' competition he has worked for long periods in such shows as *The Generation Game* and *Play Your Cards Right*, none of which extends him very much. An all-round entertainer, able to dance and play the piano well, he appears content to remain becalmed in game shows despite occasional forays into the sitcom world. His lack of conviction in such shows as *Slinger's Day* is largely an effect of his inability or unwillingness to subordinate his aggressive stage personality to the co-operative demands of an acting rôle.

Roy Castle is another multi-talented performer who also appears on game shows and such specialist programmes as *Record Breakers*, which is aimed at the school-age audience. Castle spent a number of years working on the stage with master comedian Jimmy James in order to hone his own comic timing, even though he was already established as a solo act.

Leslie Crowther presents *The Price Is Right*, a show whose popularity increases in direct proportion to its rising fatuousness. Crowther has also appeared in a number of mediocre sitcoms but the runaway success of this particular game show presumably means he is happy to remain in the undemanding world where the public does all the work.

The laboured repartee displayed in most of these shows suggests that very little is

Ted Rogers (top left) has succeeded where many performers from British TV have failed: with American audiences. In Britain, however, he is best-known for his appearance on 3-2-1, a game show which he devised.

John Inman (left) reached his widest audience through the sitcom Are You Being Served? He is also a popular dame in pantomime, an area of showbiz which was once threatened but rescued by the simple yet effective device of putting top TV names into the starring rôles.

Leslie Crowther (above, when young) forsook sitcoms to host The Price Is Right.

Jim Davidson (right) first appeared on TV as a stand-up comic before moving into sitcoms such as Home James!, *which showcase his brash Cockney character.*

The lasting popularity of Mike Yarwood (left) is a tribute to his achievement in lifting the craft of the impressionist out of the rut of endless movie-star parodies to include politicians, sportsmen, union leaders and even TV weather forecasters. All are now likely targets for accurate, sometimes rather acid, lampooning.

Bob Monkhouse, quickest-witted of British comics.

ad-libbed. Were he to return, Groucho would have the field almost to himself with perhaps the only serious challenge coming from Bob Monkhouse. By far the quickest-witted of the comics to feature in Britain's game-show scene of recent years, Monkhouse started out as a scriptwriter (originally in partnership with Denis Goodwin, with whom he wrote for Bob Hope). He has also been a stand-up comic and occasional sitcom performer. He suffered a bad press in his early years from critics who disliked his manner. Audiences seemed much less aware of any shortcomings, real or imagined, and he proved a huge success on *The Golden Shot, Family Fortunes* and *Bob's Full House.*

As a chat-show host (*The Bob Monkhouse Show*) he, like Des O'Connor in his show, makes a point of bringing to British audiences top-line American comedians, new and old, who are virtually unknown outside their own country. In such encounters Monkhouse happily gives his visitors their heads but if drawn into a verbal exchange shows himself

difficult to top. Interestingly, Monkhouse has made it clear in interviews that although those early criticisms still rankle he is continually looking for new ways to expand and develop his comedy, even after 40 years in the business. In a 1986 *Radio Times* article he revealed his regret that he had never made an audience feel nervous or insecure in the way that such artists as Judy Garland and Tommy Cooper could: 'If you give the audience more, let them see you're vulnerable, you're not letting yourself down: you're giving an extra dimension to comedy.'

Among the ways in which new artists can perform before a national audience is the talent show. In Britain Hughie Greene's *Opportunity Knocks* followed the pattern of Carroll Levis's radio show, on which Barry Took was 'discovered', and his later television shows, and the Major Bowes show in America. Among the many artists who were given an early break on Greene's show were Les Dawson and Freddie 'Parrot Face' Davies.

Another talent show, *New Faces*, also helped boost the careers of numerous comics including Lenny Henry, Jim Davidson and Marti Caine, one of the few female successes in the field of solo comedy. She has subsequently hosted a later version of the show.

Lenny Henry began as an impressionist before demonstrating a much wider talent. In *Three of a Kind* he worked with two other young artists, David Copperfield and Tracey Ullman. Henry, Caine, Ullman and Davidson have all extended their range by taking part in sitcoms. Caine made *Hilary*, Ullman was in *Girls on Top* and Davidson starred in *Up the Elephant and Round the Castle* and *Home, James.* The demands of the sitcom, notably the subordination of personality to character, script and fellow actors, have doubtless helped them polish their stage personalities.

The move made by these three also suggests a possible trend: after years of actors playing in situation comedies, perhaps the comics are now coming back. If they are to move from their usual acts into sitcoms successfully they will have to remember that even if they are the stars, they are just one member of a team. Obviously, those with powerful egos will have more trouble making this adjustment than others.

Among other latterday TV comedy acts which continue an old tradition brought to television in the 1950s are the impressionists and ventriloquists.

Impressionists have always relied heavily upon comics for their routines and, while by nature a supporting act, they frequently achieve star status. Among the impressionists who have been given their own shows are Lenny Henry, Bobby Davro, Freddie Starr, Faith Brown, Russ Abbot and Mike Yarwood.

The best of this bunch is Yarwood, whose forte is the accurate depiction of particular characteristics which often are then picked up by other impressionists. More than anyone in Britain Yarwood, like Rich Little in America, has extended the impressionist's range — into politics, for example, and other walks of public life. In some cases this has, however, resulted in endless impressions of James Cagney giving way to endless impressions of current political figures.

In terms of comedy, the perennial problem for impressionists is that the very nature of their work inhibits originality. Consequently, the minor talents among them are doomed to spend their admittedly well-paid years mouthing other artists' catchphrases in order to draw the quick, cheap laughs of instant recognition.

Ventriloquists can be original and, indeed, the creation of a comic character physically apart from the performer makes for an interesting diversion. In recent years there has been a clear division into two camps: those whose dolls are cute, cuddly (and frequently sickening) little animals and those whose stage partners are miniature partners in a double-act. Only the latter really follow the comedian's path. They continue a long and distinguished tradition which encompassed in the early years of television such performers as Sandy Powell and Harry Worth (who was advised by no less an authority than Stan Laurel to give up venting in favour of solo comedy). More recently, Ray Alan has had considerable success. Indeed, Alan's career covers a wide range of TV comedy. As noted earlier he wrote scripts for *Bootsie and Snudge* and he also hosts the game show *Three Little Words*.

Two more faces of Mike Yarwood.

Vent acts, like the impressionists, are among the few remaining traditions of the variety theatre to be regularly seen on TV. Essentially they, like the stand-up comic, belong to a different world from that of the sitcom which presently dominates TV comedy.

Another world or not, stand-up comics are an important part of the fabric of show business. Even if television does not always offer them the best setting for their work they are unlikely to die off – which is just as well, for it is from this breed of entertainer that much original material enters the wider world of TV comedy.

CHAPTER FIVE

JUST AN AVERAGE FAMILY

'Hi, honey, I'm home!'

The most common form of TV sitcom in the 1950s was set in the home of an average family. Today, the commonest setting is still the home, although not all the families depicted would be recognized as such by participants in earlier programmes.

In America, Ozzie and Harriet might well feel at home with the Keatons but they would surely find it hard to adjust to the peculiarities of life with Archie Bunker. In Britain, the Larkins would easily slip their feet beneath the table with Terry and June — but could they cope with the Young Ones?

In the beginning, the family as mainstay of American sitcom-land was popular with sponsor, network and public — in that order.

The sponsor liked it because it offered on-screen the kind of unit at which he was aiming his off-screen products: a husband with a job and a wife ready and willing to spend the fruits of his labours.

The average sitcom family of those early TV days consisted of a husband, his wife and their children. He was the nominal head of the household, working 9 to 5 to provide the money; she was a happily scatterbrained stay-at-home who would spend the money on their gadget-filled, wall-to-wall-carpeted, seemingly unmortgaged home, on their bright and cheerful young children, on him and (but only if there was anything left over) on herself — and then it was usually a fluffy triviality like a hat because that, in sitcom-land, was the sort of thing women really wanted out of life.

As for the children, in the early years of sitcom they were often there simply to make up the numbers. The youngest kids in those days had little to say and when a line of dialogue was tossed their way it was generally delivered in a squeaky monotone while the child stared rigidly off-camera at, one supposes, either an idiot-card or a doting, showbiz-fixated parent-cum-coach.

The oldest children, while having similarly little to say, were used more frequently as a plot device to allow Mom or, more usually, Dad to deliver the Moral.

The work the husband did was seldom relevant to the show; it was enough that he had a regular job. (Ozzie Nelson was something of an odd man out in this respect; what *did* he do for a living?) In his attitude towards his wife and family the husband was quaintly anachronistic, even in the 1950s, and steadily became even more so as times changed and he didn't. He was, and remains in many shows, the protectively traditional breadwinner going bravely out into the wide world every day. In many instances the job is necessary in order to get the husband figure off the set so that the plot line, which generally pivots around the wife, can progress. In *I Love Lucy* in 1950s America Desi Arnaz did at least have a job that was helpful in terms of the show: he was a bandleader and a scene showing him at work could therefore make an entertaining interpolation, a musical interlude and, not infrequently, an opportunity for further exploits on the part of the wife/star. Thirty years on in suburban Britain, the husband's job in

Wendy Craig, star of many highly popular comedy series.

Butterflies is still irrelevant and Ben ventures dolefully to his dental surgery merely to give Ria an opportunity to mope around the house devising ways in which she might manoeuvre herself into a moment of painfully chaste contact with her boyfriend.

In the earlier traditional family-oriented sitcom the Little Woman usually stayed home content in her cocoon and with nothing more serious to trouble her pretty little head than whether or not the chocolate chips would melt before the cookies were baked. It says much for the power exerted by centuries of male domination that some understandably aggravated females didn't bomb a few network headquarters long before Mary Richards joined station WJM-TV in Minneapolis and set about making the first major changes in the world of women in sitcom-land in *The Mary Tyler Moore Show*.

The sponsors' approval of the subservient rôle of women in those early shows is easy to understand. For one thing, the prevailing attitude displayed towards women preserved the *status quo*. The sponsors were aware that despite their second-class rôle in American life it was women who spent the money. The format accommodated them by making TV wives generally lovable and the husbands amiably incapable of making such significant decisions as when the house needed refurnishing or the washing-machine replacing. It is no coincidence that many sitcom scenes were shot in kitchens – a cross-check with sponsors who manufactured kitchen equipment shows why. Indeed, it was often hard to see the join between the show and the commercials which similarly extolled the virtues of the consumer society.

The networks liked these shows simply because the sponsors were happy; the public liked them because, as sponsors and network well knew, the TV audience can be very easily manipulated into liking that which is predictable – or simply that which appears on the screen whichever damn button is pressed.

The problem with much of the huge mass of family-based sitcoms, shows which Marty Feldman dubbed a 'strange mongrel entertainment, sired by the comedy sketch out of the soap opera', is that it was, and still is, bland and predictable fodder for mass consumption. Feldman continued: 'Aimed at the "average" family for easy identification, it hits nowhere, since its conception of the "average" anything exists only in the minds of hucksters of one sort or another.'

The most popular early American family sitcoms remain virtually unknown to British audiences. By the time that ownership of TV sets was widespread in Britain such shows as *The Goldbergs, Mama* and *The Adventures of Ozzie and Harriet* were already losing favour. Their non-appearance in Britain was not all due to unfortunate timing; other contemporary shows (*I Love Lucy*, for example) made the transition to British TV screens. Reasons for this, discussed elsewhere in this book, included ethnicity and plain old-fashioned differences between American and British humour, which appeared to be much greater then than now.

Ozzie Nelson and Harriet Hilliard were both experienced entertainers who were married back in 1935. He was a bandleader who also sang; Harriet sang with the band.

They began their family show on radio in 1944, maintaining a semblance of reality by having him play a bandleader and her a singer. After a feature film they moved to TV in 1952, by which time the bandleader-singer rôles were no longer viable and had disappeared, leaving Ozzie seemingly without visible means of support.

The show's pace was relaxed to the point of being somnambulistic. Of Ozzie's singing with his band in the 1930s, George T. Simon, writer and critic of *Metronome* magazine, wrote: 'Falling asleep in the middle of a Nelson vocal chorus was by no means an impossibility. Sometimes I wondered if Ozzie would ever do it himself.' Crises arose, of course (how else would sitcom writers get into the commercial break?), but they were never serious matters or, indeed, anything that was likely to impinge on the lives of the general public.

The Nelsons' kids really were their own, not that this initially overcame the inevitable rotten acting, and in 1957 son Ricky sang a song on the show which promptly went into the charts. Very soon thereafter Ricky Nelson followed in Mom and Dad's footsteps to become a singing star in his own right but, being a rock 'n' roller, he was somewhat livelier than either Ozzie or Harriet. The built-in nepotism persisted when Ricky married Kris and the other son, David, married June. Both ladies joined the cast as — what else? — their wives. The show ran for 14 years and somewhere in America, thanks to the glories of syndication, it's still running.

Father Knows Best first appeared in 1954 and, with movie star Robert Young in the leading rôle of Jim Anderson, immediately picked up a devoted following. The kiddie-count went up marginally for this one. Jim and his wife Margaret (played by Jane Wyatt, who was also a movie star) had two girls and a boy. Father also knew better than Ozzie and had a comfortably middle-class job as manager of an insurance company.

The key to the success enjoyed by the series was the fact that this father really did know best, but not in an aggressive, whip-cracking manner. Jim Anderson was warm and affectionate yet manly; worldly-wise but home-loving. The family played together and thus stayed together; they shared problems and thus overcame them; Margaret and her daughters were truly feminine and agreed without demur that father, and men in general, really did know best; the son was a true chip off the old block and would one day step into dad's shoes and run his own life, family and insurance company with comparable élan. In short, the Andersons were as gruesomely unreal as it is possible to be. Worse still, every show had a Moral. Yet the Andersons somehow struck powerful empathetic chords in a substantial slice of American society.

It cannot be entirely coincidental that the 1950s were a time when the American nation underwent several major crises: war in Korea; red scares; McCarthyism. The calming paternalism emanating from the White House, where Dwight Eisenhower was in charge, was seized upon by middle-Americans as though it were a life-preserver. Jim Anderson mirrored this paternalism and focused it down into family size for easy digestion. What the show never did was engage the problems of Real Life. When boats were sinking all around them there was no way sponsors and networks would risk rocking theirs.

The show ended in 1960, which was probably just as well; Jim would have had a hard time preserving his smug equanimity in the face of hippies and flower power and would have had a coronary at the first whiff of the marijuana-laden atmosphere of the decade which followed.

Beginning in 1961, another family-based sitcom emerged on American TV which proved to have great staying power and to gain enormous popularity in Britain. Lurking beneath its seemingly 'normal' skin were several factors which made it very different from its predecessors and which were to have a lasting effect on TV sitcom in general. Nevertheless, the surface of *The Dick Van Dyke Show* suggests a broad similarity to many family sitcoms.

The similarities include the husband-wife-son family unit; even the small boy playing Richie Petrie was a typically bad, but fortunately not whining, child actor. Husband Rob Petrie, played by Van Dyke, was very much in the 'Hi, honey, I'm home' tradition; wife Laura, played by Mary Tyler Moore, was similarly traditional in that she was smart, possibly smarter than her husband, but stayed home all day while he went out to earn the money for her to spend, etc., etc.

Among the differences was Rob Petrie's job. As chief scriptwriter for a TV comic he was placed decidedly outside the 'average' occupational grouping of the audience. Scenes showing him at work were a regular feature, which added a dimension lacking in most other shows of the period. These scenes, in which he was teamed with his two scriptwriting colleagues Buddy Sorrel and Sally Rogers (sparklingly played by Morey Amsterdam and Rose Marie), provided countless well-taken opportunities for hard-edged wisecracking of the kind normally reserved for nightclub audiences, even if it was here cleaned up for home consumption.

Amsterdam, a highly regarded stand-up comic, was already a TV veteran. In 1949 he had hosted a variety show and in 1950 was host on *Broadway Open House*, a nightly show which predated *The Tonight Show*, the series which was eventually to embalm Johnny Carson in a curious kind of idolatory. Rose Marie had been a child star and was one of the few women comics to hold her own in yet another male-dominated area of show business, the nightclub scene. She also appeared on Broadway and co-starred with Phil Silvers in *Top Banana*. She based her characterization for tough-talking Sally on Selma Diamond, who wrote scripts for Sid Caesar.

The wisecracking style of writing on *Dick Van Dyke* was also a significant difference between this and other shows of the time and one which is rarely seen in sitcom scripts; indeed, such scripts do not usually contain jokes. If the best shows find their humour in the characters, with the also-rans finding it in the situation, this show managed to do both. Humour arose primarily from character but the scripts also took advantage of the 'situation' to allow the legitimate inclusion of wisecracks.

Although not apparent at the time, the major factor in stretching the boundaries of TV comedy which first appeared in the show was a member of the cast. Mary Tyler Moore was virtually unknown to national audiences when she joined the show. At least she was unknown by name, although millions saw her as the

Happy Hotpoint Elf in a TV commercial and she played Sam in *Richard Diamond*, a popular detective series starring David Janssen in which only her legs were seen. Soon, however, she was a major TV face, figure and personality. The popularity she enjoyed with Van Dyke served her well for the future.

Just as Jim Anderson's paternalism had struck chords with 1950s families, so the family of the 1960s found points of contact with Rob Petrie. The fact of his above-average job did not matter, any more than it mattered that the new occupants of the White House came from America's richest families. The Kennedys were young and vital and of today (and were fans of the show); the Petries were also young and lively and good-looking. Maybe the average Joe and Peggy-Sue watching TV could not hope to identify with the financial and social status of the families, both real and fictitious, they admired on TV but there was a sort of kinship – that of youth.

The show's success in Britain is less easy to identify, but those wisecracks might have had a lot to do with it. Thanks to Hollywood, British audiences were familiar with the snappy one-liner that hallmarked the American nightclub comic epitomized by Bob Hope. Even if the kind of life depicted in *The Dick Van Dyke Show* was no more familiar than that led by the Andersons or Ozzie and Harriet, the jokes were understandable and just as funny to alien ears.

The small break with tradition made by *Dick Van Dyke* was not generally followed. For the most part the family stereotype was maintained in American sitcoms. Marty Feldman sums up: 'Cast from what seems to be a repertory of lovable granddads, baffled fathers, capable mums and snub-nosed Juniors, and with scripts that don't seem to be written but shuffled and dealt, they are half-hour commercials for the American way of life.'

There was another stereotype living next door to most sitcom families. These neighbours were always something more than just people who happened to live next door. They were likeable if not actually lovable, occasionally testy in an endearing way, ready to pop in at a moment's notice through never-locked doors. They provided foils and friends whenever the plot needed them. These friendships never crossed the sex line. The men stuck together and so did the women. Suburban wife-swapping? Never!

Some of these neighbours became firm national favourites, Lucy and Ricky had Ethel and Fred Mertz; George and Gracie had Harry and Blanche Morton; Ralph and Alice Kramden had Ed Norton; even Samantha the Witch had the Kravitzes.

The rôle of these and other TV neighbours was, and remains, crucial. Not only are foils needed for any comic business which cannot usefully employ the marriage partner, but the neighbours, often supposedly 'normal', can be used to highlight the zaniness of the show's stars. The list of family-based sitcoms which simply would not work without a neighbour is endless, stretching as it does from *The Beverly Hillbillies* to the suburban antics of *Fresh Fields*.

In Britain some TV sitcom families followed the American pattern but changes were on the way which strikingly demonstrated a more radical approach to TV comedy.

In the 1960s two family sitcoms appeared on British TV screens which had a major impact on the direction to be taken by TV comedy in the future. One, *Till Death Us Do Part*, adopted the standard family structure but up-ended the genre in the attitudes (and language) of its central character, the magnificently monstrous Alf Garnett. This show is discussed in Chapter 11.

The other family was anything but 'standard' and completely overturned preconceptions about family life. For a start there were no kids and there was not even a wife; just two men, father and son, bound together as inextricably as any family could ever be.

Albert Steptoe and his son Harold first appeared on 5 January 1962 in 'The Offer', an episode of an unconnected series of half-hour plays written by Ray Galton and Alan Simpson and transmitted by the BBC under the umbrella title *Comedy Playhouse*. This series was a variation on the American pilot-show format which allowed audiences to see a string of 'possibles' one after the other over a period of a few weeks.

Summarizing the theme of *Steptoe and Son*

in a couple of dozen words – 'two rag-and-bone men, one old and dirty, the other his long-suffering middle-aged son, live together in squalor and squabble endlessly about everything' – leaves an impression that if the writers had not been highly regarded the show might never have got off the ground. Fortunately, Galton and Simpson had developed a substantial reputation, thanks to their scripts for Tony Hancock, and were allowed to unveil the unlikeliest pair of heroes to carve a permanent and honoured place in the history of TV comedy. In *Steptoe and Son*, Galton and Simpson pursued what Francis Wheen has called their 'theme of comic pessimism' to great effect.

Interviewed by David Nathan for his book *The Laughtermakers*, Alan Simpson remarked on the difference between this show and writing for Tony Hancock. The earlier experience 'was great. But *Steptoe* is ours. We've got two good actors but it is our thing, whereas with *Hancock* we were just Tony's scriptwriters.'

Perhaps no other sitcom demonstrates so well the oft-quoted adage that character, not situation, makes the best comedy. Certainly there was nothing funny in the Steptoes' situation. Caught simultaneously in traps of poverty, emotional blackmail and psychological interdependence, the two men, Albert and Harold Steptoe, clung together through thin and thinner.

Albert, (played by Wilfrid Brambell) was old enough to be incapable of work, but we all knew that he was a champion at the art of lead-swinging. Of course, Harold knew the old man was an 'idle old git' but he could never quite catch him out, or was too tired after his day on the round to bother. Albert's duties in their unequal partnership consisted of staying at home and carrying out the domestic chores traditionally undertaken by the wife and mother. In fact, Albert never attempted to keep the place clean and tidy and his idea of preparing a meal for Harold seldom rose above the level of sticking a frozen meat pie in the oven.

As for Albert's standards of personal hygiene, they were even lower than those he applied to the house. Who can forget the sight of his emaciated body as he bathed in a tin tub

Albert Steptoe, the epitome of low cunning and even lower standards of hygiene (Wilfrid Brambell).

while eating a makeshift snack? And when he accidentally spilled the pickled onions into the tub only to scoop them out of the grimy water and return them to the jar, stomachs heaved from Mayfair to the meanest East End back street.

In his attitude towards his son, Albert displayed the lowest cunning, only rarely leavened with suggestions of genuine parental love. In contrast to the generally soft-centred American sitcom, however, just when it seemed that Albert might be redeemed a sudden flash of genuine malice gleamed from beneath his grubby exterior.

Albert's son was portrayed by Harry H. Corbett, with such complete involvement that his subsequent career was blighted by the aura of Harold Steptoe. Past 40, Harold

yearns for a woman, for education and sophistication, for glamour and romance, and above all for escape. Night after night he sits in his sagging armchair, pointedly turned away from his father, desperately trying to improve himself through books but forever being sucked into pointless and doomed arguments with the old man.

We all knew, as did Harold, that all he had to do was walk out the door and freedom would be his; but Harold also knew, as we did, that he never could. The bonds that held Harold to his father were those that hold children to ailing parents; that keep men and women locked together in loveless marriages; that doom thousands of lives to quiet desperation from which escape is as impossible for the average person as it would be from

Try as he might, Harold (Harry H. Corbett) Steptoe could never break the ties that bound him to Albert.

one of those self-made prisons devised by Harry Houdini.

Try as he did, and heaven knows he tried hard, Harold's disgust with the 'dirty old man's' behaviour was tinged with a filial love that was as genuine as Albert's occasional and conveniently timed 'heart attacks' were false.

Albert: 'Die', that's what you were going to say, wasn't it – 'Why don't you die?'
Harold: No, I wasn't.
Albert: Yes, you were. You can't wait to hear the first shovelful of dirt hit the coffin, can you? I wouldn't be mourned, I know that. You'd be dancing on my grave. Well, I'll tell you, it'll be a relief to go, get away from this hell-hole.
Harold: You die? Don't make me laugh. You'll get your telegram from the Queen, don't worry.

In its structure, *Steptoe and Son* was about as perfect as anything as imperfect as TV drama can be. The absence of a woman in the family was not merely a one-off joke, it was the solid core of the piece. Of course women appeared from time to time, but Harold's regular attempts to have a permanent relationship with a girl, or even one that extended beyond a one-night stand, were doomed not only by Albert's determination to let no one come between him and his son but also by the writers' awareness of the dangers such a move would pose. To have brought a woman into this all-male family would have been not only to jeopardize the relationship between the principals but to cause the characters themselves to collapse.

But was the show really a comedy? Was it really funny? Of all the many dissimilarities that separated *Steptoe and Son* from other family-based sitcoms and indeed from sitcoms generally, the most significant is that at its heart this was not a comedy but a tragedy. What made the show so successful was that it

Rodney and Del are in accordance for once in Only Fools and Horses, *but Granddad looks dubious (Nicholas Lyndhurst, David Jason, Lennard Pearce).*

Del-boy shines beside his dim brother Rodney, although Uncle Albert (Buster Merryfield) seems happy at the latest scheme.

was a tragedy with which, in its essence, many could identify. The laughter the show evoked was often uncomfortable. How many middle-aged men and women glanced uneasily across the room at their own 'Albert' as the show unfolded?

This identification was not an insular matter reflecting only life in Britain; in time the *Steptoe* concept was relocated in America and, as *Sanford and Son*, enjoyed a comparable success.

Several years later, another British sitcom took a broadly similar base but wrung from it interesting and successful, though not always quite such deep, variations. The absence of a mother/wife figure, long the staple of domestic sitcoms, had by this time become acceptable and was no longer startling. *Only Fools and Horses* centres on two brothers who eke out a living in a manner only one sagging rung above the level endured by the Steptoes. Del is barrow boy-sharp while his younger brother Rodney is as dim as a 25-watt lamp. Like Harold before him, Del (David Jason) knows he could do better for himself if only he didn't have to look after a relative for whom his feelings are ambivalent. Unlike those of the Steptoes, the feelings of the dependent pair are closer to those of genuine familial affection. Certainly Rodney (Nicholas Lynd-hurst) not only needs his older brother, he also admires and seeks to emulate him. There is another dependant in this sitcom: Del has also to take care of their Granddad (Lennard Pearce). (After the death of the actor in the grandfather's rôle, another ageing relative, Uncle Albert, played by Buster Merryfield, joined the brothers.)

Like Harold Steptoe, Del has no chance of breaking those invisible, restrictive bonds. Here also it is the characters that make the humour, not the situation. Indeed, the situation is one of sadness but stops a long way short of the tragedy of the Steptoes. Even the setting is a little closer to everyday reality, although the flat occupied by the brothers and usually stacked ceiling-high with the stock-in-trade of Del's latest get-rich-quick scheme, has a peculiar garish hideousness that is all its own.

Despite the ground-breaking changes evidenced by *Steptoe and Son*, most British family-based sitcoms in the 1960s were far from being very different from their American counterparts. Generally, practitioners of the form elected to retain a measure of cosy domesticity, despite the existence of the occasional rebel.

One such rebel was Anthony Newley, who in 1960 began a new series with a typical sitcom family seated around a table. The script followed audience preconceptions. Then, after a few minutes, his audience now lulled into a false sense of security, Newley's character, Gurney Slade, suddenly announced his dissatisfaction with it all, walked off the set and was followed by the cameras into a strange world of his own imagining in which he talked to animals and inanimate objects. The sound of TV sets being switched off rolled like thunder across the nation. Newley and ATV's *The Strange World of Gurney Slade* were before their time.

No such risks were taken in the string of successes from the 1960s and the next two decades which starred an actress who came to personify a curiously Victorian concept of middle-class morality.

Wendy Craig appeared in *Not in Front of the Children*, a BBC series, and subsequently moved through the 1970s in *And Mother Makes Three* (written by Richard Waring for Thames), then *And Mother Makes Five*, before taking what was substantially the same character in a broadly similar setting into the 1980s with the BBC's *Butterflies*.

The realization in the 1970s that the juvenile audience was growing in size and, significantly, in spending power, forced programme-makers to give the likes and dislikes of children rather more thought than they had in the past. Given the dominance of situation comedies as the principal outlet for comedy it was inevitable that the rôle of children in family sitcoms would increase to the point where it looked as though children had inherited TV Planet Earth.

One of the first American TV sitcoms to feature a child was the shortlived *Wesley*, which appeared on CBS in the 1949-50 season. The first to have any measure of success was 1957's *Leave It to Beaver*, which proved its popularity by running on until 1963. Beaver, real name Theodore Cleaver (real-life name Jerry Mathers), lived with his parents

Happy Days: *life in the 'fifties as seen through rose-tinted specs (Anson Williams, Ron Howard, Henry Winkler).*

Ward and June Cleaver (played by Hugh Beaumont and Barbara Billingsley) and went through all the growing-up problems adults imagine children to have experienced. That such antics bear no relation to reality raises questions about the kind of life TV programme-makers had as children. But in the relative innocence of the late 1950s American audiences did not ask such questions; they simply sat back and smiled appreciatively — and, presumably, laughed too.

The first successful TV sitcom aimed directly at American teenagers was *The Many Loves of Dobie Gillis*, which starred Dwayne Hickman in the title rôle. First aired in 1959, the show ran for four years and traced the trials and tribulations of an average teenager who wanted a girl of his own to love. He didn't want sex with her, of course, just love and affection and platonic companionship. Who says TV has to reflect real life to score a hit? This show can lay claim to having provided a lift-off pad for a number of young actors who went on to bigger things. The first target of Dobie's on-screen affections was played by Tuesday Weld and in order to have these returned he had to fend off a rival played by Warren Beatty. That eccentric actor Michael J. Pollard also made a few appearances on the show.

The real breakthrough for teenage sitcom came in 1973 with the arrival of *Happy Days*. As usual, Hollywood had been pioneering the trail with such movies as *The Last Picture Show* (1971) and *American Graffiti* (1973). Set in the recent past, these movies had looked at life through the eyes of teenagers and had both attracted critical acclaim and good audiences. So TV took the plunge too.

Probably the most astonishing thing about *Happy Days* was its massive success. Also surprising was the fact that in episode after episode, month after month, nothing much ever happened. Despite these seemingly fundamental drawbacks, the show made a star out of an unprepossessing young actor named Henry Winkler.

Like the movies of the same era (but without their style) this show was not set in the present. Although there is no rule which says TV sitcoms have to be set in the times in which the show is being made and screened, very

few are period pieces. The success of those near-past movies prompted the decision to make an exception and *Happy Days* was set in the 1950s. As its title suggests it looked back with nostalgic pleasure to those not-so-far-off days.

Perhaps it was a reflection of the view that the 1950s was the last innocent decade for America. Maybe it was a vestige of the love affair many Americans had with the 1950s. It could have been the simple fact that, human memory being what it is, the past always appears better the further away it drifts. By 1970, for example, many Americans had conveniently forgotten the Korean War and Senator McCarthy. Whatever it was, the show had an appealing ambiance for a wide span of the available audience.

Originally the show focused on the Cunningham family and in particular young Richie (played by Ron Howard). Richie had parents, a brother and a sister, and school pals. The show barely gathered an audience but there was also a character named Arthur Fonzarelli who stood out from the clean-cut crowd all around him by wearing motorcycle leathers and taking a serious, not to say sexual, interest in the two great pursuits of American teenagers — machines on wheels and girls. Yes, American youth's interest in cars and motorbikes did have a sexual connotation in the 1950s — and maybe still has. Arthur Fonzarelli — 'the Fonz' — struck resonant chords in many minds. Maybe he was nothing more than a much-diluted Wild One, but the young ones liked him and so too did those who had been young in the 1950s.

Soon the swaggering, leather-jacketed Fonzie was up-thumbing his way through every episode delivering uncultured pearls of supposed wisdom and gathering a following that might very well have got him elected president. But, like most politicians, Fonzie's cocksure strut concealed a hypocritical view of life. In one episode he rejects an approach by an attractive married women who implies she wants to ball with the statement, 'I got some rules I live by ... and one is I don't take what ain't mine...' The studio audience cheered. Perhaps they were an average cross-section of humanity and just as riddled with hypocrisy as the Fonz. Or maybe they really believed that they had been like him back in the innocent 1950s.

As the show's popularity grew it became apparent that the reasons were largely the popularity of the Fonz, and from being a minor character he gradually became the centre of attraction. If he never actually reached better than second billing to Ron Howard, there was no doubt that Henry Winkler was the star of *Happy Days*.

In time Fonzie became a live-in member of the Cunningham family and Winkler a runaway star, even if his occasional movies served largely to demonstrate how difficult it is for an actor, especially one who is limited and highly mannered, to shake off a successful and long-running TV part.

Happy Days gave rise to other successes, also aimed at the teenage market: *Mork and Mindy* and *Laverne and Shirley*. Among the young actors who appeared in *Happy Days* was Scott Baio, who later became very nearly as popular as the Fonz had and was given his own show, entitled *Charles in Charge*, to prove it.

Another teenage phenomenon is Michael J. Fox, who brought a measure of amiability to his essentially irritating rôle as Alex Keaton, the know-it-all son of the house in *Family Ties*. Doted on by Mom and Dad Keaton (Michael Gross and Meredith Baxter-Birney) and tolerated by his younger sister Jennifer (Tina Yothers), Alex takes himself very seriously indeed. In fact, he seems to have bypassed adolescence on his way to becoming an adult in disguise.

Although Alex is generally beset with such problems as persuading his best friend to ditch his new girlfriend in order that their regular Saturday-night practice of watching John Wayne movies can continue unaffected, the show did occasionally aim slightly higher. In one episode Alex's older sister, Mallory (played by Justine Bateman), is the target of a pass made by a much older man well-known to the family. The subject, one which must have been a real-life problem for many in the audience, was treated intelligently if a mite glibly.

The central point of *Family Ties* — a 1960s liberal-hippie couple seen twenty years on coping with an arch-conservative son — was a good starting-point but not as strong as it might have appeared at first sighting. Thanks to the presence of Fox, whose lack of height hasn't stopped him from becoming a movie mega-star, the show stayed in production after the ideas had run out.

Another know-it-all teenager is Matthew, played very unappealingly by Jason Bateman in *It's Your Move*. The best that can be said about this show is that the other actors should be complimented for their restraint.

In every episode Matt's declared aim is to ruin his widowed mother's chances of having a meaningful relationship with a man. Eileen and Norman (Caren Kaye and David Garrison) smile patiently and refrain from strangling him. W. C. Fields would have made short work of the little twerp.

Hidden beneath the surface glibness lies something not explored but which might have emerged had the show been titled *Oedipus Wrecks*.

Two other American sitcoms in which the family revolves around a central child character (both of which happen to be black) are *Diff'rent Strokes* and *Webster*. These shows are examined in Chapter 10.

The prominence of children in latterday sitcoms demonstrates the commercial view taken by the makers of TV shows through the years. As for the continued popularity of sitcoms of all kinds in the 1970s, this ensured a rise in their numbers. In terms of writing and acting the British shows frequently outdid their American counterparts but formulas became steadily more predictable. One promising sign, however, was that amidst the mass of merely average comedy shows which dominated British TV in the 1970s there were enough gems to keep even the more discerning viewers glued to their sets.

CHAPTER SIX

THE 'SEVENTIES SURVEYED

'Lookin' go-o-o-d.'
Freddie Prinze

Like the two previous decades, the 1970s bore witness to a large amount of televised dross that purported to be comedy. Fortunately, there was also a substantial seam of fine material which seemed good then and which from the standpoint of the late 1980s gleams like lost treasure.

The confidence displayed in 1960s television comedy bore substantial fruits in the course of the new decade, giving rise to a string of successes in both Britain and America.

America had *All in the Family, Happy Days, The Mary Tyler Moore Show, M*A*S*H, Maude, The Jeffersons* and *Rhoda*, all of which are discussed elsewhere, and *Barney Miller, Taxi, Chico and the Man, Soap* and *Alice.*

Apart from the top-quality shows on British TV viewers were offered a seemingly endless stream of mediocre sitcoms, many of which were really one-joke shows; some of these ran for so long that those members of the audience who liked to encounter an occasional change of face, plot, scene or dialogue were forced to conclude that the shows' inanity was but one small step away from galloping insanity.

Those who liked their sitcoms raucous had LWT's *On the Buses*, starring Reg Varney, a comic actor who deserved much better than he was offered in sitcoms. The show's comparatively quiet moments featured innuendo served up as jokes. *On the Buses* was thin on character, heavy on situation, and filled to the brim with noisily unlikable stereotypes.

Contrastingly, Granada TV's *The Cuckoo Waltz* offered mild, quiet and newly-married Chris and Fliss Hawthorne: he presentable but doleful, she sparkling and pretty. They take in a male lodger to help make ends meet. He is Gavin Rumsey, dashing and handsome and more than capable of sweeping the pretty sparkler into his king-size bed. But of course he doesn't. Well played by David Roper, Diane Keen and Lewis Collins, the show had a certain charm and with good scripts by Geoffrey Lancashire and John G. Temple it was OK for a short run. After five years, by which time Collins had begun to believe his own publicity and had moved on to more rugged things, the single-joke premise had more than run its course.

The BBC's *Are You Being Served?*, set in an antiquated department store, achieved massive popularity that endured for ten years without ever rising above end-of-the-pier repartee. The cast consisted of grossly stereotyped characters who were about as lively as the wax dummies in the store displays. As Mrs Slocombe, Mollie Sugden, who must be one of the busiest sitcom actresses in the world, backcombed her hair even higher, sprayed on yet more lacquer and snapped out predictable lines about the condition of her pussy. Across the floor, John Inman as Mr Humphries camped wildly, making a television career out of inside-leg jokes and the catchphrase 'I'm free!'

The BBC had the lion's share of the best shows of the 1970s. Among its successes were

Compo and his wrinkled-stockinged inamorata, Nora Batty, in Roy Clarke's whimsical
Last of the Summer Wine *(Bill Owen, Kathy Staff).*

two shows which fell outside the usual settings for situation comedy.

Some Mothers Do 'Ave 'Em starred Michael Crawford as an accident-prone dimwit. In any other hands the premise could have been an embarrassment because the central rôle of Frank Spencer bordered on being simple-minded. Although he coated his character in enough mannerisms to keep TV impressionists occupied for years, Crawford managed to avoid most of the traps that might have claimed a less sensitive actor. Once the dialogue ended and Frank got down to his weekly encounter with malicious machinery, the show changed direction and offered some of the best-timed sight gags since the Keystone Kops held sway.

Although not performed live on set,

Crawford's routines surpassed even Charlie Drake's in the extent to which the actor risked limb and sometimes life, dangling over cliffs, flying aeroplanes, riding motorbikes backwards or, on roller-skates, getting towed through the streets precariously attached to a London bus.

The other show which fell outside the usual form for TV sitcoms was *Last of the Summer Wine*. Perhaps best described as typically English whimsy, it traced the meanderings of body and mind of three retired men living in a village in the north of England. Written by Roy Clarke, the show was slight on action and jokes but built its characters carefully. Rather than raising laughter, it encouraged its audience to smile appreciatively. The trio of actors chosen to play the leading rôles of

In Porridge, *Chief Warden Mackay was eternally suspicious of Fletcher, Slade Prison's most anarchic inmate (Fulton Mackay, Ronnie Barker, Richard Beckinsale).*

Blamire, Compo and Clegg comprised Michael Bates, Bill Owen and Peter Sallis. Bates' death brought in Brian Wilde as Foggy, and although different from this point onwards, the show maintained its style and standard. Much later Wilde was replaced by Michael Aldridge, whose character, Seymour, was unbelievably eccentric and who began to pull the show off balance. After more than a dozen years, the strain on writer Roy Clarke's inventiveness became extremely noticeable as Compo and Clegg were drawn into yet wilder adventures.

The open air of *Last of the Summer Wine* contrasted strikingly with the tightly enclosed prison environment which provided the setting for *Porridge.* This show was built around one of the most carefully conceived and de-veloped characters to appear in sitcoms in any decade. Although Ronnie Barker had done good things before, and later created other excellent characters, the rôle of Norman Fletcher, denizen of Slade Prison, is surely the paramount achievement of his career as a comic actor. Barker built his performance upon splendid scripts by Ian La Frenais and Dick Clement and was ably supported by a fine cast of actors including Richard Beckinsale as his young cell-mate Godber, Brian Wilde as prison warden Barraclough, and a superbly judged Chief Warden Mackay from Fulton Mackay.

The prison confines and the unchanging daily routine obliged the writers and actors to explore the inner layers of each character. As a result the comedy sprang naturally from this

Corner-shopkeeper Arkwright of Open All Hours, *another finely crafted rôle for Ronnie Barker.*

detailed examination of human beings under pressure. For example, the laconic Fletcher, observing the manners of prison society, remarks to his fellow prisoners: 'I don't know how to put this gently, but there's a thief among us.'

The idea of a sequel to *Porridge* probably seemed logical at the time, but in practice it failed to measure up to its predecessor. *Going Straight* picks up Fletch's tale after his release from Slade Prison and shows, in serial form, how he tries to come to terms with life on the outside. He also does his best to keep others from a life of crime, although not always with much success. When he does, on one occasion, manage to divert someone from the criminal path, he is delighted but cynical:

I bet missionaries feel like that. I mean, it can't be all beer and skittles out in the jungle with the heat and the titsy flies. Then one day in come a group of young warriors, throw down their spears and say 'We want to learn the catechism.' Then they eat him.

Despite the consistency of scripts and central performance, the freedom of the unrestricted setting resulted in a weaker vehicle for Barker's talents. No one would wish Fletcher back in the nick but for audiences that was certainly the best place for him.

Ronnie Barker also appeared in *Open All Hours*, as Arkwright, a late middle-aged corner-shopkeeper who divides his time between squeezing every last penny from his customers, and every ounce of effort out of his assistant Granville (played by David Jason), and lusting after Nurse Gladys Emmanuel (Lynda Baron), who lives across the way. There are occasional glimpses of a Steptoe-like relationship between Arkwright and Granville, his semi-legitimate nephew. Barker's portrayal here was so different in both style and physical appearance from that of Fletcher that it might almost have been another actor in the rôle. The show, which depended for its humour mainly on Barker's almost non-stop stream of comic patter, came from *Summer Wine* writer Roy Clarke.

The barest-boned of sets provided the background for Yorkshire TV's *Rising Damp*, which starred Leonard Rossiter as the egregious Rigsby, landlord of a decaying house split into bedsits. The setting, like that of *Steptoe* before it, is seedy in the extreme; none of the characters seems to have any money, nor is there much to suggest that either Rigsby or his unfortunate tenants will ever escape their lack-lustre existence.

The awful Rigsby patrols his little empire, embittered, snobbish, ignorant and on occasion ingratiating, his dialogue laced with wicked one-liners and a fair smattering of Alf Garnett-like jabs at anyone who does not conform to his concept of British perfection. The fact that he is as unappetizing in mind as he is in body never occurs to him as he lusts after the spinster Miss Jones (very well played by Frances De La Tour, who brought disturbing hints of suicidal frailty to the part), reviles Richard Beckinsale's hopelessly inept medical student, and sneers at the black tenant (Don Warrington) who, a prince in his own country, is the only one likely to get out alive. If Rigsby is aware of this he gives no hint of it: to him 'black' means inferior and he doesn't care who knows it.

Philip and Alan are for once encouraged by the awful Rigsby, but Miss Jones has come prepared for a different kind of party (Don Warrington, Richard Beckinsale, Leonard Rossiter, Frances De La Tour in Rising Damp*).*

Just as the setting reflected that of life with the Steptoes, so there was similarly no real humour in the situation. Only Rigsby's jokes produced the laughs; without them, the fate of the characters, especially that of Miss Jones, was more the stuff of tragedy. Fortunately, Eric Chappell's scripts kept the scales tipped towards comedy and the show was blessed with an unsurpassable actor in Leonard Rossiter, who relished every moment of his rôle.

Rossiter also had the lead in the BBC's *The Fall and Rise of Reginald Perrin*. Although very different in every respect, this was another gem of the 1970s. Reggie Perrin, a middle-aged business executive at Sunshine Desserts, is, when the show begins, on the brink of a nervous breakdown. Unlike most sitcoms,

Perrin was a serial and although individual episodes could be seen and enjoyed in isolation the build-up of the story over the weeks gave it an extra element of interest. Reggie's decline towards an eventual faked suicide and his return as a 'new man' was beautifully charted by Rossiter from David Nobbs' excellent scripts.

Perrin was filled with comic characters and if all but Reggie's wife (played by Pauline Yates) were far too eccentric to be mistaken for real life, there was always the possibility that the characters were exaggerated not by script or performer but by the mental decline of Reggie Perrin. John Barron played Reggie's boss, C. J. ('I didn't get where I am today...'). In another fine supporting rôle Geoffrey Palmer played Reggie's ineffectual army

Reginald Perrin, caught between nervous breakdowns (Leonard Rossiter).

cluttered by extraneous characters including a typical Jewish mother and a pair of gays. Their problems cause her more trouble than all her readers' letters put together.

A strong central performance from Ms Lipman helped the series over its basic problem of having a theme capable of only limited development. Making Jane Lucas suffer some of the problems her readers expected her to solve with pithy replies in her column almost made this a one-joke show, but the potential dangers were overcome by many more jokes in the scripts.

The most striking and devastatingly funny sitcom to burst upon the British public in the 1970s was *Fawlty Towers.* Created and written by John Cleese and Connie Booth, both of whom also starred in the show, *Fawlty Towers* was set in that time-honoured British institution, the seaside hotel.

Run by manic-depressive Basil Fawlty (Cleese) and his termagant wife Sybil (Prunella Scales), with the frequently disastrous assistance of Spanish waiter Manuel (Andrew Sachs), regarded by Basil as 'a waste of space', and the sensible but often-exasperated Polly Sherman (Booth), the hotel, Fawlty Towers, is the scene of every horror ever inflicted upon the long- and silently-suffering traveller through Britain.

For every guest the appallingly snobbish Basil fawns upon in his desire to raise the tone of Fawlty Towers, there are dozens he treats with condescension or outright incivility ('Have they no consideration? Don't they realize I'm trying to run an *hotel*?').

Basil's snobbishness is frequently undermined by his ignorance, a facet of his character which emerged in a conversation with guest Mr Walt (James Cossins).

Basil: It's always a pleasure to meet someone who appreciates the boudoir of the grape. I'm afraid most people we get in here don't know a Bordeaux from a claret.
Mr Walt: A Bordeaux is a claret.
Basil: Oh, *Bordeaux* is a claret, yes, yes, but they wouldn't know that.

Whether attempting to have building alterations done on the cheap, getting rid of a rat Manuel is keeping in the mistaken belief that it is a hamster, trying to hide the body of a guest

officer brother-in-law Jimmy, forever scrounging a free meal: 'Sorry, Reggie, another cock-up on the catering front.'

By the end of the second series, Reggie is rich and famous, having made a success out of trying to fail with the worst idea he could imagine – a nationwide chain of Grot Shops selling rubbish at outrageous prices. All the other characters in the serial are now working for him. When he prepares to fake his second suicide, they all go with him. In this not-quite-a-sitcom, fantasy follows fairly closely behind real life where, too often for comfort, nothing succeeds like garbage.

For LWT's *Agony*, TV-land followed the unreal world of newspaper agony aunts. Created by Len Richmond and Anna Raeburn, herself a newspaper columnist of the kind portrayed in the series, *Agony* had the benefit of generally good scripts with some excellent one-liners. Its main character is Jane Lucas (played by Maureen Lipman), whose life is

Jane Lucas listens to her mother's advice in Agony *(Maureen Lipman, Maria Charles).*

who has had the temerity to die in his hotel, or concealing from her friends the fact that Sybil has left him, Basil commits every social blunder under Torquay's pale sun.

Almost every episode of *Fawlty Towers* was a classic. Carrying out fire drill is, for Basil, a boring duty to be quickly completed, and with which he will allow nothing to interfere — not even the fact that Manuel managed to set fire to both the kitchen and himself. Basil's attempt to improve the status of the hotel by holding a gourmet's evening is ruined when the chef drinks himself into a stupor. Basil has to drive to a friend's restaurant for the meal — in a car which breaks down and has to be beaten with a branch ripped from a tree. A crack on the head on another occasion when some German guests are staying at the hotel sends the already dangerously unbalanced Basil into a hysterical parody of Hitler, goose-stepping around the dining room.

With Mrs Richards (Joan Sanderson), an elderly, domineering and very deaf guest, Basil runs riot, even if he is obliged to shout at her, most of the time, during a confrontation in her room.

Mrs Richards: Now listen to me, I've booked a room with a bath. When I book a room with a bath I expect to get a bath.
Basil: You've got a bath.
Mrs Richards: I'm not paying £7.20 per night plus VAT for a room without a bath.
Basil: There is your bath.
Mrs Richards: You call that a bath? It's not big enough to drown a mouse. It's disgraceful.
Basil (quietly): I wish you were a mouse. I'd show you.
Mrs Richards: And another thing, I asked for a room with a view.

Basil (quietly): Deaf, mad and blind. *(He peers through the window and starts shouting again.)* This is the view as far as I can remember, madam. Yes, yes, this is it.

Mrs Richards: When I pay for a view I expect something more interesting than that.

Basil: That is Torquay, madam.

Mrs Richards: Well, it's not good enough.

Basil: Well, may I ask what you were expecting to see out of a Torquay hotel bedroom window? Sydney Opera House perhaps, the Hanging Gardens of Babylon, herds of wildebeest sweeping majestically...?

Mrs Richards: Don't be silly. I expect to be able to see the sea.

Basil: You *can* see the sea. It's over there between the land and the sky.

Mrs Richards: I'd need a telescope to see that.

Basil: Well, may I suggest that you consider moving to a hotel closer to the sea? *(Quietly)* Or preferably *in* it.

Mrs Richards: Now listen to me, I'm not satisfied but I've decided to stay here. However, I shall expect a reduction.

Basil: Why? Because Krakatoa's not erupting at the moment, or...?

Mrs Richards: Because the room is cold, the bath is too small, the view is invisible and the radio doesn't work.

Basil (quietly): No, the radio works, you don't.

Although the small number of episodes made, six in 1975, six more in 1979, make this one of the shortest-running successful sitcoms in the history of the genre, there is some satisfaction in the knowledge that the series' high standards were never compromised by over-extension.

While it lasted *Fawlty Towers* offered object lessons in conception, development, writing and performance. The show's casting was well-nigh perfect, with Cleese the epitome of the arrogantly snobbish innkeeper most people have had the misfortune to encounter at one time or another. However offensive any Spanish viewer might have found the much put-upon Manuel, Andrew Sachs never allowed his stupidity to make him unsympathetic. (When the show was dubbed for Spanish consumption, Manuel became an Italian.) Connie Booth, with the show's straightest rôle, gave some balance to the eccentricities of the rest of the cast.

As Sybil Fawlty, Prunella Scales casually upstaged everyone whether cackling into the telephone or delivering a penetrating 'Basil!' from off-camera whenever her husband transgressed too far or one of his *sotto voce* remarks caught her ear. Occasionally she misses one: 'You're only single once', Sybil tells a young man. 'Twice can be arranged,' Basil mutters in the background. Launching an attack after a hapless Irish builder's incompetence has brought the hotel to the brink of structural collapse, Sybil is withering:

I have seen more intelligent creatures than you lying on their backs at the bottom of ponds. I have seen better organized creatures than you running round farmyards with their heads cut off.

The depth of characterization, slightly over the top for the real world of seaside hotels but not so far as to be unrecognizable, the inventive plots, good sight gags and laugh-packed scripts made the series one of the best of the decade. Many of the longer-running shows of the 1970s, and later, could have learned a lot from *Fawlty Towers* as it consistently demonstrated that the unlikely combination of Whitehall farce and rapid-fire wisecracks was not only possible but sustainable — at least for a lucky dozen episodes.

While the most successful American sitcoms of the 1970s are discussed elsewhere in the book, there were other shows that met with qualified approval from British audiences.

Chico and the Man made its début in 1974 and was brought to an abrupt, if not final, halt on 28 January 1977 when the show's star, Freddie Prinze, killed himself. The show was a rarity within rarities among American television situation comedies. Not only was it about a member of an ethnic minority but that minority was one that seldom made it to prime-time TV. Like Desi Arnaz's Ricky Ricardo two decades before him, Freddie Prinze's Chico Rodriguez was a Latin American: to be more accurate, Chico was a Mexican-American, while Prinze's ancestry combined Puerto Rico with Hungary.

Co-starring with Prinze was Jack Albertson, a show-business veteran whose path had crossed that of Phil Silvers back in the days when they worked the Borscht Circuit in the Catskills; in his time he had also worked with Milton Berle. Albertson played Ed Brown, the 'Man' of the title, a tetchy garage-owner who was one of the few surviving American-Americans in the Los Angeles barrio. The

Basil welcomes another unwary guest (Fawlty Towers, *John Cleese*).

The Man with Chico (Jack Albertson, Freddie Prinze).

show underwent several shifts of emphasis designed to accommodate protests from groups who considered it demeaning to, among others, Puerto Ricans.

In its better moments *Chico and the Man* demonstrated good interplay between a performer who had done everything and a youngster who appeared to have come out of nowhere. In fact, before *Chico*, Prinze had worked in fringe theatre and had studied dance. However, nothing he had done prepared him for the massive fame he experienced and he proved utterly incapable of coping with the pressures. His character's catchphrase, 'Lookin' go-o-o-d', belied the pressures on Prinze's own troubled mind: drink, drugs and a broken marriage brought him to a low ebb which fame and fortune could not overcome. When he shot himself he was 22 years old.

After Prinze's death the show continued for a while with Gabriel Melgar playing the rôle of another young man, Raul Garcia, but the qualities that had made *Chico and the Man* such a success were missing and the show folded in 1978.

Comic New York cops in uniform had had their day in the early 1960s thanks to *Car 54, Where Are You?* and in 1974 it was the turn of the plain-clothes division of the NYPD. *Barney Miller* was an unexpected success for NBC. Unlike its predecessor, it took few liberties with the real police. Cops were not made fun of in *Barney Miller*; rather, the show's makers realized the potential for humour lying not far beneath the unpleasant and sometimes violent surface of big-city life. In a way, this show was a comic counterpart to *Hill Street Blues*, which laced drama with comedy. *Barney Miller* sprinkled its comedy with enough reality to give the characters credibility, and because they were fully developed the humour — of which there was certainly no shortage — could flow all the more easily.

The show starred Hal Linden in the title rôle with Abe Vigoda and Gregory Sierra in support, both of whom were to qualify for the accolade of their own shows. Vigoda, who had played a villainous Mafia bigshot in the movie *The Godfather*, was Detective Phil Fish, whose character was later spun off into *Fish*. Sierra was Detective Sergeant Chano Amenguale. Along with Detectives Wojohowicz (Maxwell Gail), Yemana (Jack Soo) and Harris (Ron Glass), these men made the 12th Precinct the most racially integrated unit in police history. Every minority figured in the show and no one seemed to mind because the fun was not directed at any particular group. Rather it was society at large which came in for its share of witty condemnation.

When a lady, visiting the city for the first time, has her luggage stolen she is understandably upset as she talks to Detective Harris:

Lady: You know, I watched all those 'I Love New York' commercials back in Youngstown, with all the Broadway actors singing and dancing. They're so exciting and colourful. But they never mention the people with knives.
Harris: Well, they only have a minute.

New York also provided the setting for *Taxi*, which was first aired in 1978. As for any series set in the workplace, the writers took care to ensure that the Sunshine Cab Company's employees were a mixed bunch.

The solid centre is Alex Rieger (played by

Some of Barney Miller *'s deliberately ethnic cross-section: Max Gale as Wojo, Gregory Sierra as Chano, Jack Soo as Yemena, Abe Vigoda as Fish.*

Alex and Elaine from Taxi *(Judd Hirsch, Marilu Henner).*

Judd Hirsch), against whom most of the other characters bounce their problems and laughs. Creator of most of the problems, and most of the laughs, is the Napoleonic Louie De Palma. As portrayed by pint-sized Danny De Vito, Louie is everyone's nightmare boss.

Tyrannical, unfeeling, coarse and in any context other than a TV sitcom a contender for an early death, Louie's main butts are the staff he supervises, but he is never averse to insulting a customer, especially over the telephone:

Ma'am, you say one of our drivers was rude to you? … What is it he said to you? … I see, well, how fat *are* you? … I want you to know that we expect our cabdrivers to be kind and courteous to our passengers. Especially to you blimpos.

He isn't too complimentary to his mother either – who, he assures everyone, would be good-looking 'if she'd shed a few pounds and get rid of the warts and the moustache.'

Astonishingly, thanks to De Vito's skill, as awful as Louie is there's always a fleeting impression that his spiky exterior conceals a sad and empty life.

The drivers are mostly ordinary individuals, although each has his or her problems. Elaine Nardo (Marilu Henner) is trying to raise her child, which means holding down two jobs; Tony Banta (Tony Danza) is a canvas-backed prizefighter; Bobby Wheeler (Jeff Conaway) is a would-be actor with little talent and no confidence.

There are two true eccentrics in the cast of characters. One, Latka Gravas, is a recent immigrant with pop-eyes, a shuffling gait and a sing-song voice. Played somewhat grotesquely by Andy Kaufman, he proved to be one of the show's most successful characters, although the reasons for his popularity are at best obscure. The other eccentric came into the show after the first year. Christopher Lloyd played the burned-out wreck of an ex-hippie, Reverend Jim Ignatowski, whose brain is still clouded with the fumes of a decade's inhalation of marijuana. Slightly disconnected from reality — he is always half a conversation behind everyone else — Reverend Jim also walks as though instructions from his disintegrating brain were having a hard time finding their way along his nervous system to his legs.

Although the script for *Taxi* was one of the best in American TV sitcoms at the time of its arrival, it suffered more than most from the soft centre which mars so much of the genre. Sentimentality was rife in *Taxi*, weakening what was otherwise a high-quality product. Given the usually high standard of scripts and acting, especially by Hirsch, De Vito and Lloyd, the show could have been great.

Another extra-terrestrial landed in America in 1978. This was Mork from the planet Ork. Mork first materialized in an episode of *Happy Days*. Wait a minute! Wasn't that a show about real life in 1950s America? Perhaps it's best not to ask what a creature from another world was doing in Milwaukee. What mattered to the network was that Mork's visit was popular and *Mork and Mindy* was a smash. The show also made a star out of Robin Williams, who played Mork, but failed to achieve comparable status for Pam Dawber who played Mindy. Perhaps this was because she was a common-or-garden earthling with no special talents, while he was an Orkian whose extensive knowledge of planet Earth was based on the old movies beamed out nightly by American TV companies. As a result Mork was on the same wavelength as most of his audience. Additionally, Mork was played by an actor with boundless enthusiasm and a fair talent for impressions — especially of old movie stars. One-joke show or not, at least *Mork and Mindy* had the benefit of an energetic and almost original talent, which more than made up for the frequently sentimental script.

Among the TV shows Mork and the other Orkians doubtless saw in great numbers were the soap operas. If any kind of TV show deserved lampooning it was surely the soaps, therefore the really strange thing about *Soap* was that it took so long before someone came along who was prepared to ridicule them by way of another show.

When *Soap* first appeared in 1977 it ran into a lot of flak. In fact, the flak was flying before it even opened. Like so many sitcoms before it, *Soap* was about a family. Well, two families, actually — the Tates and the Campbells. But there any similarity to any other TV sitcom family came to a shuddering stop.

Between them the Tates and the Campbells have every problem imaginable and a few that aren't. Jessica Tate (Katherine Helmond) is not too intelligent, her husband Chester (Robert Mandan) sleeps with anything in a skirt and one of their daughters sleeps with anything in pants. The other daughter is much more restrained. She does, however, score a sitcom first by seducing a Roman Catholic priest. The Tates' other children are relatively normal, even if one, Billy (Scott Baio), is pretty obnoxious. Jessica's father is a crazy ex-army man who doesn't know the war is over (the first war, not the second), and the family employs an irritable black butler named Benson (Robert Guillaume) who has a well-honed line in insults, trading on 50 years of servile rôles for blacks in movies and on TV.

The Campbells are no better, Mary, Jessica's sister (played by Cathryn Damon), is fairly normal, at least at the start. Her husband Burt (Richard Mulligan) has killed her first husband, while her two sons are far from average: one works for the Mafia, the other, Jodie, is gay.

One way or another pretty nearly every sexual variation is practised by the Tates and the Campbells. Before the show ran its course pretty well everyone had tried to sleep with pretty well everyone else, in many cases successfully. There were murders and at one point Burt's body was taken over by an extra-terrestrial who then discovered the joys of human sexual activity — and so did Mary, who for years had been obliged to put up with her husband's impotence.

With death, random sexual activity and various forms of psychiatric illness, to say nothing of outright insanity prevailing, the flak attracted by *Soap* was to have been expected. What may have surprised some casual observers was that the show's originator was a woman, Susan Harris. There was still some

The Tates take tea in Soap *(Arthur Peterson, Katherine Helmond, Robert Mandan).*

distance to travel before a show about and starring only women, and largely produced and written by women, would become the smash hit of American TV sitcoms. Even those casual observers might not have been surprised to note that when *The Golden Girls* appeared in the late 1980s to sweep the popular audience and the critics before it, Susan Harris's hand was involved there too.

But, even by the late 1970s, the rôle of women in TV comedy, on and off the screen, had changed dramatically from the early days.

The overall quality of situation comedy in the 1970s was very high indeed and augured well for the future. Unfortunately, somewhere along the line complacency, allied to growing demands for volume, confounded expectations. Not for the first time in show business, quantity and quality proved incompatible.

CHAPTER SEVEN

WOMEN AND THE SEXUAL REVOLUTION

'Some old ladies are real pains.'
The Golden Girls

It will come as no surprise to anyone who has reflected upon the subordinate rôle of women in society at large that their rôle in television comedy has been similarly undervalued. Their position 'on-stage' today has improved, just as it has in the real world, but there is still a long way to go both inside and outside show business.

Generations of music-hall and vaudeville comics treated women as objects of ridicule. Women, especially wives, were there to be deceived, or were feared, or were simply excluded from male preserves.

The women in the lives of such comics fell into neat stereotypes. If a woman was the comic's wife she was a sharp-tongued termagant; if she was young and attractive (often a barmaid or engaged in a similarly 'servile' capacity) she had loose morals and was a sex object. And heaven help her if she happened to be the comic's mother-in-law. There was one thing a women never was: an equal.

This lack of equality made it difficult for a female entertainer to establish a realistic persona. On the halls a woman could be attractive if she was a singer or was a male entertainer's assistant, but if she sought to extend her rôle into the realms of comedy she was usually obliged either to be aggressive or to adopt male characteristics, which often amounted to being simply vulgar. One effect of this stereotyping was to classify female entertainers as undignified. Not only was this unfair, but it also displayed a marked lack of perception on the part of audiences and impresarios alike.

One of the first women to make a real breakthrough in the field of stand-up comedy was Phyllis Diller, who entered the American nightclub scene in the 1950s. Her deliberately outrageous physical appearance was doubt-less designed to placate those males who felt that as a female comic was essentially abnormal she had to look that way too. More recently Joan Rivers, not an especially 'glamorous' lady, has chosen to appear in a more overtly feminine guise although pepper-ing her routine with jokes that heap ridicule upon her own – and others' – looks. In fact, her stream of repetitive jokes about face-lifts and breast sizes scorns masculine ideals of female beauty. Despite being very much a performer of the 1980s, Rivers maintains the aggressive-ness of her forerunners.

Attacks by female comedians undoubtedly induce in some males a hint of fear that in some subtle way they are being emasculated. As TV is dominated by men, it is not surprising that such fears long kept women in their approved rôles as homemaker and staunch supporter of their bread-winning partner.

In the early years of American TV sitcoms the path followed was largely that of the woman in American humour at large. A streak of anti-feminism permeates the writing of James Thurber and Robert Benchley; neither W. C. Fields nor Groucho Marx could find anything complimentary to say about women in their movies and stage shows.

The path was trodden into a rut by Hollywood and TV offered few if any innovations. Women in American TV drama were either single or married or single-again following the death of their partner. Divorce was as unmentionable as four-letter words. If drama couldn't clamber over the rim of the rut, comedy certainly wasn't likely to try.

If single and young, women were generally in that curious teenage that never quite reaches nubility. If single and old (in this context 'old' means over 35), they had to be unthreatening to the sitcom's central marriage and were usually given such passing rôles as maiden aunts or spinsterish librarians. In either case they had acid tongues (and in Hollywood were usually played by Eve Arden), which gave them most of the best lines – some compensation, perhaps, for the stereotyping.

The married woman in sitcom-land was generally dizzy and totally dependent upon her husband for money, security, fatherly advice, and assistance in those exclusively male preserves where mechanical knowledge was required – such as changing wheels on cars or washers on taps.

Doyenne of these dizzy dames was Lucille Ball, who set the pattern against which all successors were gauged (her career has been examined at length in Chapter 2). But for all her dominance there were a couple of years in prime time and thereafter in syndication when Lucy was given a run for her money by *I Married Joan*, which started in 1952.

The star of the series was Joan Davis, who began her career in vaudeville before forming a double-act with her husband Sy Wills. She made numerous movie shorts and several feature films in Hollywood, in all of which she engaged in raucous knockabout comedy which made no concessions to femininity. Fanny Brice reportedly wanted Joan Davis to portray her on the screen. When the time came, with Joan long gone, Hollywood, as usual, cast wildly against type and gave the job to Barbra Streisand. Joan also tried radio, where she had a highly successful series, *Leave It To Joan*, before coming to television with a show she herself produced.

Although not immediately well received, *I Married Joan* quickly picked up a following against competition from *The Adventures of Ozzie and Harriet* and *The Life of Riley* and was soon high in the ratings. Joan, playing the rôle of Joan Stevens, worked hard, using her ungainly body like a battering ram as she charged around the set – frequently taking the kind of pratfall that only a veteran of the vaudeville stage could accomplish.

Co-starring as husband Judge Bradley Stevens was Jim Backus, a solid character actor. Backus's career spanned vaudeville, the movies, radio and TV in both comic and straight rôles. He also wrote several books and scripts for TV and radio but learned to live with the knowledge that his greatest claim to international fame (and, doubtless, some compensatory fortune) lay in his providing the voice for the cartoon character Mr Magoo.

Week after week, the signature tune of the series heralded half an hour of frenetic comedy played flat-out and entirely dependent upon Joan's astonishing vitality. The show wore her out and she retired in 1955. A later attempt to return to TV was unsuccessful and she died in 1961 at the age of 54.

The single woman as unthreatening spinster appeared in *Our Miss Brooks*, which began in 1952. Although not a librarian, Connie Brooks was a middle-aged schoolteacher which came close enough to the stereotype. Fortunately, a possible marshmallow disaster was saved by the casting of the central rôle. Connie Brooks was played by Eve Arden, who, in her early career, had played on Broadway with Fanny Brice. Eve played numerous small rôles in Hollywood movies, among them *Cover Girl* (1944) and *Night and Day* (1946). In such films she was given little to do except drift across the set and drop devastating acidic one-liners. Few actors could drop-gag like Eve. The only comparable talents that come readily to mind from the same era of film-making are Lucille Ball and Oscar Levant. Eve's timing and technique were perfect and she was blessed with a voice which gave even her occasional kindly remark a sandpapery edge.

Our Miss Brooks was produced by Desilu, the company owned and operated by Lucille Ball and Desi Arnaz, and co-starred Gale Gordon as the malevolent school principal, Osgood Conklin. Gordon subsequently became a mainstay of the later Lucy shows, for

Acid-tongued Eve Arden in Our Miss Brooks.

which his character was noticeably softened, even feminized.

Miss Brooks' character also changed from being a hunter of men to being their quarry. She never succumbed, however, which probably accounts for the show's continued success in the ratings after syndication. With the passage of time perceptions of women had begun their laborious change and, thanks to Eve Arden's sardonic delivery, Miss Brooks stood up well in the new atmosphere. In 1956 Eve starred in a big-screen version of her TV show.

Eve Arden apart, the other shows of the 1950s which centred on women featured dizzy dames. The success of Lucy and Joan Davis was not generally followed up but, by the mid-1960s, network bosses felt brave enough to risk basing a new series on a woman. Initially, however, they erred heavily on the side of caution – which is to say they continued to underline stereotypes. One show from the period was *That Girl*, starring Marlo Thomas (Danny Thomas's daughter) as a young single woman living alone and trying to make it as an actress but, judging from her apartment and the extent of her wardrobe, still heavily dependent upon Dad for funds.

It was the 1970s before a major break-through occurred for women. This came with *The Mary Tyler Moore Show*, which began in 1970 and ran until 1977. Mary Tyler Moore had become a national favourite thanks to her rôle as Mary Petrie in *The Dick Van Dyke Show*; now, in collaboration with her husband Grant Tinker, she set about evolving a sitcom format which took into account the fact that she, an attractive young woman, could own a TV production company in real life. True, Lucille Ball had been in exactly the same position, but her TV character hadn't enough savvy to have a TV set repaired without encountering disaster, let alone own a company that made programmes. Mary Tyler Moore reasoned that reality could be made to work: but it was a risk, and the network chiefs needed a lot of convincing. It also required some persuasion to establish on-screen other important changes which had occurred in real life.

Back in the days when Lucy ruled the airwaves marriages were made to last. They weren't necessarily any better at that time, but divorce was not so widespread and marital stability on screen reflected the norm. Now, divorce was rife and so were all manner of marital irregularities. Sleeping around was in. If the network bosses were not wholeheartedly in favour of leaping on to the quickie-divorce bandwagon, they at least had the nous to accept that audience identification was a key factor in success. Those men and women, especially women, who had identified with Lucy were now twenty years older and a whole new generation of viewers (and consumers, don't forget) was watching TV. They wanted something which reflected life as they knew it; with which they, not their parents' generation, could identify. They got what they wanted with Mary.

In establishing the format for the show, the producers planned further important changes to preconceived notions of the rôle of women. Mary Richards, the character played by Moore, was not supported financially by a man but had a job of her own. Furthermore, the series would concentrate upon her working life rather than her home life, but this would not exclude scenes showing Mary at home. This was an important break with tradition. Not many women portrayed on TV had lives outside the home, and those who did had nothing to do with that male bastion, the workplace. Those few women who worked, like Our Miss Brooks, had a limited home life if they were allowed one at all. Mary Richards had a lot more going for her than any other TV sitcom female before her. Of course, there was compromise: Mary's colleagues at work were all men, while her neighbours at home were all women: only rarely did the twain meet and mingle.

Mary's job was also upgraded beyond those usually permitted TV women. She was an associate producer in the newsroom of a local TV station, a job which automatically carried considerable cachet in the public mind. Even more significant and groundbreaking was the fact that Mary Richards was single, and although over thirty was still well short of middle age. Mary Tyler Moore had wanted her character to be divorced, but this was still untrodden ground. Neither was she widowed, the customary alternative cop-out. Being

A crisis in the newsroom at Station WJM-TV (Gavin MacLeod, Edward Asner, Mary Tyler Moore).

single and independent was a considerable advance. Even more unusual, there were occasional hints that Mary Richards slept with the men she dated. In one episode of the show Mary accidentally revealed to her mother that she was on the pill. A single girl taking oral contraceptives? Whatever next?

What next? Well, not very much actually, but the freedom displayed by this TV woman, while decidedly limited by latterday standards, was extraordinary for the time. To the surprise of the network, which had fought a rearguard action against all these innovations, the show rapidly clocked up a huge audience. Even more surprising was the fact that the average age of this audience was low. Mary Richards' adventures at Station WJM-TV were watched eagerly by marginally post-teens and by young singles and married executives in their twenties and early thirties.

Surrounding the central character was an array of strongly developed minor rôles, each excellently cast. Playing Lou Grant, Mary's boss, was Edward Asner, whose career until this time had concentrated upon dramatic rôles. Gavin MacLeod took the rôle of wisecracking Murray Slaughter, while Ted Knight played Ted Baxter, the vain and dim newscaster. The scenes which took place at Mary's apartment were enhanced by a gallery of engaging neighbours: Valerie Harper as Rhoda Morgenstern, Cloris Leachman as Phyllis Lindstrom and Betty White as Sue Ann Nivens.

Subsequent spin-offs from *The Mary Tyler Moore Show* were *Lou Grant*, which forsook the comedy format for that of a straight drama, *Rhoda, Phyllis and The Betty White Show*. Additionally, there was *Paul Sand in Friends and Lovers*, which took up a character who appeared in only a couple of episodes of the parent show.

The writing for the show was literate and maintained a remarkably high standard, descending only rarely into the bathos that damages so many American sitcoms. Indeed, one outstanding episode centred upon a funeral yet managed to avoid being maudlin. This was the episode entitled 'Chuckles Bites the Dust', about a popular children's TV clown who died as a result of a freak accident. As one character says, 'He went to the parade dressed as Peter Peanut — and a rogue elephant tried to shell him.' Mary grows steadily angrier as everyone uses the clown's bizarre death for one tasteless joke after another:

'Lucky the elephant didn't go after anyone else.'

'That's right. You know how hard it is to stop after just one peanut.'

The jokes continue right into the church on the day of the funeral, when the gang finally agrees to cut the wisecracks. Then, as the preacher delivers his solemn oration which incudes one of Chuckles the Clown's own lines ('A little song, a little dance, a little seltzer down your pants'), it is Mary's turn to break up and start giggling uncontrollably.

Within a few months of the show's début another sitcom began which stole much of the limelight. This was *All in the Family*, and if, rightly, this show can be regarded as the means by which American TV sitcom rose to the levels of adult entertainment British audiences had been enjoying for some years, this should not conceal the value of *Mary Tyler Moore*. Perhaps *All in the Family* dealt with 'issues', but *MTM* dealt with life in a remarkably realistic way. In Rick Mitz's words, 'It was the first sitcom in which the characters lived in the Real World, not a dream world.' Yet it was still a world away from the circumstances in which the show's audiences lived.

Of the show's spin-offs, *Rhoda* demonstrates many of the difficulties of maintaining good intentions. Rhoda Morgenstern was Jewish, which had until then been something of a no-no for the networks. Of course, she had a typically Jewish mother: the rôle of Ida Morgenstern was marvellously played by the deadpan Nancy Walker — who was no more Jewish than was Valerie Harper who played her daughter Rhoda.

Apart from being a Jew, Rhoda was also single. This was the factor the top-brass at CBS most distrusted. The fact that Mary Richards had got away with being single was not enough assurance for them to take the risk. Part of the problem, as they perceived it, was that Rhoda would be seen mostly in her home. She needed a boyfriend, they decided, and in came Joe Gerard (played by David Groh). Then it was decided that she should settle down, so she married the guy — but that proved restricting, so they separated and were eventually divorced. Inadvertently, because it wasn't intended this way, Rhoda's divorce was really a breakthrough for TV comedy.

The show's confusion deepened when the home setting proved too restricting. This was partially solved by involving Rhoda more closely in the little business she had started some time earlier. The writers were obliged to wheel in numerous eccentric neighbours, so

Valerie Harper in the title rôle of Rhoda.

many in fact that the building where Rhoda had her apartment must have been next door to the local fruitcake factory. Among the more amusing occupants of the building were Rhoda's sister Brenda (Julie Kavner) and Carlton, the unseen doorman (Lorenzo Music) whose messages slurred through the intercom to herald yet another visitor.

Ida: There's a drunk in the lobby, so you'd better tell the doorman.
Rhoda: Ma, that *is* the doorman.

Eventually, the confusion felt by network executives showed in the scripts and *Rhoda* fell apart under the weight of all the indecision.

If *Rhoda* failed to capitalize upon the advances made by *The Mary Tyler Moore Show*, a spin-off from *All in the Family* took enormous strides forward. In one episode of *All in the Family* Edith Bunker was ill and her cousin, knowing Archie's ineptness at everything, came to take care of her. The cousin was Maude Findlay and she was everything Archie Bunker was not. She was a liberal; she was liberated; and she was middle-class. One thing they did have in common: neither was afraid to speak out against anything that offended them. Naturally, the things that offended Maude were vastly different from those that upset Archie. It is unlikely that Norman Lear, who had adapted *All in the Family* from BBC TV's *Till Death Us Do Part*, would have expanded a bit part into a full-scale series had the rôle of Maude not been played by an actress of uncommon skill and talent — and this one, with years of Broadway experience behind her, had a way with a one-liner that would make even Eve Arden jealous.

Beatrice Arthur brought to *Maude* a powerful personality which matched her tall frame. And, as if responding to his leading actress's physical characteristics, Lear introduced topics with as much depth and weight as featured in Archie Bunker's conversations. In *Maude*, however, the responses were appropriately free of the bigotry which had made Archie (and his British predecessor Alf Garnett) so mesmerically awful. *Maude* dealt with real life but, unlike that displayed in *The Mary Tyler Moore Show*, this was a world in which unpleasant things happened and had to be faced.

Sex featured in *Maude*, but this time it was the kind of sex that brought unwanted pregnancy and abortion. Episodes of the series also dealt with the menopause and alcoholism, not as the butt of cheap jokes but as a means of saying important things with dignity and humour.

In some respects *Maude* was a one-woman show. One episode, 'Maude Turns Fifty', really was that, in much the same way that *Till Death Us Do Part* was a one-man show for Warren Mitchell. But the supporting rôles were invaluable and excellently played. Among these were Rue McClanahan as Maude's friend Vivian and Bill Macy as Maude's husband, Walter, whose transgressions invariably caused Maude to call in help from on high: 'God'll get you for this!'

Despite the quality of the supporting rôles it was the central character that the audiences wanted to see and hear. In Beatrice Arthur they had a performer who gave them everything they wanted — and then some.

Until *Maude*, the way in which women were portrayed on American TV had varied wildly in terms of its intelligence quotient. After *Maude* it would stay down for a while. Coincidentally, when women eventually reached the top the most important of the sitcoms, *The Golden Girls*, starred three of the actresses who had participated in some of the revolutionary shows: Betty White from *The Mary Tyler Moore Show* and Beatrice Arthur and Rue McClanahan from *Maude*.

After *Maude*, in 1975, Norman Lear produced *One Day at a Time*, starring Bonnie Franklin as Ann Romano, a divorced mother of two. Like Archie Bunker and Maude Findlay before her, Ann Romano dealt with real issues in an adult way. Unlike Archie and Maude, who stood for the right and the left of centre respectively, Ann took the middle ground, the one most real-life people find they occupy. The show was low-key, bringing smiles rather than outright laughter, and was decidedly feminist in ethos. However, this was not the aggressive feminism that demands equal rights at the coal face or on the rugby pitch but reasoned, intelligent comment that took stands in such a way that it won converts.

A year after *One Day at a Time* came *Alice*,

Beatrice Arthur, eponymous heroine of Maude.

Another problem to be solved in Alice *(Linda Lavin, Liberty Williams).*

which owed its origins to the 1975 movie *Alice Doesn't Live Here Anymore.* Like *M*A*S*H* before it, this was a case where the original format lent itself readily to the confined space of the sitcom. Set almost entirely in Mel's Diner, the show centres on the interrelationships between three waitresses and Mel.

The girls were Alice Hyatt, Flo and Vera. As played by Linda Lavin, Alice is a quiet, responsible individual, if a slightly subdued person, much like Ellen Burstyn in the movie. This allows the other players to bounce their more aggressive styles off her. Most aggressive of the girls is Flo, played by Polly Holliday, although she comes nowhere close to the gloriously foul-mouthed portrayal given in the movie by Diane Ladd. Thanks to one of TV's little ironies, when Flo proved so popular she was awarded the accolade of her own series (entitled – surprise, surprise – *Flo*); she was replaced in *Alice* by a character named Belle. Hired to play Belle was none other than Diane Ladd. Sadly, if predictably, Belle's

dialogue as written for home consumption was a much diluted version of that spoken by Ms Ladd's original screen character. The third waitress is dim Vera, played by Beth Howland, who can barely find her way to the kitchen wherein the owner of the diner, Mel (Vic Tayback), presides.

The scripts were well-seasoned with snappy one-liners (one of the show's writers was Arthur Marx, son of Groucho). Most of the best come from Flo/Belle and Mel, who have a love-hate relationship, which in this case means they love to hate one another. ('Mel, you can kiss mah grits!')

Underneath all the surface wisecracking is a solid core of sensible, low-key comedy from Alice, who becomes a sort of agony aunt for the employees and customers of Mel's Diner. This gave the show an ambience missing from many sitcoms and allowed it to be easily overlooked as just another piece of American tack. In fact, as Rick Mitz astutely observes, *'Alice*'s humour didn't strive for the high of a

Nerys Hughes and Polly James in Carla Lane's The Liver Birds.

M*A*S*H or *Taxi*, where every one-liner told you ten things about the person who said it. But underneath *Alice*'s sometimes corny jokes and slapstick routines, there was something on the show that was missing from so many sitcoms: compassion.'

Also very much an all-girl affair was *Private Benjamin*, starring Lorna Patterson as a wealthy young woman who joins the US Army. The show was based upon the character created by Goldie Hawn for the 1980 movie, but milked the army for numerous not-too-original situations for comedy. In the movie the army had been the means of turning a well-heeled, male-dominated dumb-ish blonde into an independent woman. The show put her right back where TV wanted her.

Just like their American counterparts, women on British TV underwent a similarly switchbacking time. There were occasional females who dominated their menfolk much in the manner of a praying mantis, notably Mildred Roper (played by Yootha Joyce) in *Man about the House* and *George and Mildred*. A few years earlier Yootha Joyce had played a similar rôle as the ever-frustrated fiancée of mother-dominated Bunjy (Milo O'Shea) in *Me Mammy*. Planning a weekend in Paris, Bunjy offers to show her the sights but she has other things on her mind:

'I'll show you the Eiffel Tower.'

'Something like that.'

Several sitcom women at least matched their mates. A surprisingly early example of equal status in both billing and script was Jack Rosenthal's *The Lovers*. This starred Paula Wilcox and Richard Beckinsale as two naïve teenagers, Beryl and Geoffrey, she clinging on to her virginity and he desperately trying to lose his.

Gemma (Felicity Kendal), the heroine of Solo.

Some years later Patricia Hodge in *Holding the Fort* and Judi Dench in *A Fine Romance* also matched the rôles given to their screen partners but generally speaking it was rare for a leading female character to be able to display reasonable intelligence and potential depth of personality.

Of those shows that did contain important rôles for women, a high proportion were the creations of writer Carla Lane, whose work fits the sitcom definition only marginally. It is perhaps best described as mildly humorous light drama peopled with characters who gaze ruefully upon a passing world and idly dream of better things which, with a little bit of ginger, they could readily achieve.

An early example was *The Liver Birds* (co-written with Myra Taylor and Lew Schwartz), which centred upon the antics of two working girls who share a flat in Liverpool. The Birds were plunged headlong into improbable situations and, worse, unlikely characterizations. Thanks to the portrayal by Nerys Hughes, Sandra had some measure of real humanity. Her rôle, as a helplessly naïve virgin at a time when Britain was reputedly swinging through its most permissive era ever, had depth and an undercurrent of pathos. Sadly, the scripts usually undercut her rôle, leaving her looking faintly foolish when, in fact, she should have been sympathetic and someone with whom the young female audience could identify. Her flatmate Beryl (played by Polly James) was deliberately zany, as was her successor Carol (Elizabeth Estensen), in a way that few people in real life are. Thus, from the start, the series suffered from a dichotomy of purpose. Had both girls been zanies the show could have gone the way of, say, the much later (and much worse) *Girls on Top*; had they both been a little closer to life the show might have had a chance of becoming a female counterpart to *The Likely Lads*. As it was, however, the show and its characters lacked the essential realism of the *Lads*; its ambiance was always uncertain and it was ultimately less funny. The Liver Birds were as unsure of their roots as they were of their shifting accents.

After *The Liver Birds* Carla Lane moved into a different social class for shows such as *Butterflies, Solo* and *The Mistress*, which took potentially rich ground and mined from it a succession of sub-soap opera clichés which, thanks to good production values and first-class acting, proved to be enormously successful with the viewing audience. In this respect the ground occupied by Carla Lane closely resembles the literary territory over which Mills & Boon hold sway, a sort of never-never-land in which the dreamy princess wakes one day to find Prince Charming by her bed — but not in it. Her subsequent return to working-class life, in *Bread*, resulted in more uncertainty as self-consciously comic characters infiltrated the unfunny dole queues of Liverpool.

In *Butterflies* the leading rôle of Ria was played by Wendy Craig, an excellent actress with a long record of success on stage and television. An attractive woman fighting middle age, Ria is unashamedly middle-class. She isn't exactly unhappy, but she isn't happy either. Or, to be a little more precise, she is dissatisfied with what she has. Viewed from outside, what she has seems pretty good by most standards, but what Ria wants is not the appurtenances of middle-class comfort. Ria wants romance, and she finds it in the park where she happens to meet Leonard (played with diffident charm by Bruce Montague); with him she forms a romantic attachment that matches her daydreams in its patently unreal atmosphere.

At home, her life continues in its routine (or rut, as she would think of it) although her

dreaminess eventually raises questions in the mind of her husband, Ben. As written and played by the superb Geoffrey Palmer, whose face could have been designed by Walt Disney on a good day, Ben merely questions, then understands.

The chinzty urbanity of the series irritates most because the ideas and the writing and especially the performances all offer much greater potential than is realized. Most notably, just as *Butterflies* failed to advance the rôle of the family in TV sitcoms, so the rôle of women is not helped one iota by Ria. If Ria is believable it is because Wendy Craig is believable; the character most certainly is not.

In *Solo* and *The Mistress* the potential is again greater than the achievement.

Solo's leading character is Gemma, who lives by herself, prefers it that way, and is permanently feuding with her mother, who thinks she should not live alone, and her cloddish boyfriend, who selfishly holds the same opinion. In this respect *Solo* cleaves much closer to real life than did either *The Liver Birds* or *Butterflies*, but there is still about it an air of escapism.

In *The Mistress*, the leading character is Maxine, who is precisely what the series title suggests she is. No scarlet woman, Maxine is liberated yet still ever-so-slightly dependent upon a (somewhat wimpish) man for warmth and comfort.

What Gemma and Maxine seek is much what Ria wanted: romance. They also have poor taste in men and an enviable ability to maintain uncrumpled and unstained sheets.

Both *Solo* and *The Mistress* starred Felicity Kendal, a talented actress with many fine straight rôles to her credit on TV, the stage and in films. Unfortunately, during her long stint in the earlier comedy series *The Good Life*, she found a note of determined winsomeness which she seems unable to shake off. What started out as a delightful characteristic has become merely wearisome, quite out of keeping with the potentially deeper and more rewarding nature of her rôles as Gemma and Maxine.

Would-be adulterers form the one-joke central premise of *Duty Free*, a well written and ably performed sitcom from YTV which should have been dropped after its first, very

Jack Galloway and Felicity Kendall as Maxine, in The Mistress.

A Spanish package of would-be adultery in Duty Free *(Neil Stacy, Joanna Van Gyseghem, Carlos Douglas, Gwen Taylor, Keith Barron).*

funny, series. Written by Eric Chappell and Jean Warr, the show proved very popular and was brought back for more; the subsequent series revealed just how thin the original premise had been but was fortunately sustained by the script and excellent ensemble playing from the actors.

Two couples meet on holiday in Spain and the man in one, David (Keith Barron), and the women in the other, Linda (Joanna Van Gyseghem), are attracted to one another. The will-they-won't-they go to bed together routine is played as briskly as any Whitehall farce, with the obligatory hiding in wardrobes and beneath beds, but is well-laced with snappy one-liners. Balancing David and

Linda's hopeful flirtations are their more straight-laced other halves: Neil Stacy as Robert and Gwen Taylor as David's long-suffering wife Amy. The show was given rather more depth than it had any right to expect by Gwen Taylor, who made her rôle genuinely sympathetic through an understated melancholic acceptance that although there was never any danger of David leaving her for Linda it was not because she was herself still attractive to him.

If adultery is an awkward problem for sitcom writers to handle and stay funny and credible, then the depiction of homosexuality is a real minefield.

Male homosexuality was preceded on

Gunner Beaumont (Melvyn Hayes) in an untypically warlike mood in It Ain't Half Hot,
Mum.

television at a cautious distance by male effeminacy. As noted earlier, the character played by Gale Gordon in various shows with Lucille Ball skated round the edges without ever risking the really thin ice.

In Jimmy Perry and David Croft's *It Ain't Half Hot, Mum*, the sergeant major's despairing cry that the entire concert party platoon is made up of 'a load of poofs' is patently untrue. It strikes a comical chord because Sergeant Major Williams (Windsor Davies) is the kind of man who probably thinks of all actors as being precisely that. The subject was given a much deeper resonance by the performance of Melvyn Hayes as Gunner Beaumont, who in uniform is only slightly camp. Made up for one of the concert party's shows he becomes 'Gloria' and is the epitome of the typical female star of a Hollywood musical. Although the actor took his Gloria character well over the edge, he managed to retain a considerable measure of believability and pathos. If Gloria remained a stereotype, it was by no means an unsympathetic one.

Homosexuality in *Soap* existed only because it was one of the great unmentionables, taking its place alongside all the other unmentionable subjects the show featured.

In *Agony* homosexuality managed the difficult task of being both overt and free of stereotyping. The homosexual lovers are involved in the show's humour as both makers and butts of jokes. Unusually, if not uniquely until this time, they are not made the butt of jokes *because* they are homosexual. In a real sense, their sexual proclivity is beside the point, which in practice gives the humour in which they are involved greater strength than that achieved by any earlier gay stereotypes; indeed, one of these characters commits suicide – perhaps the first time this has ever happened in a sitcom.

Contrastingly, John Inman's outrageously camp Mr Humphries in *Are You Being Served?* made no attempt to avoid the stereotype.

In *Brothers*, a show made for cable TV in America, homosexuality really came out of the comic closet. Here the main thread of the series is a family's attempt to come to terms with the fact that the youngest son is homosexual. Though founded on a one-joke situation, the show had considerable potential

for inventive expansion and for the most part succeeded in offering a view of sexuality which had hitherto been absent from American TV screens in anything other than straight drama, and not often there either.

ABC and NBC had already rejected the show because of its theme before it was picked up by Showtime, who wanted it for the very same reason the networks didn't. It proved very popular, especially among gays, and producer Gary Nardino won an award from the Alliance of Gay and Lesbian Artists in the Entertainment Industry. Possibly surprising to many, and certainly to ABC and NBC executives, was its popularity with straight audiences, whose ignorance and prejudice were to some extent attacked by the show.

As portrayed by Paul Regina, Cliff Waters, the homosexual brother, wears none of the stereotypical trademarks. He dresses, speaks and walks 'normally' and his wrists are not threatened with incipient limpness. But this avoidance of the obvious did not mean that the show was ducking issues: far from it, in fact, for Cliff and another gay kiss on-screen and, much more significantly, one episode features the family's responses to a friend they learn is suffering from AIDS.

Despite such advances there are still some no-go areas in sitcom-land. Lesbianism has yet to be taken up as a serious subject for humour, perhaps because of its potential for damaging the egos of the males who still dominate television. Similarly slow in coming to the front of the bus is sex between the black and white races in comedy, although Diahann Carroll and Ken Howard have had an affair in *Dynasty*.

Norman Lear's view of sex on television today may have changed, but in 1979 he observed:

If you care to know where the only real sex is on American television, it is on the commercials. See the beautiful young model, running her tongue over her teeth on an extreme close-up, and panting about the fresh taste in her mouth. Watch what the other young model is doing with her soda pop bottle, as she extols the yummy taste of the product. She wants you to know that that brand of soda is her friend – and so, as she handles it, is the bottle.

Among the few female-dominated shows on

British TV in the 1980s is *Victoria Wood — As Seen on TV*. This is not sitcom. Its structure harks back to the older-style revue while accommodating contemporary attitudes and techniques. The show follows a simple format: an opening monologue from the star, a series of sketches of varying length, a comic song at the piano, and into the finale.

Largely written by Ms Wood and enacted by a highly accomplished team of regular players including Patricia Routledge, Celia Imrie and Julie Walters, there are, as in any revue, bits that don't quite come off, a solid core that is good, and a few moments that are absolute gems. The opening monologue suggests that Victoria Wood is a better writer than she is a performer, possibly due to her misconceived deliberately artless delivery.

The sketches bear witness to Ms Wood's generosity in giving the best lines to her supporting cast. Certainly Julie Walters, who first came to national prominence with Wood in their Wood and Walters double-act, is allowed to send up many of the stock butts of music-hall humour, including the decrepit waitress, alongside such latterday targets as the aggressive TV-show presenter. As for the soaps, they are mercilessly parodied with every visit to 'Acorn Antiques', where the scenery wobbles as alarmingly as the actors.

Also provided with gems of barbed humour is Susie Blake as a TV continuity announcer who always says what everyone imagines such people would dearly like to say in real life: 'We would like to apologize to viewers in the North. It must be awful for you.'

In America, the 1980s brought important rôles for women in a number of shows, not least in *Cheers*, which includes two strongly characterized female rôles. More cheers for *Cheers* will be found in Chapter 13.

Kate and Allie, which appeared in mid-season 1983-4, became one of the surprise successes on prime time, although it failed to repeat the achievement on its British showing. Starring Susan St James as Kate and Jane Curtin as Allie, the series follows the lives of two divorced women who decide to make things a little easier by sharing a house. The fact that each has children who do not necessarily hit it off all the time gave the show some of its storylines but, coming as it did hard

on the heels of the kiddie-saturation which afflicted the late 1970s, the show concentrated upon the adults. As suggested earlier, Lucy succeeded thanks to assured assumptions about marriage; Mary knew that the life led by single women would give the show an understanding following; Kate and Allie have a similarly assured outlook but theirs is the assurance that sooner or later divorce looms for a steadily increasing percentage of the population.

Very ably acted by the two principals and with the kids taking fortunately subordinate rôles, the show looks at how women respond to the circumstances into which they are plunged by divorce. For one, the self-assured Kate, a child of the liberal 'sixties, it is an opportunity to make a new life for herself, and she calls up endless reserves of drive and ability. For Allie, a traditionalist, it is a revelation of how totally dependent upon a man she had become. The relationship the two women have may be one of much-needed interdependence, but together they are formidably capable.

Similarly interdependent but collectively independent and twice as many in number are *The Golden Girls*, which came as a breath of air and helped answer with a resounding 'No!' those who wondered many times — and with good cause — during the early 1980s whether television comedy was finally dead.

By any standards Susan Harris's *The Golden Girls* was a remarkable achievement. The fact that it centred upon four women, three of them well past middle-age and one in her eighties, makes its success almost beyond belief.

There had been other shows about the elderly. Back in 1954 Spring Byington starred in *December Bride*, a show in which she had appeared earlier on radio. Lily Ruskin, the character Miss Byington played, was capable and intelligent, warm and understanding. In fact she was everything fantasy grandmothers are supposed to be. In this the character reflected the times in which the programmes were made. America was not then strong enough to withstand the shock generated by the kind of old lady Ruth Gordon would project in numerous movie rôles, including that of Clint Eastwood's Ma in *Any Which Way*

Surprising how suddenly TV can age comics. Julie Walters and Victoria Wood after a hard day in the make-up department.

You Can. December Bride ran for five years, achieving good ratings, a devoted following and an early TV rôle for Harry Morgan (as the next-door neighbour), but failed to persuade anyone to build upon the foothold it had achieved for the next thirty years.

In 1985 Susan Harris, who had earlier shocked some sensibilities with *Soap*, came to her new project fully aware of the difficulties she faced. 'A woman's worth is tied into what she looks like. At 82 Cary Grant could … be a romantic lead. But on television, a woman over 50 is cast as an axe murderer.'

A show about four elderly women therefore had the odds against it from the start. Imagine the first meeting the programme's makers had with the network: 'We have this great idea for a sitcom. There are these four old ladies — well, three are somewhere between 55 and 65 and one's over 80 — and they live together in Florida and …'

How on earth did they ever get it made? Perhaps it is best not to ponder too much on the question and simply be thankful that they did.

Taut, witty and well constructed, the scripts are a dream for any actress, and to have four such excellent parts in one series is truly remarkable. That they should be cast and performed so well is a tribute to all concerned.

The house where the four ladies live is owned by Blanche, a fading Southern belle who echoes Blanche Dubois not only in name. Contentedly nymphomaniacal, Blanche fights off middle age with determination and clearly sees no reason to allow any diminution in a sex life which has already made Tennessee Williams look like a compiler of primers for the under-tens. Portraying Blanche with sashaying enthusiasm is Rue McClanahan.

One of the ladies with whom Blanche shares her home is Rose, a middle-American in all senses. Of Swedish ancestry and with a picture-book rural background, Rose is one of life's innocents. Not exactly dumb, she is always the last to see the point of anything, especially the jokes her companions fire at her. But Rose, beautifully drawn by Betty

One Kate and Allie *episode is a potted history of sitcom. At left, Allie dreams that she is Lucy and Kate is Ethel Mertz. At right, she is Rhoda while Kate becomes Mary Richards (Jane Curtin, Susan St James as Kate and Allie).*

White, has great depths of emotional uncertainty. She is a widow whose husband died while they were making love. This, and the fact that a similar death occurs when Rose dates a middle-aged man, gives her status in Blanche's eyes: 'What do you *do* in bed?'

Providing the show's powerful centre is Dorothy, played by Beatrice Arthur, who brings to her rôle echoes of Maude Findlay but is here much more relaxed – even if, inside, Dorothy is constantly plagued by uncertainties. She worries about her height and whether or not she is, or has ever been, attractive to men and she worries about the fact that men tend to be afraid of her. Her appearance of physical strength makes her two friends turn to her for help when the going gets tough. They invariably get the help they seek, but as they do so the true vulnerability of Dorothy is revealed and the character becomes anything but the stereotype it might well have been in the hands of insensitive writers or of a less skilled actress.

Dorothy also worries about her mother, Sophia, which is the last thing she need do. At 80 Sophia is a tough old broad who came to America from her native Sicily and acts, talks and looks as though she could go ten rounds with Groucho Marx and come out with a points decision. Sophia doesn't like old people. ('Some old ladies are real pains.')

While the other actresses in *The Golden Girls* were already familiar to TV audiences, Estelle Getty (who is nowhere near as old as the rôle she plays) was a virtual unknown. Notwithstanding her considerable success on Broadway in *Torch Song Trilogy*, this is the part she must have been dreaming of ever since she became an actress.

In a script that positively bristles with superb one-liners of the kind Eve Arden used to deliver with such aplomb, everyone gets their share of the good ones but Sophia gets the zingers. 'Sicily was full of dark alleys. How do you think I came to marry your father?' Significantly, because the show constantly pulls towards the ever-present soft centre that bedevils American comedy, it is Sophia who interrupts the others in time to prevent the slide into sentimentality.

Often directed by British-born Terry Hughes, many of the show's scripts are written by women and women are also heavily involved in the production team.

In an episode which skated confidently on the edge of bad taste, Rose has a new boyfriend but never brings him home. When she is eventually persuaded to do so, Dorothy and Blanche quickly discover the reason for their friend's reluctance: the boyfriend is a midget. There follows a barrage of unintentional slip-ups, mostly from Blanche, who takes some convincing that he really is a midget and not a small boy Rose has dressed up as a practical joke. At one point Blanche sashays into the room with a plateful of canapés. 'Shrimp?' she enquires. Rose and her beau eventually go out to dine where they can talk quietly about their future. With every member of the audience wondering how on earth the scriptwriters can get Rose out of this without causing offence to any susceptibilities, on-screen or off, *he* dumps *her* because she isn't Jewish.

Another episode has Blanche recounting a time when she braved the wrath of her small Southern town neighbours by flouting convention with her choice of the man with whom she would attend a ball. Thanks to an earlier conversation, Dorothy and Rose mistakenly assume that Blanche's date was black and applaud her strength of character. Blanche is shocked when she realizes the depth of their misunderstanding: 'Hell, no,' she declares, 'he was a Yankee.'

Blanche's Southern upbringing is given free rein in an episode in which her father, whom she insists on calling Big Daddy, comes to visit. Fortunately, her friends are there to keep a lid on her romantic day-dreaming.

Blanche: Oh, as far as I can remember people from all over the county would drive up to Twin Oaks, that's the name of our house, to ask Big Daddy's advice on one thing or another. And while the men were discussing business on the verandah, the ladies would retire to the shade of an old magnolia to sip mint juleps and exchange prize-winning pecan pie recipes.
Dorothy: Tell me, Blanche, during any of this did the field hands suddenly break into 'Dem Old Cotton Fields Back Home'?

Blanche brushes this off with a smile and moments later prepares to leave.

Blanche: I got a million things to do before Big

Daddy gets here. I have to go pick up his favourite food, his favourite brandy and cigars. I want to make him feel right at home.

Sophia: Then get the Millers across the street to tar and feather their lawn jockey.

With all its virtues it comes as no surprise that *The Golden Girls* has gathered a trunkful of awards, among them numerous Emmys. It displays TV sitcom at its very best and demonstrates that the adage 'Quality is no guarantee of success' doesn't always hold good. Moreover it gives the rôle of women on TV a major boost, even if they are still being treated like not very bright second-class citizens in the commercials which interrupt the show. Here at least are women, and older women too, who are allowed to be funny without ever having to resort to male preconceptions or play second fiddle or lose their dignity.

Most important of all, *The Golden Girls* has restored faith at a time when the death of situation comedy on television seemed nigh. The obituary writers will have to wait a while.

CHAPTER EIGHT

WAR IS HELL . . . ON THE RATINGS

'M*A*S*H isn't really a sitcom.'
Alan Alda

War is nothing to joke about. Aware of this, when TV has made wartime comedies it has, like the movies, tended towards shows about servicemen (rarely women) engaged in light-hearted activities well behind the lines rather than showing war as it really is.

Modern wars have been regularly attended by comics, both old hands touring to entertain troops and new faces emerging from the ranks. A substantial crop of latterday British entertainers served their show-business apprenticeship defending their country: Spike Milligan, Peter Sellers, Harry Secombe, Eric Sykes and Jimmy Edwards among them. Inevitably, both the old and the new have used the military way of life as a butt for their humour but for the most part it was not war itself that provided the laughs. The bureaucratic blundering that is an inseparable part of anything involving the military has always provided a surefire laugh. So too has the food, and among the first tasks of any comic arriving at an army camp with ENSA or the USO was that of learning the names of the Adjutant or Executive Officer and the cook, which would then be slotted into the appropriate joke.

Much wartime humour stems from the simple fact that when people recall their wartime experiences they tend to shut out, consciously or not, its horrific aspects, retaining only those memories with which they can live. The shortlived feeling of togetherness generated in wartime both in and out of the armed forces was sufficiently

removed from bloody reality to allow humorists to work without the danger of treading on too many susceptibilities. While soldiers might often appear in TV comedies, therefore, what they are really engaged in – killing – seldom appears on screen.

Despite the pitfalls, Hollywood has from time to time used a reasonable facsimile of the realities of war as a backdrop for comedy. An early example is Buster Keaton's *The General* (1927); now regarded as a masterpiece, the film was a financial failure at the time of its release, partly because it included scenes of soldiers being killed in battle.

In 1942, when Hollywood was not wholly committed to maligning – or even naming – Nazis in serious dramas, let alone comedies, Ernst Lubitsch made *To Be Or Not To Be*, a glittering black comedy which starred Jack Benny in his best screen rôle. This film used its barbed humour to deal not only with Nazis but with what was really happening in Poland: 'Ah, so they call me Concentration Camp Ehrhard.'

Few other film-makers tried making comedies which gave an honest picture of war until 1970 and the appearance of *M*A*S*H*. Directed by Robert Altman from a screenplay by Ring Lardner Jr, it was set at the time of the Korean war, and released at a time when America's involvement in Vietnam gave the movie a positive and intentional relevance.

As a background for TV sitcoms, war has been featured rarely and handled with

Snudge (Bill Fraser) and Bootsie (Alfie Bass) of The Army Game.

caution. Sometimes it has failed, often miserably; once it succeeded gloriously; at all times its use has raised the highly problematical and decidedly idiosyncratic matter of good taste.

American shows such as *McHale's Navy*, which appeared in 1962 and starred Ernest Borgnine, followed the path of using war merely as an excuse for a tale about a group of men. In this series they were loose in the South Pacific, where their only serious enemies were their own top brass. From 1965 the show's setting was changed to wartime Italy but with no appreciable increase in the reality content.

The year 1965 also saw the appearance of *Hogan's Heroes*, set in a prisoner-of-war camp. The series bore sufficient resemblance to the play *Stalag 17* (which became a movie in 1953) to allow the playwright to win a plagiarism suit. In *Hogan's Heroes* the prisoners run the camp as if it were their own and use it as a base for conducting behind-the-lines attacks on enemy installations. They are aided in this by the good fortune of having as camp commandant a joke-German named Colonel Klink. This rôle was played by Werner Klemperer, whose performance suggested he had seen and greatly admired Jack Benny's in *To Be Or Not To Be*. Klink has an even jokier German assistant in Sergeant Schultz (John Banner). Not surprisingly, the prisoners – under the leadership of Colonel Robert Hogan (Bob Crane) – always come out on top and seem thoroughly to enjoy their captivity.

Like their American counterparts, many of the British films and TV shows which touched upon matters military featured peacetime armies. Especially prominent were the National Servicemen who served the cause unwillingly and, like their regular army counterparts, tend to remember only the good moments of their time in uniform.

Of the early shows by far the best was Granada TV's *The Army Game*, which in 1957 brought to public prominence such actors as Alfie Bass, Bernard Bresslaw, Bill Fraser, Charles Hawtrey and Michael Medwin. William Hartnell, who played RSM Bullimore for the first couple of years, was one of the screen's longest serving non-coms

Snudge finally has the squad from Hut 29 where he wants them (Bill Fraser with, left to right, Alfie Bass, Ted Lune, Harry Fowler, Mario Fabrizi).

with a military record stretching back over numerous war films. He even earned a place in comedy-film history with the title rôle in the first-ever *Carry On* film, *Carry On, Sergeant*. He was finally demobbed in 1963, when he became the first Dr Who.

The Army Game, which was modelled

upon the film *Private's Progress*, was not about war; indeed, for most of the time it was not obviously about the army. What each episode of its five-year run presented was a succession of dodges devised by a group of conscripts to avoid responsibility and any potential hazard. One character, Bootsie, as his nickname suggests, even avoids wearing regulation footwear and slouches about in unlaced plimsolls.

The dozen years since the ending of the war were not so far distant as to have removed all memories of army life from viewers' minds, and with conscription looming on the horizon for most of the nation's young men, *The Army Game*, was good-natured escapism. Its characters were well-drawn and strong enough for two of them, Bootsie and Snudge (Alfie Bass and Bill Fraser), to have their own series, in which, finally out of the army, they worked below stairs in a seedy gentlemen's club.

In choosing the Home Guard as the subject of their enormously successful series *Dad's Army*, the writers Jimmy Perry and David Croft found the ideal balance between reality and comedy and were never hampered by the danger of falling victim to bad taste.

Although well-intentioned and in the context of the times a valid contribution to the war effort, the Local Defence Volunteers, later the Home Guard, were a body of men that included those who were too old to serve, those who were too young and some who had minor medical incapacities. Some of their number had previously military experience gained in long-forgotten wars, while others were complete innocents.

Both during and after the war the Home Guard was the subject of jokes, but these were always affectionate – ridicule played no part in them. Like Robb Wilton with his wartime monologues, Perry and Croft successfully trod the narrow path between laughing at and laughing with the originals behind their comic creations. However often the *Dad's Army* platoon – based at a fictional but realistic south coast resort – find themselves in a ridiculous situation, the humour is always warmly indulgent and never malicious.

Blessed with a perfect cast of mostly elderly British character actors, many of them veterans of stage and screen (and a few real wars, too), the BBC's *Dad's Army* soldiered on for many years of delightful encounters with rival platoons, outraged local citizenry, one another and, very occasionally, a real German who had the misfortune to drop into Walmington-on-Sea. Interestingly, on those few occasions when Germans do appear in the show, they are not the jokey kind.

Commanding the platoon is Captain Mainwaring, who is also the local bank manager. Played with superbly judged pomposity by Arthur Lowe, Mainwaring revels in his quasi-military authority. The power which his uniform and service revolver give him is never abused beyond his commandeering items in the national interest: the vicar's office, a horse on which to ride at the head of his men, the air raid warden's motorbike and even the butcher's van, which on one memorable occasion is converted into a

Wartime Britain's first line of defence taking a well-deserved rest (left to right, Arnold Ridley, Ian Lavender, Arthur Lowe, Clive Dunn, John Le Mesurier, James Beck in Dad's Army).

Captain Mainwaring and the unfailingly polite Sergeant Wilson (Arthur Lowe and John Le Mesurier).

gun-carrier with hidden ports through which, on Mainwaring's command, the platoon thrusts its rifles.

Fortunately, any excess of authority Mainwaring might attempt to exercise is always undercut by his platoon sergeant, who is also his assistant manager at the bank. The rôle of Sergeant Wilson was played by John Le Mesurier, who gave his unfailingly polite character a slightly distracted air of harmless rakishness.

Among the other ranks was John Laurie as Private Frazer, the undertaker, whose mournfully pessimistic tales of terror transfixed the platoon: 'We're doomed. Doomed!' Clive Dunn played Corporal Jones, an aged veteran of a war in which the other side had used spears against the British Army's bayonets: 'They don't like it up 'em.'

Too old to be of any use whatsoever, even coming to attention half a beat behind everyone else, Corporal Jones is also the platoon's alarmist: 'Don't panic! Don't panic!' But as he is the local butcher and can be relied upon at moments of crisis to supply his commanding officer with an extra pair of under-the-counter sausages or some similar small bribe, he may be said to justify his existence.

Arnold Ridley played Mr Godfrey, an extremely old 'typical' English gentleman of private but limited means whose sister Dolly provides the platoon with a continuous supply of fairy cakes. Godfrey's greatest failing in Mainwaring's eyes is his inability to go very far between visits to the lavatory. James Beck played Private Walker, the wide boy who has somehow managed to avoid being called-up by the proper army and who is never without a black-market fag. Ian Lavender played young Frank, the bank clerk who always comes on parade in the muffler his mother insists he wears. This, together with many acts of startling ineptitude, earns him Captain Mainwaring's eternal wrath and the epithet: 'Stupid boy!'

Aided and abetted (when not actively opposed) by Bill Pertwee as the air raid warden, Frank Williams as the vicar and Edward Sinclair as the verger, the Walmington-on-Sea platoon happily took its endless opportunities for humour with both hands. Many of the storylines were founded in real experiences of the Home Guard; others were close enough to have been real. Even if events were sometimes pursued to improbable conclusions, there were always the solid performances of the cast to carry the day.

Despite being realistic in many respects, Dad's Army never came into conflict with the fact that in war people die. In avoiding this, the writers and programme-makers managed not to give offence to those who suffered in the war. Indeed, they never even hurt the feelings of the ex-Home Guardsmen in their substantial audience. Most often, Dad's Army left behind it a warm glow of affection for the series' participants and revived happy memories of a period of recent history when people pulled together and when, despite the fact that the British were at war and had their backs to a crumbling wall, it was still safe to go to bed at night with the door unlocked.

The doubtful area of what is or is not good taste was opened up in 1984 with the appearance on the BBC of 'Allo 'Allo!, a series set in occupied France during the Second World War and centred upon the activities of the French Resistance.

Although the long-term political ambitions of some Resistance members has been the subject of debate and dispute in the years since the ending of the war, few would question the fact that for the most part these were men and women of considerable heroism who risked torture or death if caught in acts of sabotage or aiding Allied service-men and others to escape. In some parts of France (as elsewhere in Europe) reprisals were taken by the German army. At Oradour-sur-Glane, a village near Limoges, 642 out of the 652 inhabitants were shot or burned to death and the village razed to the ground in one such act of reprisal.

When the war was over collaborators were sought out and many went into hiding for years. Those who were found suffered varying degrees of punishment: some women had their hair shorn; other collaborators, men and women, were executed on the spot.

It is against such a background that any comedy about the Resistance has to be measured. Even after making allowances for the passage of time and present-day accept-ance of jokes about almost anything, it is hard to find any saving grace in 'Allo 'Allo! Yet this sitcom has proved to be enormously popular.

Although the cast includes several British character actors of some merit, the whole thing is hammed-up and the characters are no more than stereotypes.

Almost as puzzling as the fact of the show's success with audiences is that one of its writers is the same David Croft who co-authored Dad's Army. The witty charm of the older series has been replaced with end-of-the-pier humour which relies totally upon innuendo so heavy-handed that it makes the Carry On films seem sophisticated.

The leading character is René, a French café-owner (played by Gordon Kaye), who complies with the requirements of stereotypes by being intent only on getting into the knickers of various young Frenchwomen. The latter, as portrayed here, appear to be permanently on heat as they gambol about the place dressed in revealing underwear and, as often as not, caressing a phallic pistol. The Germans are all of the jokey variety, with Richard Marner and Sam Kelly playing the part of amiable Wehrmacht officers. This pair are presumably the good Germans while Herr Flick, a member of the Gestapo (played by Richard Gibson), is wildly signalled as being the bad German. The Gestapo officer occasionally tumbles a female German soldier (Kim Hartman) who favours underwear liberally decorated with swastikas.

A wearisome sub-plot centres upon the search for a stolen painting, 'The Fallen Madonna', which is referred to as the 'Madonna with the Big Boobies'. That such a line should get a laugh once is just about understandable; that it is repeated *ad nauseam* and always gets its laugh says little for the viewing public's powers of discernment.

The reasons why the show should have been made at all and why it has achieved success are difficult to fathom: is it the distance in time or is it the physical distance at which the events take place that enables the situations presented to be rendered 'comic'?

It is more than 40 years since the circumstances that provide the background for *'Allo 'Allo!*, Occupied France, existed. Perhaps it is unfair to expect those members of the show's substantial audience who are under 50 to make the intellectual connection between the real-life events and the TV show. But what about the older members of the audience, and the writers, to say nothing of those younger viewers who have read or, more likely, watched serious television documentary programmes about what happened and absorbed the implications? Can these significant others really find it all so amusing?

Then there is the physical distancing. In *'Allo 'Allo!* the British are writing about the German oppression of France. If an American TV company were to make a show in similar style which uses as its setting the imprisonment of the British by the Japanese in the same war, would British audiences laugh so heartily?

Clearly, the general public has forgotten what really happened in Occupied France. What is staggering is that the BBC appears to have forgotten too. In 1987 *'Allo 'Allo!* was among the shows being offered to potential buyers on the Continent.

Today, Oradour-sur-Glane stands as the Germans left it – a grim memorial to the dead. If *'Allo 'Allo!* were ever to be screened in France, British holidaymakers might be well-advised to give this silent place a wide berth.

That a comedy series such as this should hold the attention of several million regular viewers, and attract further thousands when a stage version was mounted in London's West End towards the end of 1986, suggests that a massive and lamentable decline in standards has occurred in recent years. That this should have happened after the efforts of some comedy writers and TV programme-makers of the recent past makes *'Allo 'Allo!* even more deplorable than it seems at first glance.

The shining highlight of those improvements in standards, which allowed writers, directors, producers and actors to lift their craft to the point where even war could be made the subject of a high-quality comedy, is the TV version of *M*A*S*H*.

The Korean war wasn't really a war. Carefully euphemized by the Pentagon as a 'police action', it began in June 1950 and ended in July 1953, by which time the toll of American dead, wounded and missing exceeded 140,000. British and Commonwealth soldiers were also heavily involved and thousands more were added to the casualty lists. On the other side, North Korean and Chinese casualties were estimated at 1.3 million with some half million Korean civilians also falling victim.

Some police action!

Of course, these statistics pale into significance beside those of the First and Second World Wars and those of the Vietnam war. They do, however, clearly indicate that this was no minor occurrence about which joking was permissible. It was a very serious and deadly business, yet the creators of book, film and TV series were able to find humour without stumbling over the line between good and bad taste.

That the show should prove so immensely

116

*M*A*S*H, a shining highlight of TV comedy (left to right: Alan Alda, Loretta Swit, Gary Burghoff, Larry Linville, Wayne Rogers).*

successful and run for eleven years (251 episodes) without ever crossing into dubious areas was an extraordinary feat demonstrating remarkable skill and judgement. To make matters better, *M*A*S*H* only rarely fell foul of the propensity American sitcoms have for opening up to reveal a marshmallow middle. True, it often preached, but not about American values such as Mom and Apple Pie but rather the basic rights of men and women, about understanding, and about dignity.

The initial letters of *M*A*S*H* stand for Mobile Army Surgical Hospital, a front-line medical unit whose job it is to patch up the slightly wounded and get them back into the fighting, or patch up the severely wounded so that they will live long enough to be evacuated to a proper hospital. The surgeons in MASH units (the asterisks are a Hollywood addition) and their counterparts in all armies are not only required to be first-rate at their job but also to have the ability to do it under fire. The self-deprecating term they hang upon their work is 'meatball surgery'.

Apart from the control imposed on the quality of their work, the surgeons and nurses rarely have time to rest or play or enjoy any of the benefits they expected when they chose their professions. The Americans in Korea were mostly drafted when in their mid-twenties. They brought to the war — sorry! police action — elements of the casually macabre humour of their student days and allied to them a thin shell of deliberate cynicism to separate themselves from reality in this bleakest of situations. In the circumstances in which they were forced to work a sense of humour was not out of place; it was often all that stood between them and nervous or emotional collapse.

Richard Hooker's original novel upon which the movie was based was not, despite its subject matter, notably anti-war. In real life the author was Dr Richard Hornberger, who was never too happy about the dramatized versions of the story of his first-hand experiences. The shift in emphasis to make *M*A*S*H* anti-war and anti-establishment began with the film and continued with, and was emphasized by, the TV version. This was almost entirely a result of timing. When the movie appeared America was involved in Vietnam and some were already questioning the rights and wrongs of the matter. When the TV version began on 17 September 1972 the questioning was considerably louder. Three months to the day before the début a burglary had taken place at the Watergate building in Washington and America's attitudes to the war, its government, even its president, were undergoing a dramatic change.

The timing, then was perfect. But the show could still have gone disastrously wrong. Fortunately, thanks to the carefully chosen team of producers, directors, writers and cast, everything came out right.

Although those who loved the movie might well disagree, the cast changes were an important factor in the TV version's success. For the most part these were not made out of any disregard for the actors in the movie but simply because producers Gene Reynolds and Burt Metcalfe doubted that big-name stars like Elliott Gould and Donald Sutherland would be interested in a TV sitcom. In the event this proved to be a distinct plus for the show as the replacements were so good that later viewings of the movie cause those excellent but very different performances to pale beside those of their small-screen counterparts.

The lead in the TV *M*A*S*H* went to Alan Alda, who tackled the rôle of Captain Benjamin Franklin 'Hawkeye' Pierce as if it were the one he had waited all his professional life to play. His first co-anarchist was Captain 'Trapper John' McIntyre, played by Wayne Rogers and, as in the movie, he and Hawkeye were of equal status. As time went on, Rogers became greatly concerned that his rôle was not developing as were the others in the series and Trapper John was steadily becoming just a sidekick for Hawkeye. Rogers bowed out and was replaced by Mike Farrell as Captain B. J. Hunnicutt. The officer in command of MASH 4077 was originally Lieutenant Colonel Harry Blake (McLean Stevenson) and later Colonel Sherman Potter (Harry Morgan). Chief among those who disapprove of Hawkeye's antics are the inept and malicious Major Frank Burns (Larry Linville), later replaced by music-loving snob Major Charles Emerson Winchester III (David Ogden Stiers) and Major Margaret 'Hot Lips' Houlihan (Loretta Swit). Others in a continuing

Captain Benjamin Franklin 'Hawkeye' Pierce, surgeon and anarchist (Alan Alda).

gallery of excellent supporting characters (and players to match) were Corporal Walter 'Radar' O'Reilly (Gary Burghoff, the only actor from the movie to transfer to TV), Corporal Maxwell Klinger (Jamie Farr) and Father John Francis Mulcahy (William Christopher).

To describe M*A*S*H as a situation comedy is more than a mite inaccurate as some episodes, deliberately, contained no laughs. For the most part, however, even the most serious episode had its humour. Just as important, there was always something serious even in the funniest episodes of M*A*S*H. If the humour was often black, it served only to enhance the reputation the show acquired as it slowly built a following.

The slow pace of its rise in popularity led to fears that it would be dropped after the first season, but the network, CBS, persisted and also largely refrained from demanding too many changes or too much toning down of the show's anti-war ethos.

The remarkably high level of writing and a related consistency in characters and character development stemmed from the presence of Larry Gelbart as co-creator and principal writer. Although sheer pressure of work caused Gelbart to ease back in later years, his contribution at the outset was enormous and he eventually wrote more than a third of the show's scripts. Gelbart had been one of Sid Caesar's writers and after M*A*S*H he continued writing for television and the movies and had co-writer's credit for the screenplay of the 1982 Dustin Hoffman movie Tootsie.

By the end of the second season of M*A*S*H the ratings had begun to make it apparent that CBS had a winner, although few can have expected the show to become an integral part of American popular culture.

Along the way, in one episode after another, Hawkeye fought his battles against authority, war and the prevailing insanity of the situation. Also, as the series progressed M*A*S*H had something to say about prejudices: racial, sexual and class. Especially notable (although not in the earlier episodes) was a strong element of feminism. None of these subjects was much catered for in TV sitcoms of the time and even today is less well-served than should be the case.

By the time it was eight years old some of the people involved in M*A*S*H were beginning to fold their tents and quietly steal away. But another three years of success followed and for the final episode, which ran for two-and-a-half hours, the national audience was phenomenal. The final show, 'Goodbye, Farewell and Amen', which was screened in 1983, drew an audience estimated variously as between 85 and 125 million viewers.

Most significant of the qualities of M*A*S*H is the way in which the characters, Trapper John and perhaps Frank Burns apart, grow as their stay at the 4077 MASH continues. Radar is a helplessly naïve country boy at the start but, like so many similarly immature servicemen, leaves the war zone an older and wiser young man. Winchester, a pompous Bostonian when he is first posted to the unit, finds some measure of humility. Max Klinger changes most noticeably on the surface when he stops wearing women's clothes (his way of trying to swing a discharge on a 'Section 8' — which would categorize him as being crazy).

Even Hawkeye changes, although the wise-cracking surface never alters. 'Frank, if I could yawn with my mouth closed you'd never know just how boring you are.' Underneath, however, Hawkeye hardens, though continually fighting against the absurd policy that requires surgeons to patch up young men so that they can be returned to the firing-line.

Most significant of all the changes in character is the development of Margaret Houlihan. In the early years of M*A*S*H she is, like so many sexually attractive women, the butt of routine jokes, but gradually, and largely due to Loretta Swit's determination, Margaret grows as a woman. Creditably, the scriptwriters, encouraged by Alan Alda, showed a comparable maturity in adopting a more feminist stance in the later years.

Out of the 251 episodes few ever fell below 'very good' (although everyone connected with the show admits to one, 'Major Fred C. Dobbs', being a disaster) and most were worthy of the numerous nominations for awards the series received over the years.

Many of the shows gave opportunities for actors in the series to write or direct (or both). A story written by McLean Stevenson was nominated for an Emmy. This was 'The Trial of

Henry Blake', in which Henry faces a court-martial for consorting with the enemy, a charge brought by Frank Burns, aided and abetted by Hot Lips.

In 'Abyssinia, Henry' Henry Blake finally gets to go home. But as the episode ends Radar comes into the operating theatre to announce that the colonel's aircraft has been shot down – and there are no survivors.

'Mulcahy's War' finds Father Mulcahy chafing at the limitations of his power to bring comfort to those who come to him for spiritual guidance. He insists on going to the front to discover what it is really like and ends up carrying out an emergency tracheotomy with the aid of Hawkeye's radioed instructions.

'Fallen Idol' is the episode in which Radar grows up when he is wounded and operated on by Hawkeye, who later gets drunk. Radar criticizes his hero, which brings down on his head all the surgeon's pent-up wrath. 'How dare you!' shouts Hawkeye. 'To hell with your Iowa naïvety! To hell with your hero worship! And your teddy bear! And while I'm at it, to hell with you! Why don't you grow up, for cryin' out loud? I'm not here for you to admire. Now cut it out, you ninny!' Radar is broken up on hearing this and later, when the unit's anger sends Hawkeye back to apologize, it is Radar's turn: 'To hell with you!' he yells. In due course they patch up their friendship but it is then set on a more equal basis, no longer that of hero and hero-worshipper. Indeed, when Radar is awarded a Purple Heart he also receives from Hawkeye an accolade that even a general has never been given – a salute.

In 'Old Soldiers' Colonel Potter returns from an unexpected visit to Tokyo and throws a party for the gang. When they arrive at his tent he is wearing his First World War uniform. He tells them how, back in 1917, he and four comrades made a vow: the five would preserve a bottle of brandy liberated from a French château and when four of them were dead the survivor would drink a toast *in memoriam*. The last survivor has just died in Tokyo and Potter wants his new friends to share the moment: 'As much as my old friends mean to me, I think you new friends mean even more.'

The clear evidence of friendship which permeates M*A*S*H on screen was matched by the off-screen relationships of the actors and those behind the camera. All were warm, and reputedly, with one exception, the actors matched their screen rôles. The exception was Larry Linville, who off-camera was not at all like his character, the thin-lipped Major Frank Burns, forever on the receiving end of well-aimed wisecracks.

Frank: Why do people take an instant dislike to me?
Trapper: It saves time, Frank.

It is no wonder that Frank can never balance his relationship with Hawkeye and Trapper:

Hawkeye: Hi, Frank.
Trapper: Hello, Frank.
Frank: That'll be the day.

Inevitably, the personal warmth and comradeship seeped through the screen to include the audience, and when it was time for the last, long episode it was as if millions were gathered to say goodbye to old friends, not just a TV show.

That final episode of M*A*S*H contained several storylines (as do most ordinary-length episodes, which rarely have less than three concurrent plots). Grimmest of all is the story of a woman who deliberately smothers her baby to prevent it crying out and revealing the presence of a busload of refugees and soldiers. Among the soldiers is Hawkeye, and the experience is almost enough to tip him over the fine dividing line between mental stability and insanity. As the war lumbers towards its end, B.J. starts for home but is brought back when the 4077 is unable to find a replacement surgeon to cope with the results of the last outbreak of heavy fighting. One storyline concerns Max Klinger's decision to marry Soon-Lee, a decision which leads to his opting to stay behind at the war's end in the country from which he has spent years trying to escape.

Another storyline in this final episode demonstrates the refusal of the makers of M*A*S*H to ignore the reality of war, as well as their determination not to allow the series to end on a note of false optimism. Charles Winchester has inadvertently captured some prisoners as a result of a group of Chinese soldiers surrendering to him. Discovering they are musicians, he sets about teaching them Mozart's Quintet for Clarinet and Strings. By the time the prisoners are moved out they have achieved a passable degree of competence. Hours later, Charles is called to attend to a newly arrived batch of wounded. One, seriously hurt, is the sole survivor of his musical group. For Charles, who has just learned that he has been appointed head of thoracic surgery at a Boston hospital, this is a final blow in the succession that began when he was first sent to Korea. Apart from his work, music is the dearest thing in his life; but now, he says, 'My life will go on as expected. For me, music has always been a refuge from this miserable experience; now it will always be a reminder.'

M*A*S*H was nominated for numerous awards and won many of them, including Emmys for Gene Reynolds, Larry Gelbart and Alan Alda in 1974, Reynolds again in 1975 and 1976, Gary Burghoff and Alda in 1977, Alda again in 1979, Harry Morgan and Loretta Swit in 1980, Alda and Swit in 1981-2.

Tee-shirts and mugs, bubble gum and beer, towels and hats, toys and badges, sleepwear and posters were among the items of merchandise that spun off from the show, which also precipitated a barrage of magazine articles and essays and Susan Kalter's excellent The Complete Book of M*A*S*H.

Few sitcoms have run as long; and of those that have, none has approached the consistently high standards of writing, production and performance which M*A*S*H achieved and maintained.

War may be hell, but here, at least, it gave birth to a hell of a good TV show.

CHAPTER NINE

ALTERNATIVE TO WHAT?

'Much of British TV humour now seems to be disappearing down the toilet in its own swill.'
Herbert Kretzmer, **Daily Mail,** *February 1987*

The sophisticated West End revue style of comedy has enjoyed an occasional fling on television. In the 1960s Alan Melville hosted a series of shows in which he demonstrated his elegant wit. These and other revues included comic monologues, songs and sketches that were sometimes funny and often frankly sentimental. Joyce Grenfell, Beryl Reid and Dora Bryan were among the theatrical personalities who brought their polished performances to television by this means.

The revue format was also adopted by two innovative shows of the 1960s, *That Was the Week That Was,* which brought satire to British television for the first time, and *Not So Much a Programme, More a Way of Life.* In the 1980s, another innovation brought us 'alternative comedy'.

Everyone knows what satire means. After all, it's been around for a long time. Almost 2,000 years ago Juvenal wrote, 'It is difficult to live in these times and not write satire.' The word is also defined in the dictionary: 'the use of ridicule, irony and invective, ostensibly for the chastisement of vice or folly.'

But what is alternative comedy?

The 1960s satirists had behind them a long and honourable tradition of political lampooning, stretching back over several hundred years. The TV satirists, largely from the universities, came to wider attention following the huge popular success of Alan Bennett, Jonathan Miller, Peter Cook and Dudley Moore at the Edinburgh Festival in 1960 with their revue *Beyond the Fringe.*

All four subsequently moved into television, although not always exclusively as performers. The *Fringe* quartet and The Establishment, the London club which played host to them and many others during the London run of *Beyond the Fringe,* which began in May 1961, created an atmosphere for a new comedic style, but it was one that was decidedly elitist.

In 1962 Ned Sherrin brought several specimens of this new breed of performer to television with *That Was the Week That Was.* Political comment, most of it acerbic, became the order of the day and no politician was safe thereafter. Indeed, it wasn't until politicians learned an old showbiz lesson — that even bad publicity is better than no publicity — and started co-operating, even with such potentially damaging caricatures as those in the later *Spitting Image,* that the jokes began to wear thin.

The most visually obvious departure made by *TW3* was the fact that the studio and the audience were visible for much of the time. This refusal to attempt to imply that the show was anything but a show strengthened its satirical content and especially those segments which examined news items in telling, if occasionally subversive, detail.

Fronted by David Frost and with a team of regulars that included Kenneth Cope, Roy Kinnear, Lance Percival, Millicent Martin and William Rushton, *TW3* mixed 'news reports' with sketches, songs and interviews. The latter, in the hands of Bernard Levin, strayed

Thanks to its acerbic wit, TW3 *became required viewing. Among the regulars were (left to right) William Rushton, Kenneth Cope, Millicent Martin, Al Mancini, David Kernan, Lance Percival and David Frost.*

far from the previously accepted parameters of polite conversation. The show's producers, writers and performers were also unsparing of any individual in public and political life whom they felt should be taken to task for his or her actions. Targets as diverse as Home Secretary Henry Brooke and Norrie Paramor, A&R Manager for Columbia Records, were savagely attacked for real or assumed divergences from 'acceptable' behaviour. Brooke's controversial decisions regarding the granting of political asylum were fair game, while the attack on Paramor's alleged use of the 'B' sides of current pop records as a depository for his own songs might be regarded as something of an overreaction. Television's cupboards have their fair share of skeletons, after all.

Inevitably, there were those who thought

TW3's behaviour unacceptable and it was itself attacked by a wide range of individuals, including Richard Crossman and a whole string of fellow politicians of all stripes; one memorable assailant was the man who emerged from the audience one night and delighted millions by pushing Bernard Levin off his stool.

As the show's title indicates, there was an up-to-the-minute immediacy about it, especially most of the news and political sketches, all closely geared to the week's, even the day's, happenings. The team's abilities and liberal sympathies were perhaps best demonstrated in the show which immediately followed the assassination of President Kennedy; in comparison most other TV coverage paled into shallow insignificance.

TW3 ran until the end of December 1963

(1964 was a General Election year and Hugh Greene, then head of the BBC, was prevailed upon to discontinue the show that so consistently and effectively debunked the country's politicians). Although the programme gave birth to numerous other shows and careers, its special feeling has never been repeated. Not everyone, however, fully understood the significance of what was happening on their screens.

In a sketch written by Keith Waterhouse and Willis Hall to close the first series a pair of average television viewers sit staring at their TV set.

He: Well, it was satire, wasn't it? What we call satire.
She: All jokes and skits and that.
He: Yes, mucky jokes. Obscenity. It's all the go nowadays. By law, you see, you're allowed to do it. You can say 'bum', you can say 'po', you can say anything.
She: You dirty devil!

Twenty years later the also political but much less subtle, not to say vicious, *Spitting Image* came along. In this show puppet heads garishly caricature politicians among other well-known personalities and hang them by their own words, mannerisms, greed, villainy and incompetence. With variable scripts which do not always measure up to the venomous accuracy of the puppets themselves, the series created by Peter Fluck and Roger Law has a reputation that is hard to maintain consistently. Like many shows which adopt a revue format it is good in parts, and it is at its best when it tackles individuals who too often get away with murder rather than the obvious dimwits who abound in the programme's chosen target area. The most obvious analogy for the show comes not from television but from the fading art of the sharply pointed political cartoon that yesterday's newspapers regularly printed with telling effect.

The target of *Whoops Apocalypse!*, another 1980s comedy series, was also political incompetence, but it used actors to portray its often outrageous political caricatures. As this comedy saga rushed helter-skelter towards the Third World War and a nuclear holocaust, the sight of a recently lobotomized US president (played by Barry Morse gave

Whoops Apocalypse! *took TV comedy into World War Three (Geoffrey Palmer, Richard Griffiths).*

an uncomfortably chilly real-life undercurrent to the comedy.

Among the performers who rose to prominence during the late 1960s were a group of post-*Fringe* university graduates who made inroads into the *Fringe's* elitism. John Cleese, Eric Idle, Graham Chapman, Michael Palin, Terry Jones, Graeme Garden, Bill Oddie and Tim Brooke-Taylor were among them. The first five of these became *Monty Python's Flying Circus*, while the remaining three became *The Goodies*. Also included in the *Python* team was Terry Gilliam, an admirer of the work of Ernie Kovacs, who had died in 1962. Gilliam helped restore the cartoon to its proper place in adult entertainment.

Of course, *Monty Python* was not satire, but its anarchy and irreverence paved the way for the later alternative comedians. *Python* was essentially a string of unconnected sketches, and no attempt was made to hang them together in any noticeable pattern or structure: 'And now for something completely different . . .' suddenly became a link no continuity announcer dare use ever again. As with any revue or sketch-based show there were bad bits and good bits (and a fair few naughty bits). When they were bad they were very, very bad, but when they were good they were hilarious.

Anyone and anything could be a *Monty Python* target. Sketches included a race to decide who was 'upper-class twit of the year' (reputedly Prince Philip's favourite), a harangue against British holidaymakers in Spain, and skits based on the army, TV game shows, psychiatrists and politicians.

The deliberate destruction of form was not a *Python* invention. Terry Jones acknowledges that Spike Milligan was ahead of them with his shows *Q5, Q6*, and so on. The *Python* team succeeded in bringing to the screen a more widely acceptable form of verbal lunacy not too far removed from that of Milligan and Company's *Goons*. Like Milligan, *Python* happily terminated sketches which were dwindling away by having a character (usually Graham Chapman's senior army officer) walk on the set and demand an end to it on the grounds that it was becoming 'extremely silly'. Unlike Milligan, who often abruptly ended his sketches by walking off muttering to himself, *Python*'s actions were clearly deliberate. Why else would Chapman have been dressed in uniform? The implication with Milligan was always that he had just that moment decided he didn't think much of what he had written and was performing and wanted to get on with something better. Audiences, conditioned to accept form, were made uneasy by Milligan; with *Python*, they simply laughed.

If the lack of a punchline to some *Python* sketches suggested inadequate comic thinking, the great majority of the show's routines tell a very different story.

In one sketch John Cleese as an irate customer harangues shopkeeper Michael Palin about his failure to have in stock any single brand of cheese known to man, despite his being the keeper of a cheese shop; and in another, set in a pet shop, the argument is about Palin's having had the temerity to sell him a dead parrot – which, Palin claims, is merely pining; but Cleese will not stand for this:

It's *not* pining, it's passed on! This parrot is no more! It has ceased to be! It's expired and gone to meet its maker! This is a late parrot! It's a stiff! Bereft of life, it rests in peace. If you hadn't nailed it to the perch it would be pushing up the daisies! It's rung down the curtain and joined the choir invisible! This is an ex-parrot!!

Parodies of other TV shows, driven into the

Bruce Montague as the power-crazy Middle East connection in Whoops Apocalypse!, *with David Kelly.*

126

Monty Python's Flying Circus. *Opposite, above: Terry Jones. Opposite, below: Michael Palin, Carol Cleveland and Terry Jones. Above: calm before chaos, with Terry Jones, Michael Palin, Terry Gilliam, Eric Idle and Graham Chapman.*

ground by too many inept latterday comic performers and impressionists, are also a feature of *Python*. Game shows come in for well-deserved contempt: in one, contestants are required to summarize Proust's *A la Recherche du temps perdu* in fifteen seconds (the prize eventually going to 'the girl with the biggest tits'); in another, viewers are blackmailed into paying over huge sums of money to stop films of their sexual indiscretions being screened. It is tempting to suspect that some post-*Python* game shows have had their revenge by pursuing such parodies even further.

The Goodies tended towards a slightly more structured show and the programmes were perhaps marginally more consistent, although they only rarely touched the heights of *Monty Python*. One show which did achieve such a standard was much less juvenile than the norm. This was a devastating attack on apartheid in South Africa, and featured a piano with only white keys.

Marty Feldman, who had appeared with John Cleese in 1967 in Rediffusion's *At Last the 1948 Show*, wrote and starred in *Marty*, making excellent use of his physical appearance to add an unsettling air of menace to his always very funny shows.

The concept of *TW3* was revived in much-diluted form in the late 1970s with the appearance of *Not the Nine O'Clock News*, which starred four newcomers to television: Rowan Atkinson, Mel Smith, Griff Rhys-Jones and Pamela Stephenson. Again the targets included politicians and other establishment

Not the Nine O'Clock News, *the show that started the TV careers of Mel Smith, Rowan Atkinson, Pamela Stephenson and Griff Rhys-Jones.*

figures and extended the attack to television itself. Trendy TV clergymen came in for parody in a Rowan Atkinson sketch:

Are you a gay Christian? No, that's all right, I don't mind, I don't mind at all if homosexuality is your thing, if that's the bag you're into then that's great, fantastic. Don't be ashamed. Stand up, come out of the toilet as the phrase has it and stand up and say, 'I am tempted to be a homosexual' and if you do and you feel you can do nothing about it and you've been to a psychiatrist and you've had aversion therapy and you've tried tying metal weights to your private parts and you still feel these tendencies then I'm afraid it means that God just wants you to have a rotten life. God's like that. He hates poofs.

TV game shows, personalities, newsreaders and commercials were all lambasted, with often sharp and accurate lampoons. Such attacks do not demand originality however, and this was the show's greatest weakness. Despite generally strong performances by the cast, all of whom went on to other if not always better things, *Not the Nine O'Clock News* always left behind the feeling that each show was never quite as much as the sum of its parts suggested it could have been.

Among the later TV shows made by members of the cast of *Not* were *The Black Adder*, a send-up of every rotten costume movie Hollywood (or Pinewood) ever made, starring Rowan Atkinson. He also appeared in London's West End in a series of highly successful one-man shows. Mel Smith and Griff Rhys-Jones made *Alas Smith and Jones*, generally good but heavily reliant upon the audience's total acceptance of the pair's often limited charm, and *The World According to Smith and Jones*, which took a good idea (the use of clips from Hollywood movies to trace a comedy history of the world) and made a mess of it. The pair have also appeared separately, both trying their hands at straight rôles. Pamela Stephenson has been less successful in her subsequent comedy rôles, and her occasional appearances on talk-shows have often been embarrassingly crass. She has also turned to straight acting, with rather more success.

The BBCs *Not* was countered on the independent network by *Over the Top*, a late-Saturday-night show that evolved out of a Saturday-morning show for children. These origins were glaringly obvious. True, it had some adult humour, mainly from Alexei Sayle, a comedian with an edgy attacking style, but it was mostly a rag-bag of ineptly written and performed sketches presided over by the embarrassed producer, Chris Tarrant. The studio audience, showered as it was with coloured balloons and paper streamers, responded to the brightly-lit party style with vociferous enthusiasm. Like so many comedy shows before it, *OTT* lost sight of the fact that the viewing audience is not partying but is sitting at home, possibly alone, waiting for someone to reach out a hand and offer the release of laughter. This is an admittedly difficult feat and needs thought, intelligence and care. Pouring buckets of coloured glop on to female members of the studio audience who have been persuaded to appear topless isn't the way to do it.

OTT's format, which mixed sketches with stand-up comedy and a measure of studio-audience involvement (all elements that can be traced back to *TW3* and *Not the Nine O'Clock News*), is perpetuated in several late-1980s shows including *Saturday Gang* and *Who Dares Wins*. The former brought forward several young comics, among whom Gareth Hale and Norman Pace have more potential than most of their contemporaries.

Like so many other shows of its kind, *Who Dares Wins* is very good in parts but occasionally falls flat on its face (or bottom, for it is not above anal jokes). The team gathered for this show comprises Rory McGrath, Philip Pope, Jimmy Mulville, Tony Robinson and Julia Hills. Once again TV itself comes in for a fair bit of flak, especially interviewers. Julia Hills demonstrates an unerring ability to display the edge of panic on which most interviewers must live. For her, interviewees actually do go insane or die on-camera. In 1987 she joined Ernie Wise and Lulu for the stage musical *The Mystery of Edwin Drood*.

Insanity is never far from the surface of Kenny Everett's TV shows. His comedy is often carelessly aimed and neither consistency nor believability appear to worry him too much as he plunges from one manic portrayal to another. At his best he succeeds in persuading adults to let their hair down and join in his lunacy. At his worst he can be childishly unfunny.

Much of Everett's work is scripted by the experienced Barry Cryer, a first-rate comic talent. Unfortunately, Everett himself doesn't always know when to stop. Given Cryer's support, more care and fewer Benny Hill-type gags, Everett might well prove capable of pushing back the boundaries of televisual comedy — not far, maybe, but anything is better than nothing.

As Spike Milligan and *Monty Python* in their day pushed out the limits of what was and was not permissible in the way comedy shows were structured, so *Not* and *OTT* and others tested the boundaries of what could or could not be shown and said. In so doing the performers involved appeared to be more concerned about how far they could go rather than how funny they could be.

In the end, many simply resorted to yelling vulgarisms for their own sake (and, amazingly, getting laughs — from their generally young audiences who appeared to think they were witnessing some new and significant breathrough). Obviously the audience, and very possibly the performers too, can't have heard of Lenny Bruce.

Of course, Lenny never had a TV show — and if he had it would not have been a sitcom. Neither would he have been allowed to stay the way he was for long. Writing on Lenny and Mort Sahl, Marty Feldman observed, 'Television buys the name on the package and tries to change the contents.' Lenny was unchangeable and he had to go. He left a gap that has yet to be filled and in the meantime the forces of those who hounded him have shown no signs of diminishing energy, whatever some of today's young comedians might like to think to the contrary.

By the mid-1980s a horde of young and a few not-so-young comics were on TV happily coarsening comedy even though they fell well short of using the words that sent Lenny to jail. As they did so, they beamed with self-pride at their courage and determination to confront the forces of repression. The trouble was, and is, that most often they are not using language as Lenny had used it but were back to the mindless mouthings of the street swearer who can't be bothered to think of another adjective — even supposing he knows one.

Interviewed in 1969 for *Television Quarterly*, the American entertainer Steve Allen observed that 'there was a great difference between the vulgarity which Bruce employed and that to which the average night-club comic will resort. Your Las Vegas man will use dirty material simply to make an audience laugh. Lenny didn't do that at all. When he entered the area of sex or scatology, it was always to make a philosophical point.'

There is very little sign of such maturity in the work of any of the latterday comics. Among the ways in which vulgarisms are used is the childish nudge-nudge form, the 'Look, aren't we brave — using language like this?' school of humorists. If they know anything about comedy, or even about life in the real world, it is not very apparent. Indeed, most wear their ignorance like a badge of honour and trot out their material as though it were some kind of unholy writ when in fact it has neither depth nor wit nor any sign that they understand what it is they are doing.

However obscene Lenny Bruce might have appeared (and obscenity is very much in the eye and ear of the beholder), he invariably sought to make that philosophical point. Many of those who appear to think they have inherited his mantle wouldn't know a philosophical point if it hit them between the legs.

The young British comedians involved in these supposedly innovative areas of comedy have had hung upon them the term 'alternative comedians'. The term would seem to have been introduced to describe those writers and performers (many perform their own material) who offer a sharp contrast to traditional forms of humour. In practice it seems to mean those individuals who can cram into their patter the highest possible number of buzz words, to be greeted by their audiences as being hilarious in themselves. Alf Garnett used 'bloody' because it was part of his natural speech pattern; those amiable souls who used 'bum' did so in order to tease a laugh from their supposedly sophisticated audiences; Lenny Bruce used 'fuck' as a verb in just the way it is used by millions. Taken out of such contexts and peppered through routines that are otherwise bereft of real humour these words, their derivatives and companions become mere appendages to witless, unfunny material. In the past, comedians learned their trade *before* being granted an opportunity to appear on TV. While there may be a degree of evidence that some very good comics were kept down thanks to the prevailing prejudices of the day, this system was infinitely superior to that of letting those with decidedly limited talent practise the craft of comedy, very badly, in full view of millions.

What passes through the minds of surviving veteran masters of comedy such as Tommy Trinder and Max Wall, should they take the trouble to watch such shows as *Saturday Live*, can only be imagined. However, in an interview with Michael Freedland, Max Wall recalled, 'Arthur Askey said to me two days before he died, "I think we've seen the best of it." And I'm inclined to agree.'

At first glance this sounds like the unperceptive opinion of two old-stagers who had become as relevant as dinosaurs. After watching and listening to the alternative comedians it is depressing to discover that they may well be right.

Curiously enough, alternative comedians have entered the usually bland world of situation comedy. As might be expected, their sitcoms ignore the traditions of the genre, but while this is certainly no crime, the results often are.

Shows like *The Young Ones*, *The Comic Strip*, *Girls on Top* and *Filthy Rich and Catflap* have a good following, largely among the under-21s. Among the writers and performers are latterday comedy idols Ben Elton, Rik Mayall, Adrian Edmondson, Jennifer Saunders, Dawn French and Nigel Planer. Their antics often appear to be founded in temporary insanity, but these are not the amiable loonies who peopled the world of the old-time gagsters. Rather, as in a street-corner encounter with a belligerent drunk late at night, these performers generate a fear that the world is full of potentially homicidal maniacs who have not only taken over the asylum but are rapidly encroaching upon the world beyond.

It is often hard to grasp that this is the comedy world of television, a world which once housed Tony Hancock, Phil Silvers, Morecambe and Wise and Jack Benny, and which still houses the talents which can produce such sitcom successes as *The Golden Girls* and *Cheers*. On the other hand, watching with alarm the pop-eyed, spittle-spraying aggression of some latter-day comics as they yell lines which acutely demonstrate hatred and anger, it becomes easier to understand the success of *'Allo Allo!*

It may be the scripts, or it could be the performers, but there is all too often an absence of intelligence and understanding. As Lenny Bruce demonstrated, these fringe areas of comedy demand copious measures of both.

As for the shock tactics of Elton, Mayall and their fellows, who do they think they are shocking? Their forebears from *Beyond the Fringe* and 1960s TV shocked a stuffy, reactionary establishment. There is still an establishment and it is still, inevitably, stuffy and reactionary. But is it, and the society which surrounds it, still so easily shocked?

In any event shock, today, seems often to be simply a matter of screaming out unfunny lines at maximum decibels. Certainly the successful use of vulgarity demands a measure of confidence in performance. A surreptitious delivery of a risqué line lends it an unnecessary sleaziness. Nevertheless, a joke that is not funny in the first place does not become so when shouted.

Jerry Lewis proved that years ago. Doesn't anyone ever learn?

CHAPTER TEN

BLACK, BEAUTIFUL, AND NOW BOX OFFICE

'You can still pick a guy's pocket while he's laughing.'
Bill Cosby

The rôle of all ethnic groups in entertainment has been and remains awkward, and is frequently misunderstood, especially by those who rule the airwaves. American and British humorists have long made use of ethnic differences as a source of humour. Unfortunately, most humorists have used ethnicity as a means of making fun of people, which is by no means the same thing as laughing with them.

Jokes about one group or another abound and go through stages, in which a different race is substituted as the butt of the joke (the jokes themselves tend to stay the same). One year it might be Pakistani jokes, the next Irish; in America it might be Polish jokes, followed by Swedish ones. Predictably, the ethnic group subjected to the jokes is usually in a minority, is often despised for no reason other than that its members are 'different', and while feared in a general sense the tormentors are seldom afraid that their ethnic targets will turn on them.

Some ethnic groups have often found a means of cultural enrichment in humour. Two such groups in America have been both the butt and the source of much humour and have contributed greatly to national and international humour and language. These are the Jews and the blacks.

Jewish humour has a very long history, dating from centuries before any Jews set foot in the New World. Persecuted for thousands of years, the Jews used humour as a kind of defence which as often as not turned in on itself and spoke to the Jews themselves with a tongue as barbed as that of any oppressor. The substantial Jewish community in America has inevitably given them a higher profile than in any other country. Millions of Jews were among the immigrant hordes of the eighteenth, nineteenth and early twentieth centuries. The presence in the ranks of the entertainment industry of many Jewish men and women led to a gradual intermingling in American humour and language of a gently self-deprecating style of joke-telling. This and the barbed witticisms, coupled with a differently accented delivery of lines, lent a strong ethnic flavour to much American humour; to outsiders, this brands it as being peculiarly American when, in fact, it is peculiarly Jewish.

The distinguished writer Leo Rosten has made a study of Jewish humour and from the hundreds of examples of phrases he has culled from everyday language are many which can be heard in varying guises in today's TV shows and on the streets of cities on both sides of the Atlantic:

Get lost.
You should live so long.
I need it like a hole in the head.
Who *needs* it?
All right already.
It shouldn't happen to a dog.
Okay by me.

Another is tailor-made for parents of would-be actors and comedy writers: 'From that he makes a living?'

The emergence through American vaudeville of several Jewish entertainers who later moved successfully into radio and TV leaves little doubt about the influence of this ethnic group in establishing a form of humour which is at the root of the divergence between Britain and America. Among the entertainers who fall into this category and who have no real direct counterpart across the Atlantic are George Jessel, Al Jolson, Eddie Cantor, Fanny Brice, Jack Benny, Milton Berle and Phil Silvers.

Although only a few early American TV sitcoms used ethnic-minority families (Jews in *The Goldbergs*, Scandinavians in *Mama*) the Jewish influence pervades much of American sitcom-land. Morey Amsterdam's wisecracks in *The Dick Van Dyke Show*, Alan Alda's Groucho-inspired delivery in *M*A*S*H*, most of the dialogue in *The Golden Girls* – all derive from the same general source. Indeed, Jewish humour is so fully integrated into American humour and speech today as to make it difficult, if not impossible, to distinguish where one ends and the other begins. Despite the divergence between American and British humour, the jokes and speech cadences of Jews are becoming steadily more commonplace in Britain. (We should be so lucky!)

Much less readily integrated but also of considerable and continuing importance has been a similarly distinctive style of humour, that of black Americans.

From the standpoint of the late 1980s, when black characters appear in major rôles in most forms of American TV drama, light entertainment, news and current affairs programmes, it is easy to lose sight of the fact that a few years ago the presence of blacks on TV was akin to that of an earlier generation's place in the motion-picture industry. In Hollywood a black person worked, if he worked at all, as a menial, off screen and on. By the late 1960s a change had begun on the big screen and it was slowly matched by the small screen. Before then, however, blacks were rare indeed – rare, but not non-existent.

In 1950-51, the season after *The Goldbergs* and *Mama*, two major black shows were shown, both of which were successful. One was *Beulah*, which, typically for the period, featured a black maid-cum-cook working for a rich New York family. The first person to play the part of Beulah was the great singer-entertainer Ethel Waters. She was replaced by Hattie McDaniel, who in 1939 had become the first black actress to win an Oscar (for her performance in *Gone with the Wind*). In turn, she was replaced in *Beulah* by Louise Beavers. The show ran until 1953, though it was in trouble with the NAACP (National Association for the Advancement of Coloured Peoples) before then. But the fuss surrounding *Beulah* was a mere storm in a tea-cup when set against that in which the most popular sitcom of that same 1950-51 season eventually foundered.

Amos 'n' Andy had begun life as a radio show in the 1920s, when the rôles were played by white actors. Even when Hollywood beckoned the actors simply blacked up and carried on as if no one cared, but even they quailed at the thought of doing the same on TV. This time the whites, Freeman Gosden and Charles Correll, were replaced by black actors Alvin Childress and Spencer Williams Jr, with Tim Moore as Kingfish, a minor character in the radio version of the show who was now upgraded to co-star status.

The characters in the show were stereotypical. This is no crime in itself; if it were, 99.9 per cent of all known sitcom writers would be behind bars. Andy was a lazy good-for-nothing and Kingfish was a larcenous con-man. Amos was actually hardworking and owned his own cab company. Thus, two out of the three principals fulfilled white stereotyping. In some respects the furore created by the NAACP and other black organizations was not entirely justified. Racial stereotype or not, as Rick Mitz has acutely observed, Kingfish was no more dishonest than Ernie Bilko.

Yet the distress displayed by the NAACP was genuine and entirely understandable. This was the first major TV show to use blacks in leading rôles, and therefore presented the first real opportunity for blacks to answer back, in front of a mass audience, to the racial abuse, from stereotyping to lynching, that had taken place in the nine decades

Before the show was pulled off the air in a flurry of protests, Amos 'n' Andy *attracted huge audiences (Spencer Williams Jr as Andy and Tim Moore as Kingfish).*

since Emancipation. The opportunity was being squandered, which was not in itself surprising since the show's creators and most of the writers and other behind-the-scenes personnel were white.

In 1953 *Amos 'n' Andy* ended but continued to be screened thanks to the joys of syndication. And so the uproar continued until 1966, when the show was finally withdrawn and laid to rest. Despite its very obvious failings, *Amos 'n' Andy* was a funny show; the problem lay in the fact that its humour drew laughter from white audiences at the expense of blacks.

The first significant departure from stereotyping of blacks on TV occurred in 1965 in a drama series entitled *I Spy* in the currently popular espionage genre. (The earlier *Harlem Detective* did not have the national exposure *I Spy* enjoyed.) Co-starring in *I Spy* were two actors who were one another's script equals in all respects, including getting the girls, the laughs (for despite being a drama the scripts were well-garnished with wit) and the action. They were the white actor Robert Culp and a black comedian and actor named Bill Cosby.

I Spy ran for three seasons and Cosby won three Emmy awards. He was also popular with audiences, and only three TV stations, two in Georgia and one in Florida, refused to take the show because of his presence. What was significant about Cosby's rôle as Alexander Scott was that it was not written specifically for a black man. If Scott had been played by a white actor almost no change in dialogue would have proved necessary. This refusal to accommodate audience preconceptions marks much of Cosby's later career in TV sitcoms.

Cosby's personal popularity was greater than the show's. In his study of blacks on TV, J. Fred MacDonald has determined that during the run of *I Spy* Cosby was the most popular TV star with the 12-17-year-olds; third most popular with the 18-34-year-old group; and eighth equal with the total audience. In the light of prevailing attitudes towards blacks on TV this was a remarkable achievement.

In 1969 Cosby appeared in *The Bill Cosby Show*, in which he played high school

Top: the barrier-busting series I Spy, *with Robert Culp and Bill Cosby. Above: Cosby solo.*

Nurse Julia Baker and Dr Morton Chegley, spotting something alarming in Julia *(Diahann Carroll, Lloyd Nolan).*

athletics coach Chet Kincaid. The show's achieved aim was to display scenes of American life which were drawn entirely from the black experience and yet were universal in their emotional appeal, and Cosby himself was executive producer. Nevertheless, the series was substantially a product of white writers and programme-makers.

Talking to Richard Warren Lewis for *TV Guide* in 1969, Cosby expressed his awareness that the show would not hold any appeal 'for people who are really militant about any story with a black person in it – black viewers included. But you can still pick a guy's pocket while he's laughing, and that's what I hope to do.' In the same interview Cosby readily admitted to a curious reversal of traditional rôles which manifested itself in the show. Here, the black characters were well-rounded and essentially 'normal' people while the white rôles were deliberately stereotyped.

The Bill Cosby Show ran until 1971 and was broadly concurrent with other shows starring blacks as American TV sought to match the changes in contemporary attitudes

towards blacks. *Barefoot in the Park*, which ran for only 13 weeks in 1969, starred Scoey Mitchell and Tracy Reed in the rôles created on Broadway by Robert Redford and Elizabeth Ashley and played in Hollywood by Redford and Jane Fonda.

Much more popular with audiences but regarded suspiciously by blacks was *Julia*, which first appeared in 1968 and ran until 1971. Developed by Hal Kanter, the show was surrounded by controversy even before it was aired. The rôle of Julia Baker went to Diahann Carroll, whose personal commitment was high. Her character was only lightly sketched out to begin with but she built up Julia's background drawing upon both her personal experience and on the wider black experience in America.

Julia, a widowed nurse, lives in comfortable and clearly middle-class surroundings and struggles with such problems as bringing up a small child. Ms Carroll, whose later TV appearances include *Dynasty*, was herself a divorcee with a child from an interracial marriage. Black criticism of the show stemmed from the fact that Julia's problems were not especially relevant to what many blacks regarded as their enforced lifestyle. Ms Carroll's response to such criticism was pointedly logical: 'I don't know of any TV programme that is a real reflection of *white* life . . . All television is divorced from reality . . .' Even the absence of a man in Julia's life was attacked as being a further castration of black males in American society. The response of the show's producers was that since the (white) males in most TV sitcoms were incompetent inferiors to their wives or girlfriends, the absence of such a black character here was a plus. This response did not stem the rising tide of black antipathy displayed towards the show.

Kanter hired more black writers than had hitherto generally been the case in TV, but the attacks continued. Diahann Carroll: 'For a hundred years we have been prevented from seeing accurate images of ourselves and we're all overconcerned and overreacting.' Ms Carroll was well aware that there was no gainsaying the fact that despite the advance signalled by the existence of *Julia*, it was still a show created by whites for white-dominated TV. Given considerable say in her character's development, Ms Carroll was able to incorporate more black attributes as the show continued but a change to an 'Afro' hairstyle was not enough to assuage black militants.

In the 1970s noticeable changes began to take place in black comedy. Like the Jews before them, blacks now mocked themselves with a coruscating lack of inhibition that sought not to overlay the years of oppression and enforced inferiority with soft, light-hearted humour but to demonstrate that, come what may, they had survived and would continue to do so. Making a considerable impact in this period was *The Flip Wilson Show*, which spoke directly and uncompromisingly about such matters as black racial characteristics. Competition, long a staple of racial humour, was accentuated, but bore hints that now success need no longer be a forlorn hope.

From the standpoint of the late 1980s, when blacks are relatively commonplace on TV, the earlier struggle to make statements about being black in the unlikely setting of a TV sitcom may appear strange. But the move to gradual acceptance, which is by no means complete today, was only a result of minor changes here, adjustments there, during the years since *Amos 'n' Andy*.

In 1973 Florida Evans, the maid from *Maud*, was given her own show, *Good Times*. Played by Esther Rolle, Florida had a hard time despite her show's title. Hassled almost as much by off-screen wrangles as by her on-screen struggles to survive in a Chicago ghetto, Ms Rolle quit the show for a while but came back for the last year of its six-year run.

In 1974 *The Jeffersons*, a spin-off of *All in the Family*, brought from that show a comparable, if reversed, display of bigotry. George Jefferson (Sherman Hemsley) might be rich but he is just as prejudiced as his former neighbour, Archie Bunker. He is also a social climber (something of which Archie can never be accused), and this desire for upward mobility became a common facet of many black characters in TV sitcoms.

1978 saw *Diff'rent Strokes*, featuring little Arnold (played by diminutive 11-year-old Gary Coleman), a black ghetto orphan moving socially (and physically) upwards when he is adopted by a white millionaire and goes to live in his penthouse apartment.

This show's situation was one which offered opportunities for handling serious subjects with a coating of humour. Only rarely were these opportunities taken and almost none of these few reflected the black experience. The show's desire to be taken seriously showed itself in a commendable episode about the dangers of drug-taking in which First Lady Nancy Reagan finally landed a rôle on prime-time television.

Benson Dubois, the butler of the earlier *Soap*, also moved upwards socially, in 1979's *Benson*. In this show he starts out as butler to State Governor Gatling (James Noble), then moves up a major step to become Assistant Governor. Like those of the whites in *The Bill Cosby Show*, the white rôles in *Benson* are largely stereotypical, but here the same comment can be applied to the central character. Although played with considerable subversive charm by Robert Guillaume, Benson bears remarkable resemblances to the 'sassy' black servants who appeared in Hollywood movies and many early TV shows. *Benson* has, however, taken occasional forays into strange regions for comedy. In a 1985 episode the show's main characters consider the problems of nuclear war. If they come to no definite conclusion this may well have been a result of the network's insistence that the writers amend their original one-sided script to offer a few pros to the glaringly obvious cons. In the end, it was left to the audience to make up its own mind. As casual reading of any newspaper shows only too clearly, that is easier asked than done.

What is most depressing about both *Benson* and *Diff'rent Strokes* is that they, like *Julia* before them, are predicated on a view that upward social mobility for blacks is dependent upon the paternalistic whim of white superiors.

The 1980s produced another tiny child actor, 12-year-old 40-inch-high Emmanuel Lewis, who played the title rôle in *Webster*. Webster did no more to advance black status on TV than had either Arnold or Benson. For all practical purposes these shows ignored race. Herman Gray, writing of *Webster* and

Cosby *stars (left to right from top) Tempestt Bledsoe, Malcolm-Jamal Warner, Lisa Bonet, Bill Cosby, Phylicia Rashad, Keshia Knight-Pulliam.*

Diff'rent Strokes, observes how they had settled 'closer to the model of racial invisibility than visibility in both setting and thematic content. The pattern that emerges from these shows suggests that race and racial issues exist primarily as a context in which other issues are developed. Race itself is not a central issue.' Hence, an episode of *Webster* which dealt with the subject of child sexual abuse, while eminently laudable, was looking at social, not racial issues.

Racial issues in Britain have rarely provided the impetus for TV comedy. In the late 1980s most black faces on British screens are in imported American shows. This may well be a result of the fact that shows such as *The Fosters* and *Empire Road*, both starring Norman Beaton, met with little general enthusiasm when they were screened in the mid-1970s. The makers' apparent refusal to pander to the general public by adjusting the heavily accented speech which, while accurate, was hard to follow, was commendable but doubtless limited the shows' appeal.

Back in 1971 Thames TV's *Love Thy Neighbour* took a fling at the method of expressing bigotry used in *Till Death Us Do Part*. With Jack Smethurst and Kate Williams as a white couple and Rudolph Walker and Nina Baden-Semper as their new black neighbours, the show tried but failed to make its statements with the necessary subtlety and wit. Johnny Speight's scripts for *Till Death Us Do Part* had used racial epithets to telling effect; in *Love Thy Neighbour* Vince Powell and Harry Driver's scripts tended to separate epithets from the comedy content of the show. Once the two male characters had finished calling one another 'coon' or 'honky' (their wives were notably free from prejudice) they got on with non-racial comic business that depended little on skin colour. Much more subtly written and performed was *Mixed Blessings*, which starred Muriel Odunton as a young black woman whose marriage, as the show's title unnecessarily indicates, is 'mixed'.

The Asian community in Britain has provided the basis for such shows as LWT's *Curry and Chips*, written in 1969 by Johnny Speight and starring Eric Sykes and Spike Milligan, who blacked up for his part. Although the practice of blacking up lingered on into the early 1970s (Michael Bates as Rangi Ram in *It Ain't Half Hot Mum*), it was later realized to be unacceptably offensive.

Asian actors were given sitcom opportunities in the mid-1980s with *Tandoori Nights*, which dealt with the rivalry between two North London restaurants, each named after currently popular TV dramas: *The Jewel in the Crown* and *The Far Pavilions*. Insufficiently funny, the show failed to reach a wide audience.

Among the American imports screened in Britain in the late 1980s is Bill Cosby's latest venture, *The Cosby Show*. In this show, which became the most popular TV programme in America in 1986, Cosby departed several steps further from accepted TV norms.

Cosby's character in the show, Clifford Huxtable, is a paediatrician who obviously enjoys a lifestyle towards the top end of America's middle class. His wife is a lawyer, she is beautiful, and they have five children who are all intelligent, lively and attractive. The ghetto is a million miles away. The scripts make no concessions to tradition and, like the

Cosby part in *I Spy*, could be played without change by an all-white cast. Since the show is a creation of Cosby's and he clearly has considerable authority over what he does, it has to be assumed that the form taken by the show is exactly the way he wants it. For all that, the show appears deliberately to overlook certain important issues which continue to confront many American blacks.

The Huxtable family demonstrates what most reasonable people already know, that given equal educational, occupational, social and other opportunities, blacks behave, work, play and could rise in society in exactly the same way as whites. Yet countless thousands of blacks in Western society live a life that demonstrates daily that they are being denied those very opportunities the Huxtables have taken and exploited.

The interaction between members of the Huxtable family follows an idealized path rather than that which is most likely followed by any average real-life family (black or white). In Mark Edmundson's phrase, Cliff Huxtable 'outwits rather than outweighs' any member of his family who seeks to oppose parental authority. Gone is the paternalism of Jim Anderson in *Father Knows Best*; gone too is the frustrated bluster of Archie Bunker in *All in the Family*. In the place of these extinct forms of family leadership is one of contemporary enlightenment. Father may still know best but he proves it with a light hand, with ironic wit, and without ever forcing his son or his daughters to lose that most valued of childhood possessions – dignity.

The care with which this show has been assembled is evident from its smoothly professional style. Well hidden from sight is the consideration given to many psychological issues. Jack Curry, writing in *American Film*, states that on the advice of the show's consultant psychologist the original concept underwent certain marginal, yet significant, changes to reduce intergenerational friction.

The importance of relationships between the generations displayed in the Cosby format is that it comes hard on the heels of a period in which kiddie-power ruled TV (and the movies) and is thus redressing a distortion in the balance of programme-making. Cliff Huxtable is the boss, but he doesn't brandish his authority as though it were a weapon. He

Father still knows best in The Cosby Show *(Lisa Bonet, Bill Cosby, Tempestt Bledsoe, Malcolm-Jamal Warner).*

also schemes to maintain an authoritarian rôle over his wife Claire (Phylicia Rashad), but applies the outmoded tenets of male superiority only jokingly. In the event, Claire lets him win when it suits her, a sitcom ploy from way back.

The subject of race rarely features in the script. Just two occasions come readily to mind, and curiously enough both are slightly awkward in manner, suggesting that they have been put in for effect.

In one show, after rather more family dissent than is usual, the Huxtables are drawn together in silent rapport by the sudden and convenient appearance on their TV set of a reshowing of Martin Luther King's 'I have a dream' speech. Though this particular scene may be justifiable on the grounds that the speech now has a place in many American hearts regardless of race, the other case is less readily settled.

The Huxtables' son Theo (Malcolm-Jamal Warner) is becoming emotionally involved with a girl. They sit together on the front steps talking about themselves and about a book from which Theo occasionally reads extracts. The book is Ralph Ellison's *Invisible Man*, a novel now more than 30 years old but which remains as valid today as ever before. Despite its undoubted literary status, its significance as a commentary on the position of blacks as determined by whites in American society, and as a rallying cry for the rise in black consciousness, *Invisible Man* most certainly is not something romantic schoolkids moon over.

Apart from racial responses there are several other qualities *The Cosby Show* does not achieve. Among them are any feelings of the kind of tension which permeated *All in the Family* or *Maude*. There is never any doubt but that the Huxtables will remain bound together with powerful ties of love. There is never any fear that issues of race or status will disrupt the family. True, the show never seeks such confrontations and, indeed, the TV sitcom may not be the place for them, but their total omission is a little sad.

As for the show's success with audiences, that is certainly intriguing. Perhaps this is how the (white) American people like to imagine those blacks who have thrown off oppression will behave if the revolution ever comes.

Given the show's popularity, its high standards of writing, its generally excellent acting (the shaky young actors of the early episodes have learned fast), and especially his own considerable contribution, Cosby could, perhaps, have caused a mild *frisson* of alarm had he chosen to offer an alternative and less bland view of life. Nevertheless, considerable credit has been earned by Cosby over the years. In this, his latest TV show, he reaches a standard of overall excellence which exceeds that of most other performers, black or white. As Robert Culp, his former partner in *I Spy*, has remarked: 'His message . . . is the most important message anyone can get across in America today. So many marriages are breaking up, millions of children are being cast adrift. It's frightening. Cosby's doing a wonderful job and I'm very proud of him.'

Culp is correct in what he says. Through his depiction of the Huxtables, Cosby is upholding the popular perception of the potential strength of the American family – idealized, perhaps, but then, what TV family isn't? What Cosby does not do is depict a *black* American family, idealized, or not. As long ago as 1950 J. Saunders Redding wrote, 'Season it as you will, the thought that the Negro American is different from other Americans is still unpalatable to most Negroes.' It appears that this view is still true.

Given the record of the past 30 years of TV comedy and drama, what Cosby has so far achieved is commendable. What remains to be done, whether by Cosby or his successors, is to build upon these foundations so that a black family can feature in TV comedy in a situation which is peculiarly black – without preaching and without playing Uncle Toms – and still gain multi-racial acceptance.

Cosby has brought that day closer, but there is still some distance to go, as may be determined from a passage towards the end of *Invisible Man* where, in a dream, the unnamed protagonist tells his enemies that he is through running. They know better and tell him: 'Not quite.'

That sets the task for future black performers in television.

CHAPTER ELEVEN

US AND THEM

'We invented the language; you're the ones that mucked about with it.'
Tommy Trinder

Humour doesn't travel too well between countries. An Englishman sitting down to watch a television comedy show from, say, Germany or Japan will probably wait in vain for something to laugh at. This has nothing to do with any difficulties over language: it's what other people find funny that causes the problem. An unprepared viewer tuning in to a Japanese game show might well be forgiven thinking he has encountered a re-run of the Burma Railway, while German jollity is usually as indigestible for non-Germans as a meal of pumpernickel and sauerkraut.

On the whole, humour has travelled much better between America and Britain than from other countries, despite the fact that, judging from the difficulties encountered by British performers over there, the prevailing winds tend to blow from west to east.

One of the reasons is easily spotted. Generations of British moviegoers grew up on a diet of American movies which made the whole frame of reference – accents, lifestyles, ideas, dreams and ambitions – relatively understandable. Many of the movies were comedy vehicles, too, from those of Chaplin, Keaton, Lloyd, Laurel and Hardy in the early days (Chaplin and Laurel were in fact British) through to the work of Woody Allen, Mel Brooks and their kin. Along the way came W. C. Fields, Jack Benny, Danny Kaye, Fred Allen, Burns and Allen and Bob Hope (another British-born star).

By the time American TV shows came across the Atlantic an entire nation was attuned to those accents and that humour – not that the British audience was a pushover for Americans. There were such matters as timing, parochial references and style. Some performers failed to make sufficient adjustments; they were quickly on the boat back home wondering where they had gone wrong.

Mostly, however, Americans succeeded in Britain. Perhaps their more relaxed style took a little getting used to but even the extended pauses used by Jack Benny were soon accepted. Indeed, the American style was quickly picked up by British comics, though not always judiciously. Parochial references were not a serious problem, of course, and it became a simple matter to translate jokes about Pittsburgh into jokes about Scunthorpe without changing anything more than the place-name. The problems arose in the delivery of the joke. As British entertainer Ray Alan has commented, after hearing an American at the London Palladium telling jokes in Brooklynese, some British comedians would rush straight off to their own engagements and tell the same jokes in, say, a north country accent, and wonder why they often misfired.

The problem of timing was mentioned by Stan Laurel in conversation with Ray Alan. British comics rushed their material, Stan observed: 'The most difficult thing to get a British comedian to do is stand still and do nothing. They've got to be busy. They even overtalk their own tag lines.'

The problems of a reverse trip across the Atlantic were much more difficult to overcome. The decline of American film comedy in the face of the popularity of TV comedy in the 1950s and 1960s was countered by the importation of British comedy films. The fact that such films as the Ealing comedies were popular among certain groups in certain cities misled many people into thinking that all Americans were similarly receptive. They were not.

That the two nations were divided by a common language was never more evident than in theatres, clubs and on TV. When Tommy Trinder, a veteran comic of the variety stage with a fearsome reputation for ad-libbing, was heckled by an American for speaking strangely, he was quick to point out that it was the Americans who had 'mucked about' with the language.

Additionally, just as an American joke which depended upon, say, a Jewish accent needed changing for British audiences so, too, much lower-class British humour depends upon the sound of the voice, the spoken accent. Unchanged, some comics found their material missed American audiences for no other reason than that they failed either to understand what was being said or, more subtly, understood the words but failed to grasp the meaning implied by the accent.

Even the highly successful Morecambe and Wise, two entertainers with a wide-based act and sufficient experience to conquer most fields, failed to make the transition. Eric Morecambe's refusal to adjust his accent even for London audiences, let alone American ones, may well have been a major contributory factor in the duo's inability to capitalize upon an appearance on *The Ed Sullivan Show*. The fact that adjustments can be made, by listening, learning and making slight accommodations on subject matter, is proved by the success in America of such performers as Freddie Sales and Ted Rogers, whose greatest fans could not pretend they are in the same class as Eric and Ernie.

Contrastingly, such 'frightfully British' performers as Terry-Thomas and Wilfrid Hyde White retained their accents and manner and fulfilled American expectations of what 'typical' Englishmen looked and sounded like.

The world of situation comedy has proved to be replete with similarly one-way traffic. An early show tried to have the best of both worlds with the (rather good) idea of a British and American family who exchanged their teenage daughters. The British scenes were shot in Britain, the American scenes in America. *Fair Exchange* starred Eddie Foy Jr and Victor Maddern as the two fathers, Audrey Christie and Diana Chesney as the mothers, with Lynn Loring and Judy Carne as the exchanged girls. The British family also had a young son played by child actor Dennis Waterman (this was in 1962). At about this time he also appeared in the first-ever TV version of Richmal Crompton's *Just William*. Many years later he became Terry McCann in *Minder*.

Some later British shows, including *Rising Damp*, *Monty Python* and *Benny Hill*, were simply transferred, mostly on to PBS, but for the most part if Americans wanted British shows they took the idea alone and reworked it for the US audience. In some cases the changes made in adaptation were slight, accents and setting apart; in other cases they were widespread.

Agony, a show about a Jewish agony aunt with a pair of homosexual friends became a show about a doctor who wasn't Jewish and whose friends were not gay. Even the original show's transvestite was not allowed to wear women's clothes. It is hard to understand why the Americans felt the need to buy the concept. Given all those seemingly fundamental changes, would anyone have noticed that *The Lucie Arnaz Show* was based on *Agony*?

Usually, of course, the changes are not quite so dramatic, although it would take a fairly earnest viewer to spot the links between *Pig in the Middle* and *Oh Madeline*. The former starred Dinsdale Landen as a husband juggling wife and mistress (Joanna Van Gyseghem and Liza Goddard) while the latter stars Madeline Kahn as a lady trying to revive a fading marriage. Unusually for the period, the late 1980s, *Oh Madeline* makes extensive use of slapstick, recalling the long-past days of Lucy.

There was no serious difficulty in tying *Reggie*, which starred Richard Mulligan, to

A problem arises in Man About the House *(left to right: Sally Thomsett, Richard O'Sullivan, Paula Wilcox, Yootha Joyce).*

The Fall and Rise of Reginald Perrin or in linking *Keep It in the Family* to *Too Close for Comfort,* in which the central cartoonist character, played by Robert Gillespie/Ted Knight, wears a glove puppet whichever side of the ocean he is on. A similarly close match is observable between *George and Mildred* and *The Ropers*, although the shows out of which these two spun underwent some not very subtle changes.

George and Mildred Roper had first seen the light of day as a supporting pair to the three principals in *Man About the House*, which starred Richard O'Sullivan as Robin Tripp, who shares a flat with two young women, Chrissy and Jo (Paula Wilcox and Sally Thomsett). Any sexual longings Robin might have felt for the girls are well and truly suppressed, despite occasional mock-lustful remarks, and if the girls are romantically interested in him they are even more subtle about it and hide their feelings well. This

deliberate underplaying of the sexuality implicit in the show's premise made it funnier and, in a curious way, it was also mildly but never overtly sexy. Indeed, the only overtly sexual moment was in the weekly credit titles which included, among the shots of shaving gear in a jumble of make-up, a shot of three china figures – a cockerel between two cats.

The American version of *Man About the House* was retitled *Three's Company* and a few marginal name changes occurred among the characters: Robin Tripp became the somewhat butch-er Jack Tripper, although he kept his job as a student chef. The Ropers hung on to their surname but became Stanley and Helen.

So far, so what? It was only when the writers took a hand that things really changed. Where the original had been good-naturedly humorous about sex, which was mostly in the mind of Mrs Roper anyway, the American version brought sex out on top.

However, rather than treating it in an honest and adult manner, the writers gave us sex with a snigger, with the jokes aiming at eight inches or so below the belt. The American cast comprised Jack Ritter (son of old-time Hollywood cowboy Tex), Joyce De Witt and Suzanne Somers (as Janet and Chrissy), with Audra Lindley and Norman Fell as the Ropers. Although most were called upon to play very different characters to their British counterparts, the actors concerned were all very good, especially Norman Fell and Suzanne Somers. The problems lay in the obviousness of the jokes.

Stanley: You gay?
Jack: Well, sometimes I'm quite depressed.

Or:

Janet: When you take a girl out and you go to get her, don't you like it if she's dressed and ready?
Jack: No, just ready.

The changes made in this particular transition from British to American screens were largely those which replaced subtlety with crudity. Given the fact that the writing team was fundamentally the same as that which had turned *Till Death Us Do Part* into *All In the Family*, these failings are hard to understand.

Till Death Us Do Part first appeared on the BBC in 1966 and by the end of the first episode it was obvious that writer Johnny Speight had created a man who would live forever in the memory, even if there were those who thought Alf Garnett was more monster than man.

Week after week Alf paraded an astonishing display of bigotry which embraced race, politics, religion and a few more topics besides. With language that might be termed forthright, although heaven knows Alf would have found a pithier term for it, he harangued his captive audience (wife, daughter and son-in-law) on anything which crossed a mind that had not entertained a liberal thought since the day it was born.

'You silly moo!' Alf Garnett berates the hapless Else in Johnny Speight's Till Death Us Do Part (Dandy Nichols, Warren Mitchell).

'Up the 'Ammers!' Alf Garnett, Britain's best-loved bigot (Warren Mitchell).

Oddly enough, Alf Garnett didn't actually hate anyone. He certainly didn't hate blacks, 'yer coons'; he just wanted them back where they came from and where he believed they would be happier – up trees in far-off jungles.

Politically, Alf was that far from uncommon working man who was the staunchest of Tories and fervently believed that espousal of any form of socialism was opening the door to communist oppression. The fact that his son-in-law was a Trotskyite made him almost as unwelcome as the fact that he wore his hair long ('Listen, Shirley Temple . . .') and came from Liverpool ('yer Scouse git'). Alf's contempt extended to all socialists and to the average British working man: 'Labour lost the last election because Michael Foot went on telly promising to put four million back to work and frightened the life out of them.'

An ardent champion of the Royal Family ('yer Royals'), he hung their portraits on his living-room wall alongside one of Winston Churchill. But Alf's support for the Conservative Party did not extend to such grammar school upstarts as Edward Heath, and still less did it encompass Margaret Thatcher. Women in Alf's narrow world had no business being anything other than a man's helpmate, 'Er Majesty excepted, of course.

In his years at the top Alf Garnett attracted a great deal of flak, but not from TV critics and certainly not from the mass audience. Attacks came from two quarters: there were those who objected to the language and spent their time counting the numbers of 'bloodys' which peppered his verbal onslaughts; and there were those who applied rather more reflective reasoning and expressed alarm that what Alf was doing was not so much holding up bigots to ridicule as underpinning them with his diatribes.

There was probably a little truth in this last point but it is hard to take it too seriously. A fondness for Alf Garnett was no more likely to have produced an increase in National Front membership than it stepped up the terrace crowds at Upton Park, where Alf's beloved West Ham United played. Conversely, it seems doubtful that those whose bigotry was buried only slightly below the surface would have thrown it off completely after hearing him in action. Maybe, instead, they buried their prejudices just a little bit deeper to avoid being thought of as a Garnett-clone. As for those who were already as bigoted as he, of course it didn't cure them. That is no criticism of the show; its purpose was to entertain, not to proselytize. As for those who are like Alf Garnett in the real world, they're incurable anyway.

Johnny Speight's scripts allowed Alf to attack just about everyone who floated across his creation's tunnel vision, often in the same rambling speech. In one example Alf surprised the family by suggesting that Enoch Powell was wrong in 'having a go at the coons'.

Yes! He ain't seen the real danger. It's not the coons. We don't want 'em over here stinking the country out with their curries, and making a row on their dustbin lids. But they're bloody harmless – not like yer bloody Russian unions and yer Chinese take-aways . . . Hot-beds of bloody fifth column, they are. But we're on to 'em, don't worry. You'll see . . . the next time one of them commy shop stewards goes in the nick, he'll rot there. All they organize them bloody strikes for is so they can get on the bleeding telly. I blame the BBC for encouraging 'em. They'll put anyone on the bloody telly they will. Rock 'n' roll vicars . . . an' sex maniacs, an' bloody Irish gunmen. Admit they put stockings over their heads first, but still . . . They only let the Queen go for one show at Christmas – I don't know what they've got against that woman. She should have her own series, 'cos she's better 'n Lulu. Blimey, she's the best thing on at Christmas.

The central performances in *Till Death Us Do Part* (and in the early days there were seldom any supporting rôles) were uniformly excellent. Anthony Booth as Mike, the son-in-law, had an air of casual insolence beneath his needling which invariably set Alf off on one of his outbursts. As Booth had less to do than anyone else, his departure from the show was predictable and not greatly missed, although comparison between the later shows and the early ones suggests that his rôle was more important than anyone appeared to credit at the time. Una Stubbs played Alf's daughter Rita, whose outrage at her father's bigotry, like the delight she took in Mike's needling, was tempered by an obviously deep affection for the old man. The importance of her presence was most apparent when the sequel, *In Sickness and in Health*, began its run. Rita did not appear in every episode and she was missed.

As Alf's wife, Else, the 'silly moo', Dandy Nichols had very little to say but her presence and delivery of the few lines she was given were a joy. Time after time she would prick one of Alf's balloons with a masterly put-down. Equally well executed were her interruptions of Alf, which in isolation were very funny indeed but when orchestrated, as they often were, built up a superb interplay worthy of the finest double-acts.

When Alf brought Lord Hill, then head of the Independent Television Authority, into the conversation, he momentarily sparked Else's interest as she recalled Hill's former rôle as the BBC's Radio Doctor.

Else: He cured my lumbago once, he did.
Alf: Look . . .
Else: I wrote to him . . .
Alf: Look . . .
Else: An' told him how I had this lumbago.
Alf: Look . . .
Else: An' he wrote back.
Alf: Look . . .
Else: Very nice letter he wrote.
Alf: Look . . .
Else: Told me what to do with it, he did.
Alf: Look . . .
Else: I think we was all a lot healthier when he was on the radio.
Alf: Look . . .
Else: What?
Alf: I lost me thread now, you great pudden!

The monster himself was played by Warren Mitchell, whose total involvement in the part became the show's greatest strength. Everything was right: accent, speech patterns, clothes, even the way he walked (a major element of characterization that is sometimes overlooked by lesser actors). Sustained by Johnny Speight's scripts, Mitchell built his character into a national monument of startling and somewhat fearsome proportions.

Speight has acknowledged the influence of Muir and Norden's Glum family on his work for Arthur Haynes and in his creation of the memorable Alf; while perceptible, this should not diminish the originality of his creation.

Some measure of the difference between writing sitcoms for actors rather than for specific comics can be gleaned from the fact

In Sickness and in Health *found time catching up with the indomitable Alf and Else (Warren Mitchell, Dandy Nichols).*

that Mitchell, today inextricably intertwined with Alf Garnett, was not first choice for the part. Other actors very seriously considered for the rôle were Peter Sellers and Leo McKern.

Later changes to the show included a series without Else, who was said to be visiting relatives in Australia, an unsuccessful solution to the problem that Dandy Nichols was unhappy. She later returned but was clearly ailing. After Dandy Nichols' death Alf soldiered on, getting older and hoarser but with his bigotry in no way impaired. The strength of the show's original central premise began to look a trifle threadbare, perhaps a result of evidence on all sides that real-life Alf Garnetts were not only alive and well but were working in the media, the police and parliament as well as just about

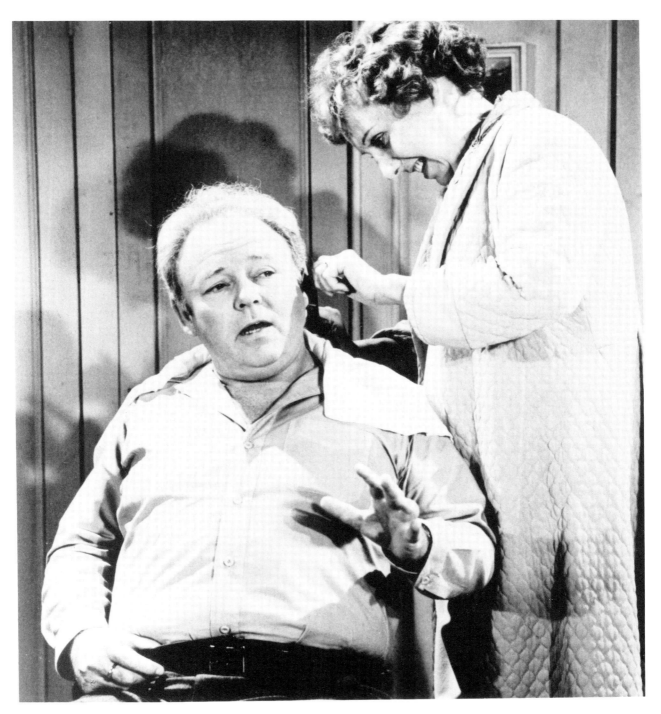

Alf Garnett's transatlantic counterpart, the equally bigoted Archie Bunker, and his long-suffering wife Edith, in All in the Family *(Carroll O'Connor, Jean Stapleton).*

everywhere else in Britain.

In some respects *Till Death* can be seen as having revolutionized British television sitcoms. But in its content if not in its language it did have forebears in television outside sitcom-land that had cast more than a few bricks at a generally complacent society. *TW3* and its offshoots had taken swings at numerous sacred cows, the Church and the State among them, and had clobbered a fair few in the process.

There were more than a handful of Alfs in America, too, and the concept of *Till Death* was taken up by Norman Lear and adapted to a slightly different set of prejudices, taboos and sacred cows.

All in the Family starred Carroll O'Connor in the Alf Garnett rôle, here renamed Archie Bunker. His wife was Edith (Jean Stapleton), his daughter was Gloria (Sally Struthers) and his son-in-law Mike (Rob Reiner). Unlike the British original, this show was branded as revolutionary.

American television, although older than its British counterpart, was still somewhat immature, even in 1970 when *All in the Family* began as a mid-season replacement. The networks were still taking care not to offend anyone through the language, content or even ideology voiced in the shows they aired, lest minds reared to respond only to slogans were unduly disturbed. Into this genially avuncular territory Archie Bunker strode like a latterday Attila the Hun. If he didn't rape and pillage he certainly laid waste any preconceptions of what could and could not be shown on prime-time TV. Above all, like Alf Garnett, he held up for contempt and ridicule those attitudes of mind which lay festering beneath the surface of a society that might have been presumed to be the melting pot of the world's emigrants – and, since 1964 at least, freed from racial discrimination. Like Alf, Archie was right-wing and suited his surname by having a bunker mentality. Absolutely sure of himself, he had no unwarranted misconceptions about melting-pot myths and civil rights. He knew that large slices of American society were comprised of 'hebes' and 'coons' and he said so, in the process nailing his colours to the Republican Party's mast.

Well, I'll tell you one thing about President Nixon. He keeps Pat at home. Which was where Roosevelt should have kept Eleanor. Instead, he let her run around loose until one day she discovered the coloured. We never knew they were there. She told them they were getting the short end of the stick and we've been having trouble ever since.

Over the years Archie and his family underwent certain traumatic experiences that his British counterparts were spared. Edith was subjected to an attack by a rapist; she went through the menopause; and she had problems with her religious beliefs. Gloria had her share of problems too, including a miscarriage and a difficult birth, while Mike underwent a vasectomy operation and suffered from impotence.

In time Archie, like Alf, found himself deserted by his family. In 1978 Gloria and Mike were written out when Sally Struthers and Rob Reiner (son of Carl Reiner, creator of *The Dick Van Dyke Show*) left for other ventures. At the end of that same year, Jean Stapleton also called it a day, but O'Connor continued in a new show entitled *Archie Bunker's Place* and was still blustering against everybody and everything as the 1980s dawned.

With a record five years in the top slot in the ratings, *All in the Family* became America's all-time favourite sitcom. Maybe Lucy wouldn't have liked it, but millions did. Whether they liked it because they saw Archie Bunker as a savage lampoon of the right-wing bigot or because they quietly agreed with what he said and stood for is as open to question as Alf Garnett's success in Britain.

Generally speaking, the glaring difference between British and American sitcoms is that slab of goo which lurks inside the crisply-baked meringue casing of most American shows. There is also a different approach to dialogue and the use, or non-use, of jokes. If *All in the Family* was largely free of the former it certainly didn't suffer an absence of wisecracks.

Writing on this point around the time that Archie Bunker began his career, Leslie Halliwell observed that '. . . Alf was wooden and witless in his ignorance and, no matter how Johnny Speight may have protested otherwise, rather endearing. Deeply ingrained in the American comedy tradition is the need for everyone to be smart. So Archie Bunker is also a wisecracker . . . Whether this will impair the durability of the original idea remains to be seen.'

As we have seen, Archie did endure and it might well be that his jokes were part of his success.

The very long run of *All in the Family,* allied as it was to the much greater number of episodes in each season (about 39 in the old days, fewer in more recent times), highlights one of the major differences between British and American television comedy shows. While in Britain a single writer, or pair, will usually write every episode of every series, in America the concept for a show is usually handed over to a team of writers. The greater output needed to satisfy demand justifies this because one man could not possibly write a 30-minute show every week for 39 weeks. Although Speight, Roy Clarke, Galton and Simpson, John Sullivan and others often manage a high output without a glaringly obvious fall-off in quality, other British writers often show signs of strain after half a dozen episodes. While the Writers' Guild of Great Britain might well rise up in arms at the thought of allowing the American system to make inroads in the UK, provided suitable safeguards could be found for creators and principal writers such a system could serve to overcome the tiredness which often creeps into British comedy series.

Another British sitcom to undergo Americanization was *Steptoe and Son*. The idea was around for some time. Two pilots were made, one starring Lee Tracy and Aldo Ray, the other with Barnard Hughes and Paul Sorvino, but to no avail. The second was the work of Norman Lear and, still liking the concept, he decided to try again. This time, he made the central characters black and promptly hit the jackpot.

The matter of skin colour apart, *Sanford and Son* stayed fairly close to the original British concept. Fred and Lamont Sanford were father and son junk merchants living in squalor in a Los Angeles ghetto.

Starring as Fred was Redd Foxx, whose real name, John Elroy Sanford, was adopted for the characters. Foxx was a veteran entertainer with more than 30 years' experience in clubs, hotels, radio and TV. Lamont was played by Demond Wilson, an actor from the 'legitimate' theatre.

Although the change from white to black gave the American show additional areas to explore, it remained fundamentally similar to *Steptoe and Son*, the bulk of the scripts centring upon the acrimonious father/son relationship. In one important area, however, the American writers, perhaps hampered by that dangerous minefield of glop, did not reproduce the powerful element of tragedy that ran through *Steptoe and Son*. *Sanford and Son* was often good but though it may often have been jokier than *Steptoe* it was never as memorable.

When *Sanford and Son* folded in 1977 a spin-off, *The Sanford Arms*, was made, featuring LaWanda Page (Aunt Esther in the original), but failed to attract an audience. Similarly unattractive to audiences was 1980's *Sanford*, which saw Redd Foxx back as Fred, who had married a rich woman and was living in Beverly Hills. It was a mistake Galton and Simpson would never have made. While it might be possible, just, to imagine Albert Steptoe marrying himself off to a rich widow, he would never have fitted into a life of luxury along the banks of the Thames at Maidenhead.

On the other hand, he might have had some fun trying.

CHAPTER TWELVE

CLASS

'I look up to him, but I look down on *him*.'
The Frost Report

Class is something of a problem in television comedy, just as it is in real life. Given the different way in which the societies are structured, class in America means something very different to class in Britain. The British should never let an American claim that his is a classless society: it isn't. If an American should ever ask a Briton, especially an Englishman, to explain the class system, confusion will reign — on both sides.

The complexities of the English class system offer numerous opportunities for humour. They also offer similarly extensive opportunities for hatred; the absence of a class revolution in English history does not mean the English are less volatile than the French, or less oppressed than the Russians were. It has rather more to do with generations of grinning and bearing it, of showing a stiff upper lip in the face of adversity, of politely taking one's turn, of queueing in the rain, of knuckling the forehead to one's elders and betters.

A classic sketch written by Marty Feldman and John Law for *The Frost Report* demonstrated several layers of the English system.

Tall, upper-crust John Cleese stands next to medium-height, middle-class Ronnie Barker and next to him stands small, lower-class Ronnie Corbett. Barker: 'I look up to him [Cleese] because he is upper-class; but I look down on him [Corbett] because he is lower-class. I am middle-class.' Cleese: 'I have got innate breeding, but I have not got any money. So sometimes I look up to him

[Barker].' Corbett's character then demonstrated the writers' awareness of the complexities: 'I know my place. I look up to them both; but while I am poor, I am honest, industrious and trustworthy. Had I the inclination, I could look down on them. But I don't.'

Understandably, comedians and comedies which depend upon the class system for their laughs do not cross the Atlantic very well.

The English working class has a strong tradition of comedy and comedians, the middle class is less noted for such attributes, while the upper classes have yet to produce a single stand-up comic, although some might think they've already done so without really meaning to.

Naturally enough, the strongholds of working-class humour and humorists are those areas of the country in which industrial employment has traditionally been concentrated. Simplistically, this means the north of England, which at one time boasted a gallery of pastmasters of the art including Arthur Askey, Norman Evans, Tommy Handley, Jimmy James, Albert Modley, Dave Morris, Frank Randle, Ted Ray and Robb Wilton.

In the years after the Second World War, as the variety theatres began to fail, most of these comics tried radio. This raised another aspect of the class system: accent. When Frank Randle burst on to a northern stage, legs, arms and eyes all ostensibly operating independently of one another or any central nervous system, and belched loudly before

'Whatever happened to . . . ?' Likely Lads *Bob* and *Terry survey the damage (Rodney Bewes, James Bolam).*

declaring, 'Eeeh, Ah've supped some stuff toneet!' he would bring the house down. In the south of England it wasn't the basic vulgarity of his humour which caused the problem – after all, London's East End had its own share of base vulgarians. Most of the time audiences simply didn't know what this supposed lunatic was talking about. And when Frank tried radio, the foundations of the BBC fairly shook.

Conversely, southern working-class comics fared well in London but often did not travel well. Doyen of this breed was the incomparable Max Miller. Although very popular across the country, it was on London's halls that he became a deity. Unfortunately, Miller's radio career was curtailed when his borderline humour got him into trouble with the BBC. The prohibitions on his radio work meant that by the time television became an option for comics, he was one of many who were bypassed.

If working-class comics, especially those from the north of England, had had their ranks drastically thinned by their experiences on radio, television continued the process. In time, there was a reversal of fortune which coincided with the growth in popularity of working-class novelists and film-makers in the 1960s and an even wider acceptance of regional accents developed. None of this meant that the class system was breaking down; if anything it was being reinforced, but for a while, at least, the seething masses were placated by being allowed to send a select few of their number across the divide.

The North-South divide, while serving as a means of drawing bitter laughter by way of occasional jokes, has not yet become an issue or a *modus vivendi* of situation comedy on television, where class presents problems for programme-makers. In an interview with *The Guardian*'s Dennis Barker in January 1987, Greg Dyke, director of programmes for TVS, a commercial station in the south of England, expressed concern at ITV's apparent inability to adjust to changes taking place in Britain as the balance of wealth shifted even more to favour the south. He was also aware of the corresponding divide between what worked north of Watford and what didn't: 'A northern situation comedy may play well in the North but not in London or the South.'

Among the very best of British sitcoms is one which, in its first flush of life, touched upon but did not depend upon the audience having some measure of understanding of the class system. This was the BBC's *The Likely Lads*, written by two north-easterners, Dick Clement and Ian La Frenais, and starring two young actors, James Bolam as Terry Collier and Rodney Bewes as Bob Ferris. The series ran from 1965 to 1969, and several years after it had ended Terry and Bob were brought back for a new series, but, unlike the many sitcoms which grow sadder and unfunnier with the passage of time, this one had matured superbly. Unlike its predecessor, *Whatever Happened to the Likely Lads?* was very deeply involved in class.

The young Terry and Bob are a pair of north country lads struggling through their awkward late-teens. Each has his own very different view of the world in which they live.

Terry is aggressive, single-minded in his pursuit of a good time and of girls – and a good-time girl is his idea of heaven. He is bright but not noticeably weighed down with ambition. This is not because he lacks self-confidence – if anything Terry is too confident for his own good – but rather because he intuitively understands that people like him have a clearly defined rôle in society. Trying to fight the system is just wasted effort. Left to his own devices, Terry would probably have worked in the same dead-end job until it was time to collect his pension.

Bob is Terry's opposite, or, perhaps more precisely, his *alter ego*. Shy and lacking in confidence, he is always slightly nervous of any scheme of Terry's that could conceivably end in a confrontation with authority. And for Bob authority could be anything from a policeman to someone with a better accent. As intelligent as Terry, Bob's lack of confidence does not prevent him from having ambitions. He believes that there is a way out of the class trap and that he can make the break if he works hard enough.

When Terry and Bob return in the later series, they are four years older and much has changed. For one thing, the writers were older and wiser (but just as good and as funny); for another, Britain's society had changed. True, it had not changed as much as it would a few years on when the north in general and the north-east in particular became a disaster area, suffering unemployment, social deprivation and urban decay on a massive scale. But those later changes would lead to a very different kind of television writing. When Alan Bleasdale wrote *Boys from the Black Stuff* in 1982 he used humour in a more devastating manner than any overtly comic writer had thus far risked. Back in 1973, it was still possible to deal with northern problems with a lighter touch.

Just as their surroundings have changed, so too have Terry and Bob. Terry's changes are only superficial. He has spent the intervening years in the army and, as for so many young soldiers, the experience has merely allowed him to enjoy the same kind of good time as before – and the same kind of girls. The only difference has been that the girls were in foreign parts and while there he has inadvertently married one. Now he regrets his marriage, he is still without ambition, and he is still convinced that there is no way out of his social class. The main change in Terry is that he is no longer prepared to spend the next 40 years in a dead-end job. He is now happy to spend them idling the time away.

The passage of time has changed Bob too. He has struggled upwards, working hard to get a better job and a car and a house of his own. As the new series opens he too is about to marry, and does so as the series progresses. In his own eyes Bob is a success. His material possessions are just one measure of that success, dining out on a Saturday night is another, and so too is the annual fortnight on the Costa Brava or on the ski slopes of some mispronounced Austrian village. Bob is happily looking forward to his future and his slow but sure rise up the middle-management ladder. Most important of all, Bob thinks he has risen out of his class. Of course, that is before Terry comes back.

The return of Terry and his subsequent onslaught against Bob's pitiful self-improvement was class humour at its best. And this was not all that the series offered. Bob's wife,

the awful Thelma (superbly portrayed by Brigit Forsyth), is everything Terry dislikes in a woman. She is bossy and intent on remaking her man in her own image of how an ideal husband should be. And then there is her sexiness – or, rather, the lack thereof. Thelma's manner always implies that sex is something not very nice which has to be occasionally tolerated, yet her veneer would seem to conceal a powerful sex drive that will never be fulfilled with the man she has chosen for her husband. Infrequently glimpsed was the barely perceptible hint that Thelma and Terry might just be on the verge of striking sparks off one another. When those moments arise, however, Thelma's innate commonsense prevails, she stiffens her resolve, and if sparks fly they are not the sexual sort.

In their other battles Thelma sees Terry as a major challenge to her control over Bob. This is not because Thelma is malicious. She simply belongs to that strong-minded breed of woman against whom comics have railed for countless years. She is the domineering wife, the model for a million seaside postcards; add a few years to her age and she will become the embodiment of every mother-in-law joke ever told.

Unusually in any situation comedy that examines the issue of class, even if only fleetingly, Terry and Bob rarely encounter people from another social group but develop their differing views on class with one another.

The more commonplace use of class in British sitcoms has been the straightforward clash between members of different classes who have no more in common with one another than if they had been born on different planets.

Thames TV's *George and Mildred*, a spin-off from *Man About the House*, and written by Johnnie Mortimer and Brian Cooke, was primarily concerned with the sexual relationship between George Roper and his wife. George, grumpily portrayed by Brian Murphy, is another archetypal seaside postcard character – the one with knotted handkerchief on head and trousers rolled up to the knees. Murphy became an expert at delivering marvellously transsexual lines of which the excuse that he didn't want sex with

George once again frustrates Mildred (Brian Murphy, Yootha Joyce).

his marriage partner because he had a headache was the most blatant. As the predatory Mildred, actress Yootha Joyce was a mass of twitchily frustrated sexuality. Unlike the female praying mantis which eats the male after sexual intercourse, Mildred tends to demolish George as an alternative to the sex act.

But sex is only one conflict in the world the Ropers inhabit; the other is class. Instead of the basement flat they occupied in the series in which they originated, their own show found them transplanted to a middle-class housing development (a posh term for a housing estate) largely peopled by rising young executives. Although Mildred revels in her new and entirely imaginary status, George hates everything about it. Working-class and defiantly proud of it, although not so proud he will actually go out and look for

a job, George's main class conflict comes with his next-door neighbour, Jeffrey Fourmile, played by Norman Eshley as if he had a permanent smell under his nose. He has — George.

Somewhat weakening the credibility of their battles is the strong element of caricature in both George and Jeffrey. Indeed, this comment can also be applied to Mildred and to Mildred's sister and her husband (Avril Elgar and Reginald Marsh), who pay occasional visits. These visits occur only when the materialistic sister has some new acquisition to wave under Mildred's envious nose. The only 'real' person in the main cast is Jeffrey's wife, Ann, who also serves as her husband's only saving grace. Gently undercutting his excesses with mildly deprecating lines, she alone brings to the proceedings a hint that there might be a real world out there in which

Class conflict at its most polished in The Good Life *(left to right: Penelope Keith, Richard Briers, Paul Eddington, Felicity Kendal).*

similar class warfare is being fought out. Coincidentally, the actress playing Ann, Sheila Fearn, had also appeared in *The Likely Lads* in the rôle of Terry's older sister, Audrey.

Perhaps as compensation for being permanently on the losing end of his battles with Mildred, George generally wins the skirmishes against Jeffrey's outrageous snobbery. He even subverts Jeffrey's determined efforts to raise his son as a carbon-copy embodiment of his own prejudices. Young Tristram (Nicholas Bond-Owen) gleefully accepts George's alternative to his father's dreary ideas on education. Learning to play three-card brag for money is for him an infinitely superior pastime to reading the latest brochure from the Conservative Party.

Just as class took second place to sex in *George and Mildred*, so it took second place in *The Good Life*, a show which was not really about class at all — but it existed just the same. While *George and Mildred's* comedy employed broad strokes for its characters, situations and to indicate class differences, the brushwork used by writers John Esmonde and Bob Larbey in *The Good Life* was remarkably fine.

The central idea of the show was simple: a young couple, Tom and Barbara Good, decide that they have had enough of the rat-race. He gives up his well-paid job with an advertising agency and they become self-sufficient. They will grow their own food, power their home with electricity they will generate themselves, they will barter food for those essentials they can neither make nor grow. So far, a good idea for a comedy series. What made the idea brilliant was that instead of pushing off to some Welsh mountainside in order to live the Good Life, Tom and Barbara decide to stay where they are — in their mock-Tudor semi in Surbiton.

The sight of the Goods' garden being ploughed up so that they could plant potatoes and cabbages and other staples is bad enough for their neighbours, but when they begin keeping pigs it is too much, at least for one neighbour. Living in the next house are Jerry and Margo Ledbetter and while Jerry, who works at the same agency from which Tom has resigned, views it all with mild amusement, and more than a touch of envy, Margo vacillates wildly between outrage and conviction that her friends have gone crazy.

The key rôles were impeccably performed by a quartet of leading stage actors, only one of whom was well-known to television audiences from earlier sitcoms. This was Richard Briers, whose wearily crumpled face and body lent texture to the rôle of Tom Good. Notwithstanding his casual appearance Briers rattles out lines like a slightly hoarse machine-gun. His earlier sitcom appearances had included *Marriage Lines*, in which he co-starred with Prunella Scales, and *Brothers-in-Law*.

Tom's wife, played by Felicity Kendal, engagingly undercuts her husband's deadly serious approach to their new life. Without ever saying so, she conveys that although she would follow the path he had chosen even if it led her to the grave, she would just as readily revert to their original lifestyle if he were to change his mind. Additionally, there are always hints that she does not expect their self-sufficient life to continue till death does them part, but that one day soon Tom will come to his senses. Nevertheless, whenever such disasters as crop failure, flooding, or the goat refusing to give milk, strike, and Tom is ready to pack it all in, she rallies him. She knows that if they are to call it a day it must be for better reasons.

As Jerry, Paul Eddington conveyed his half-amused, half-envious view of his neighbours with effortless ease. With less to say and do in the scripts than any of the other principals, Eddington contrived to make his reactions to whatever went on around him highlight the essential absurdity of the basic situation. Jerry clearly likes Tom and Barbara and although this sometimes puts him in the opposite corner to his wife he never allows their differences of opinion to degenerate into conflict.

It is through Margo that the question of class arises. Subtly played by Penelope Keith, Margo is a complete snob — but she is never unpleasant, never unsympathetic. This allowed a minor character to develop into a significant foil. As the series progressed, the key to most episodes was not so much what new scheme Tom and Barbara would devise for their joint survival, but how Margo would react to it.

Riddled with all manner of prejudices, Margo's first response to any new development over the fence is to assess how it will affect or reflect upon her. For Margo, status — how she is regarded by her other friends, neighbours and peers — is paramount. But struggling against the mass of class judgements she brings to bear on anything that crosses her path is the fact that Margo is basically a very kindly and decent woman. In her own way she loves her friends the Goods and constantly worries about them. She is especially concerned for Barbara, whom she believes to have been dragged unwillingly into the 'good life' by Tom. Margo constantly seeks ways of helping them out of the series of crises that punctuates their existence. Her idea of help is always to offer the materialistic solution they have forsworn. But this is not intended as sabotage: Margo simply doesn't know how else to show her concern.

In a classic episode Margo unwittingly sabotages her own Christmas. In a tirade against a local tradesman worthy of Alf Garnett at his best, she manages to leave herself on Christmas Eve without food or any of the other items she would normally have around her at this time. She and Jerry are invited to share the 'home-made' Christmas of Tom and Barbara, but her armour-plated reserve prevents her from enjoying herself and her behaviour soon threatens to cloud the gathering in deepest gloom. For once discarding the fun-poking stance he takes with Margo, Tom lectures her sternly and manages to get through that hitherto unpierced defence. Margo relaxes and to everyone's surprise, not least her own, she becomes the life of the party and has the happiest – and least materialistic – Christmas she has ever known.

Margo could very easily have become a figure of ridicule, but thanks to the quality of the writing, character development and especially Penelope Keith's performance, she becomes less a comic figure than a tragic one. As a result, Margo gave the series a depth it might otherwise have lacked and helped it maintain a position as one of the best and most popular domestic sitcoms to appear on British television.

After Margo, numerous rôles were offered to Penelope Keith. Predictably, she was cast in her next sitcom as a snob. The problem with this later rôle, and the series, was that while the class barriers that encased Margo had been subtly defined, they were now rigidly enforced and often exaggerated. In *To the Manor Born* she became Audrey fforbes-Hamilton, a down-on-her-luck aristocrat who has to vacate her stately home. This is bad enough for poor Audrey but, far worse, the new occupant is a man who has made his money in 'trade' and, it later transpires, isn't even British but a mittel-European who has changed his name and his accent. Audrey's response to Richard De Vere (Peter Bowles) is in line with an upgraded version of Margo but she lacks that character's charm and vulnerability. If Margo is that rare form of snob, the kind with whom it is possible to sympathize, Audrey is just a snob, full stop.

Class – its differences and conflicts, the way in which it divides Britain and inhibits the aspirations of a majority of the population – was a permanent undercurrent in *Till Death Us Do Part* and *Steptoe and Son* and also gave an edge to most of Tony Hancock's struggles to rise above the level of no. 23, Railway Cuttings, East Cheam. There's a class joke even in the address.

Class also features in occasional episodes of series which are not themselves essentially concerned with the subject. Sometimes this can prove a mistake. In the otherwise consistently good *Only Fools and Horses*, one episode has Rodney meet the young daughter of an earl; their fleeting affair brings elder brother Del into contact with the upper classes. First during a night at the opera and later at a horrific dinner party at the earl's country seat, Del capers grotesquely through every social gaffe known to man. It was a gruesome display of caricature gone mad. No one, not even an imbecile – and Del was far from that – could have behaved in such a manner. It was a rare error of judgement by scriptwriter John Sullivan.

If American sitcom has produced fewer excursions into class this is because of certain essential differences. England may be said to have three basic classes, working, middle and upper, within each of which are an infinite number of variations and stratifications. Then there are divisions according to which part of the country an individual is born and raised in, which part he currently lives in, and which part he hopes to live in when he has scrambled as far up his particular class ladder as possible. As for stepping from one class into another . . . not in a lifetime! The American class system, on the other hand, operates partially but by no means exclusively upon money and success. Racial origin also counts for a lot. Less obvious to the outsider is the matter of breeding (and, if Paul Fussell is right in his hilariously funny book, *Class*, it also has something to do with the amount of polyester in an American's clothing).

The rôle of personal wealth and success as a great American class divider is not only very different from its equivalent in Britain, it is also much less subtle. For all practical purposes it is a one-off joke which, once told, is difficult to resurrect effectively week after week. One show managed it, however, when in 1962 the Clampett family from the Ozarks struck oil, sold their land to an oil company and decided to move to Beverly Hills. Against such opposition as that offered by Lucille Ball and Dick Van Dyke, *The Beverly Hillbillies* shot to first place in the ratings and stayed pretty close to the top during its long run.

An earlier success, *The Real McCoys*, had also uprooted a family and moved them to California. The McCoys, led by triple-Oscar winner Walter Brennan as Amos, came from

The Honeymooners, *a blue-collar classic with the Kramdens and the Nortons (left to right: Jackie Gleason, Art Carney, Audrey Meadows, Joyce Randolph).*

West Virginia but their move to California still found them living down on the farm. The Clampetts, however, followed the great American tradition and if they didn't go from a log cabin to the White House, they certainly went from a tarpaper shack to a Hollywood mansion.

Starring Buddy Ebsen as Jed Clampett and Irene Ryan as Granny, the show recorded the efforts of the hillbillies to adjust to their new environment. Their attempt is doomed, mainly because they do not really want to live in Southern California but would have preferred to stay at home in their beloved mountain country. But $25 million is $25 million, so they use the money lavishly and unwisely. Material possessions abound, not that they always know what to do with them. They dine off the billiard table and Granny uses her scrubbing board in preference to a washing machine (and always has trouble telling the difference between a washer and a TV set).

Although *The Beverly Hillbillies* was usually well performed, the scripts only rarely rose to a comparable level. On those few occasions when they did, it was possible to see the show as an attack on materialism, which is at its most strident in the series' chosen setting of Beverly Hills. At its worst, and it often was, the show ridiculed country people and pretty well anyone who did not conform to the notion that the best thing in life is money. For all its numerous flaws, *The Beverly Hillbillies* was hugely popular and ran for nine years.

Another broad division of American society, that of man's employment — blue-collar workers on the one hand, white-collars on the other — produced one classic and one near-miss. The classic was *The Honeymooners*, which starred Jackie Gleason as Ralph Kramden and initially Audrey Meadows as his wife Alice.

The Kramdens first appeared in a sketch in a variety show, to which they later returned

Ed sugaring another of Ralph's bitter pills in The Honeymooners *(Art Carney, Jackie Gleason).*

after the short run of the sitcom series. In a slightly subdued way, Ralph Kramden was an early relative of Alf Garnett/Archie Bunker. He was a know-all, and was loud in airing his ignorance. He was also tireless in his search for a foolproof get-rich scheme, anything to lift him above the level to which a rigid societal structure had doomed him. Ralph earned his living driving a bus, but inside was a Cadillac-driver struggling to get out.

He was never so broke, however, that he would let Alice go out to work, a fact which irritated her.

Alice: Look, Ralph, maybe I could get a job and help out.
Ralph: Oh no you don't. When I married you I promised you'd never have to work again.
Alice: But it won't be for long.
Ralph: I don't care, Alice. I've got my pride. Before I'd let you go to work, I'd rather see you starve. We'll just have to live on our savings.
Alice: That'll carry us through the night, but what'll we do in the morning?

Thanks to Gleason, who wrote, directed and produced as well as acting in the series, the short-lived *Honeymooners* became a classic and Ralph Kramden a kind of folk hero. Ralph's conflicts with Alice, which she always won because she was brighter than he, were counterpointed by Ralph's relation-

ship with his best friend Ed Norton (played by Art Carney in his first important rôle).

Only 39 episodes of *The Honeymooners* were syndicated, but they can still be seen late at night or in the early morning on America's TV screens, where they are watched by a dedicated and nostalgic audience which runs into millions. In 1985 5,000 people attended the convention of the Royal Association for the Longevity and Preservation of *The Honeymooners* (RALPH for short). Also in 1985 these devoted souls were rewarded by the discovery in Jackie Gleason's personal vault of 67 additional episodes. Totalling 52 hours, these shows are being screened on prime-time TV and have also been released for home video purposes. There's no business like old show business.

If *The Honeymooners* was an American classic, the status of near-classic blue-collar comedy can be bestowed upon *The Life of Riley*. This had begun as a radio show starring movie tough-guy William Bendix. When the transfer to TV was first tried in 1949 Bendix was unavailable and coincidentally the part was offered to Jackie Gleason. The show bombed and Gleason forswore TV until *The Honeymooners* made him change his mind.

Another shot was taken at a TV version in the 1952-3 season. This time Bendix was available, and despite the opposition (*Ozzie and Harriet, I Married Joan, Our Miss Brooks*) the show was highly successful and ran until 1958.

In Bill Bendix's capable and hairy-wristed hands, Chester A. Riley was another maker of the mould which later produced the master-pieces of Garnett and Bunker. Unlike Ralph Kramden, Riley was not always seeking a way out of his social class. If he wasn't exactly blue-collar and proud of it, he was certainly blue-collar and unashamed of it.

Feet up, ball game on TV, beer in hand, every week Riley put the world to rights. Politically speaking, he also put it more than somewhat to the right and in so doing helped voice some of the attitudes of red-scare America in the 1950s.

A prevailing view taken by many American sitcoms which depict working-class charac-ters is that they are somehow more wholesome, more decent than their fellows from the middle classes — a view which signifies a substantial degree of condescension and therefore serves to undercut much of what passes for class comedy, making it anything but classy.

Happy Days and its spin-off *Laverne and Shirley* are two examples. These two shows, which the distinguished American writer Robert Sklar has used as examples in his work on class issues in television, offer a view which suggests that the best way to deal with the problems of class barriers is to accept them.

Like Fonzie in *Happy Days*, Laverne and Shirley (Penny Marshall and Cindy Williams) also live in the 1950s and make up in a curiously rigid morality what they lack in worldly goods or pretensions to upward mobility. Shopping in a fancy store, Laverne is overwhelmed by the evidence of wealth all around them. 'Shirl, we *do not* belong here.' Initially more belligerent, Shirley also begins to view things through class-rimmed glasses. 'Look at the price! It's a year's rent!' Eventually ejected by the store manager, who is disturbed at the tone-lowering effect the girls are having, Shirley has the nearly-last word: 'We two girls wouldn't want to buy something from a man who smells like the inside of my grandma's purse.'

For many of the contented American viewers of the series, the class element in *Laverne and Shirley* was obscured beneath a barrage of sight gags, of sexual meanderings as Shirley tried to hang on to her virginity in an increasingly permissive world, and the usually unforced affection mutually displayed between two ordinary working girls who spend their days putting caps on beer bottles in a Milwaukee brewery and for whom the future holds little if any promise.

The fact that relatively few attempts have been made to produce class comedy in America suggests an awareness of the inherent difficulties involved. After all, more than any other element which the viewer brings to television, class is very much in the experience and background of the beholder.

More inhibiting is the fact that the middle class — the class which is most nervous about status — dominates television in both countries. Its members are beset by desires to rise above their class and terrified of being pulled down a peg or invaded from below. Programme-makers are similarly nervous about upsetting the *status quo*.

Being nervous about something is a bad state of mind with which to begin exploring an area for comedy. Consequently, more often than not, it is avoided. It is probably just as well, because apart from the isolated examples mentioned the results have been much less than satisfactory.

THE 'EIGHTIES SURVEYED

'So it's good night from me . . .'
'And it's goodnight from him.'
The Two Ronnies

A trend of the 1970s which rose to the surface in the 1980s was the blending of comedy with drama. As already observed, the higher-quality comedy shows have usually had a strong dramatic core; the addition of comedy to straight, especially tough, drama also tends to improve the product.

In America, such shows as *The Rockford Files* and *Moonlighting*, both private-eye series, owed much of their success to the tongue-in-cheek playing of principals James Garner, in the first instance, and Cybill Shepherd and Bruce Willis in the second.

Most notable of the American drama-with-humour shows is *Hill Street Blues*, a product of MTM. This began in a distinctly jokey style before settling down into a more obviously dramatic format, but a high level of good comedy writing and playing was maintained in between the serious drama and the violence.

In Britain a late-1970s drama serial on BBC entitled *Don't Forget to Write* cast George Cole as a television writer suffering from writer's block and undergoing all manner of torture from his wife and his writing rival (Gwen Watford and Francis Matthews) as he struggled to work his way out of the problem. With a good script from Charles Wood and excellent playing from the principals, the show had more laughs than many sitcoms.

George Cole also starred as the shifty Arthur Daley in Thames TV's *Minder*, alongside Dennis Waterman as Terry McCann. This series, which was created and often written by Leon Griffiths, used humour extensively even in the first season when the violence was still quite thick on the ear. Later on, as the humour quota increased and the violence diminished, this became another example of a non-comedy series outrunning the genuine sitcom entries in its laughter content.

Other drama series followed suit, the BBC's excellent *Rumpole of the Bailey*, written by John Mortimer and starring Leo McKern, being a notable example .

Alan Bleasdale wrote several television dramas which contained humorous situations, among them *The Muscle Market* and *The Black Stuff*. When called upon to follow up *Black Stuff* with a series about its principal characters he surprised everyone, not least the BBC, by coming up with a major drama series, *Boys from the Black Stuff*. This exposed the bitter despair of the unemployed in Liverpool and made millions of people, especially those below the North-South divide, suddenly aware of the way in which the nation was tumbling headlong towards self-inflicted destruction. Unemployment was not the only issue Bleasdale took on; broken marriages and homelessness were the least of his characters' worries as successive episodes dealt with death, human and urban decay and insanity. Yet, through it all, the writer, aided by a superb cast and director Philip Saville, managed to inject a seemingly unbreakable thread of humour, albeit one that was usually black and occasionally manic.

The problems of unemployment were also tackled in a drama series from Central TV which used humour more overtly than had Bleasdale. *Auf Wiedersehen, Pet* was written by Ian La Frenais and Dick Clement, originators of *The Likely Lads*, *Porridge* and other successful sitcoms. Here, the series followed the adventures of a group of Geordie bricklayers who were obliged to travel to Germany to find work, where they were joined by mates from other parts of Britain. In fact, the central premise was an old one: that of gathering together a group of disparate characters in a situation of mutual antipathy, hope or jeopardy. Thanks to high-quality writing and excellent ensemble acting from a group of largely unknown young players, the series was a huge popular success. A sequel which brought them all together again was both predictable and strained by coming too quickly on the heels of the first adventure. If a few more years had elapsed, as the same writers had allowed to happen between *The Likely Lads* and *Whatever Happened to the Likely Lads?*, the result might have been better.

Regular sitcoms which enjoyed great British success in the 1980s, and which included a few that had started out at the tail end of the 1970s, were often limited in inventiveness not only in the writing but also in the concept. Several clustered around the already thin idea of grown-up children refusing to leave home or returning to live with Mum and Dad, or, conversely, of Mum or Dad coming to live with son and daughter after being widowed. Middle-aged dads brought up nubile teenage daughters at the expense of their own fading sex lives and there was also some incidence of middle-aged one-parent families meeting up with other middle-aged one-parent families, object matrimony.

In the son-returns-to-Dad format was *Home to Roost*. This starred John Thaw and Reece Dinsdale as father and son Henry and Matthew Willows. Here the grumpily contented Dad has his tranquillity disturbed when Matthew turns up, having been thrown out by his mother who, too late, has discovered that her son has inherited all those traits of character which led her to divorce his father. With father and son staring at one another

through a kind of ageing mirror, the show benefited from superior central performances and writing. In 1987 this show was picked up for 'translation' into American as *You Again*.

No Place Like Home increased the number of people involved by having Mum and Dad besieged by several grown-up children. The presence of William Gaunt and Patricia Garwood as Arthur and Beryl Crabtree helped the show achieve several series and a devoted following but can scarcely be accused of taking sitcoms a step forward.

How to relate to parents was a question mulled over by *Don't Wait Up*, which starred Tony Britton and Nigel Havers as father-and-son doctors, and *Three Up, Two Down*, co-starring Michael Elphick and Angela Thorne. They play Sam and Daphne who are Dad and Mum, respectively, of a recently married husband and wife. Sam and Daphne clash partly on grounds of who is most important to their new grandchild but mostly on matters of class. He is all boiler-suit and proud of it, while she is disdainfully pearls and twin-set.

An example of single parents with kids who are joined together in hoped-for matrimony is *Let There Be Love*, which starred Paul Eddington and Nanette Newman.

Thames TV's *Fresh Fields*, in which the kids have fled the nest leaving the parents wondering what to do with themselves, starred Anton Rodgers and Julia McKenzie as William and Hester Fields and Ann Beach as their nosy neighbour Sonia. Rather like actors in an only slightly-above-average repertory company, none of the principals made any pretence of not playing to the studio audience.

Sorry! starred Ronnie Corbett as Timothy Lumsden, a middle-aged son unable to break the family ties and escape his parents' home. Controlled by his despotic mother (Barbara Lott), the frustrated Timothy is repeatedly brought to the point of leaving, but she invariably knows the moment at which to step in and tie him down again.

All these shows have an easy-going, comfortable appeal, following a tradition which runs all the way back to *Life with the Lyons* by way of *Not in Front of the Children*.

Penny is once again persuaded by the irresponsible Vince in Just Good Friends *(Jan Francis, Paul Nicholas).*

Leading lights of the bland suburban tradition are Terry Scott and June Whitfield, who have doggedly pursued their chintzy existence through seemingly endless decades. Audiences know exactly what to expect from such friendly titles as *Happy Ever After* and *Terry and June*, both of which evoke instant images of gnome-infested suburbia.

Similarly undemanding and enjoyed by millions were *A Fine Romance, Just Good Friends* and *Ever Decreasing Circles*.

Bob Larbey wrote LWT's *A Fine Romance*, a well-crafted, literate series which featured elegant performances from Judi Dench and Michael Williams. Married in real life, the pair were unable to get it together on-screen despite the determined efforts of their friends who thought they should.

Just Good Friends, written by John Sullivan for the BBC, is another case of good acting and smooth if unprofound writing overcoming a basically improbable situation. The show starred Paul Nicholas and Jan Francis as Vince and Penny, a young couple separated by class (again) and his incorrigible desire to steer clear of matrimony. He has once left her waiting at the altar and when, some time and a few relationships later, they meet again, for some inexplicable reason Penny lets him into her life once more. Not content with that, she also admits Vince to her bed and by the end of the 1986 series had actually taken the risky plunge and married the man she could quite clearly do without. The fact that her marriage to Vince Pinner turned Penny Warrender into Penny Pinner suggest that when the series began matrimony was not on the writer's mind.

This show, like *A Fine Romance* and several others of the period, followed a growing trend towards serialization. Although certain plot elements were self-contained within each episode, each series had a developing plot line running all the way through.

Domestic situation comedy at its slickest came with *Ever Decreasing Circles*, in which Richard Briers, who has been at it ever since *Marriage Lines* a generation ago, carried on perfecting his already nigh-on-faultless portrayal of mildly eccentric and slightly neurotic suburban Englishmen. As Martin Bryce, obsessed with finicky detail and determined to maintain standards only he fully understands and which are virtually unattainable, he romped through a well-acted series. Slick though performance and staging were, only rarely did the writing match up, and at times the characters were faced with situations that were improbable even by sitcom standards. It was also very difficult to believe that Martin's wife Ann (Penelope Wilton) would have stayed with him for two minutes. Certainly she wouldn't have hung around until the arrival of Peter Egan as Paul Ryman, their new next-door neighbour, before starting to chafe at the constraints imposed by a husband of such relentless insensitivity, to say nothing of his passion for order and complete lack of passion for his wife.

Neurotic Martin up against slightly superior Paul in Ever Decreasing Circles *(Richard Briers, Paul Egan).*

Richard Briers, interviewed for *Radio Times* by Tim Heald, was understandably rather more sympathetic towards his character, observing that Martin 'is rather a pathetic character, marvellous to play, the kind who has four different kinds of spade in the garden and changes the water in the battery every three days. All to do with fundamental insecurity.'

Established comic talents continued or returned during the 1980s with varying degrees of success. Harry Worth, long a favourite performer, made *O Happy Band!*, written for the BBC by Jeremy Lloyd and the ubiquitous David Croft. Dick Emery made *Emery!*, which was unusual in being a comedy-thriller serial, a form very rarely exploited by television despite the long tradition in British films and radio, of which Naunton Wayne and Basil Radford were the best-known exponents. A failed attempt to revive their style for television was *Charters and Caldicott*, starring Robin Bailey and Michael Aldridge.

Leonard Rossiter brought his lip-curling delivery to *Tripper's Day*, which despite his performance fell a long way short of his wonderful Rigsby in *Rising Damp*. Rossiter's untimely death brought an end to a wide-ranging career which encompassed the legitimate stage, films and television drama and included two classic sitcom creations: the awful Rigsby and the manic-depressive Reggie Perrin. The decision to continue his last show under the title *Slinger's Day* and starring Bruce Forsyth was not a good idea as Forsyth's abrasive comic style needs victims, not foils.

Ronnie Barker and Ronnie Corbett, both with several sitcoms to their credit, continued

Twenty years on yet still working their magic (Ronnie Corbett, Ronnie Barker).

their long-running partnership in *The Two Ronnies* into the 1980s. The format of the show has remained virtually unchanged over its 20-year run: an opening and closing 'news' summary followed by a string of sketches featuring one or both of the stars, several of which make great use of Barker's linguistic skills. A grand finale usually involves a great deal of dressing up, and a fair bit of camping about, and always a song for which new and dextrous lyrics are written.

The durability of *The Two Ronnies* stems in part from the fact that Barker and Corbett do not appear week in week out in this guise, and in part from the sheer professionalism of their joint work.

Although in their individual sitcom work Barker has a clear edge over his diminutive partner, in *The Two Ronnies* they are somewhat closer together but with Barker still leading the way. In live performance, however, it is Corbett who comes into his own, being much more the man of the theatre than Barker, a product of television.

An all-talking style of TV sitcom emerged in 1980 with *Shelley* and continued with *It Takes a Worried Man*, both written by Peter Tilbury. Shelley, played by Hywel Bennett, is a sometimes engaging drop-out trying, with little enthusiasm and less success, to use his university education to improve his standing in the world. Working-class and not very proud of it, Shelley is frequently offensive to people less well-educated than he, for no apparent motive other than a desire to demonstrate a misplaced sense of superiority. Peter Tilbury himself took the leading rôle of Philip Roath in *It Takes a Worried Man*, somewhat stiffly delivering a doleful line in stream-of-consciousness chat during which he worries himself through the male menopause, a broken marriage and a dead-end job, all with the aid of a joke psychiatrist who is more in need of treatment than the hero.

The potentially rich territory of a man who is accident-prone was mined unprofitably in Channel 4's *Chance in a Million*, which starred Simon Callow as Tom Chance. The implied parody of other sitcoms never quite took hold. Similarly uneasy were Tom Chance's speech patterns, pared to the minimum, which were supposed to be as funny as the situations in which the hero found himself. In the event, the way Tom had of speaking ('Warning you. Not entirely happy. Tone of voice') proved even less funny than the mess he made of everything he touched. That in itself was quite an achievement.

Conversely, politics, an unlikely area for situation comedy, proved both funny and highly successful.

Yes, Minister, written for the BBC by Anthony Jay and Jonathan Lynn, began in 1979. It featured a typically inept and not-too-bright politician and two members of his staff. As Jim Hacker, the vaguely fearful MP, Paul Eddington excelled even his previous fine characterizations in sitcoms. As Sir Humphrey Appleby, Hacker's Secretary, Nigel Hawthorne made the best of the best lines, many of which were Civil Service doubletalk at its most incomprehensible. The smallest of the three central rôles, Bernard Woolley, played to perfection by Derek Fowldes, quietly and effectively counterpointed the other two.

Based upon actual parliamentary practice, the series poked merciless fun at conniving politicians and the Civil Service — and became Prime Minister Thatcher's favourite TV show. 'Its closely-observed portrayal of what goes on in the corridors of power has given me hours of pure joy,' she declared. Mrs Thatcher did not seem to be disturbed that the show revealed, as she maintained, in quite accurate detail, the extent of the procrastination, and the politics within the politics, that permeate central government.

The success of the series was such that it eventually had to move into a marginally different gear. Although never overtly orientated to any particular party, the implication was always that Jim was a Conservative serving a female Prime Minister. In a succeeding series, much to his own amazement, Jim Hacker becomes Prime Minister. *Yes, Prime Minister* continued into the late 1980s, with Jim Hacker facing up to responsibilities he is mentally ill-equipped to tackle; even Sir Humphrey's all-knowing expertise looks shaky when confronted with nuclear weapons and worldwide unrest. Though this sitcom may be reflecting real life, the programme's general adherence to a believ-

Parliamentary problems for Jim Hacker in Yes, Minister *(Derek Fowldes, Paul Eddington, Nigel Hawthorne).*

able background suggests that one day real life could imitate sitcom.

The series' quality has been recognized by a number of awards, most unusually New Year's Honours for the leading actors. Not for the first time, the rôle of the writer was undervalued. As Herbert Kretzmer observed in the London *Daily Mail*, 'Several excellent comic actors could have undertaken the rôles of Jim Hacker and his Cabinet Secretary. The only irreplaceable figures in the . . . series have been the writers. The organ-grinder's tin remains empty while his monkey has been awarded with a nut. The whole thing is absolutely daft.'

The wit and sophistication of comedy set in 1980s Whitehall is a world away from another popular show of the same period.

Set in late-1950s Britain, *Hi-de-Hi!* is seaside postcard comedy at its most obvious. Jimmy Perry and David Croft had previously explored the near-past in *Dad's Army*. They came up with another winner with this series set in a seaside holiday camp. In addition to a good basic concept *Hi-de-Hi!* had the benefit of good writing and generally excellent characterizations. Maplin's Holiday Camp is a kind of cut-price Butlin's, where all the remembered or imagined horrors of the 1950s holiday boom descended upon the heads of hapless holidaymakers, thanks to the efforts of a staff of raging incompetents. From the head of entertainments, an over-weight comic named Ted Bovis (Paul Shane), by way of the senior 'Yellowcoat', Gladys Pugh (Ruth Madoc), to the hopelessly out-of-touch camp manager in Geoffrey Fairbrother (Simon Cadell), the staff at Maplin's do their worst.

The supporting cast included several familiar faces and a few new ones. As Mr Partridge, the drunken Punch and Judy man, Leslie Dwyer was in his stony-faced element, while Diane Holland and Barry Howard as Yvonne and Barry Stuart-Hargreaves, the camp's ballroom dancers, marvellously demonstrated the class system that operates even within the ranks of show business.

Ongoing themes include Miss Pugh's desperate attempts to raise Mr Fairbrother's sexual interest and Ted's equally persistent money-making fiddles. As portrayed by Ruth Madoc, Miss Pugh is a slightly coarser sister to Thelma from *Whatever Happened to the Likely Lads?*

The show's ratings kept it running for several years, but its inventiveness wore thin. The writers began searching for ideas, always a dangerous sign, and many of the themes they explored succeeded only in exposing the limitations of the basic concept. Later cast changes did not provide much in the way of sparkle and a gradual decline in the care with which many of the surviving regulars maintained their characterizations was apparent, not that this seemed to deter either the BBC or the audience.

That excellent actor Geoffrey Palmer, whose presence has been a delight in several series including *Butterflies* and *The Fall and Rise of Reginald Perrin*, was finally given his own show. He was not allowed to escape his established persona, however. As he remarked in an interview with Stewart Knowles for *TV Times*, 'Sometimes I think I have cornered the market in dull, plodding men.'

Channel 4's *Fairly Secret Army* tells the story of a retired army officer, inept and now unemployable, who pursues his right-wing fantasies to extremes by starting up a private army. He plans to prevent the nation's continuing decline into anarchy by opposing what he sees as the unbridled activities of a bunch of swinish lefties.

Aiding and abetting Major Harry Kitchener Wellington Truscott on the loony right as he rants and raves at the loony left are some of his former rankers, some lame-brains who

A cut-price holiday camp provided good TV comedy and a touch of nostalgia (Paul Shane and Ruth Madoc in Hi-de-Hi!*).*

appear to think they're actually joining the National Front, and some who have joined up for want of any other activity with which to occupy their time. Among them are Michael Robbins, a gruff-voiced actor who long ago served as Reg Varney's brother-in-law in *On the Buses* and has never been employed to the best of his abilities, and Liz Fraser, who has been similarly underemployed in television comedy despite long service in the *Carry On* films.

Like Alf Garnett before him, but in a much less obvious manner, Harry Truscott offers his audience a few problems of identification. Is he encouraging right-wing extremism or is his ridicule of it strong enough to carry all but the lunatic fringe? The balance of this show generally carries the day for ridicule. However, some of Harry's supporters trigger the occasional realization that there are people around who would rally to the flag if a real-life Harry Truscott were to come over the horizon.

Many of the British comedy shows of the 1980s, on both BBC and the independent channels, were made not by the TV companies themselves but by independent programme-makers, bringing Britain more into line with modern American practice.

In America, the importance of the independent production and distribution companies has increased. By 1986 many independent stations were transmitting programmes and instead of paying the high asking prices for the syndication of old shows some were putting their money into new ones. In some cases these were shows which had been piloted for, but not taken up by, the networks, or which had failed to attract good ratings on prime-time and had been dropped. *Mama's Family* is one such show; *Charles in Charge* is another. Among the shows which were made specially for the independents were *Throb* and *Small Wonder*.

The latest in the line of science fiction/fantasy sitcoms, *Small Wonder,* is about a robot named Vicki (Voice Input Child Identicant). Tiffany Brisette, the little girl playing the rôle, may or may not be a good actress. As she is called upon to deliver her lines and move around as though she were made of metal and plastic (which of course Vicki is), it

is hard to tell where talent ends and artifice begins. Unfortunately, the inventiveness which would be needed to create a genuine robot like Vicki was not applied to the series. Small wonder *Small Wonder* was not heaped with critical praise. Yet audiences loved it.

Other 1980s American shows which enjoyed mixed results included *The Four Seasons*, a show based upon the Alan Alda movie of the same title. Inspired by Alda, and featuring him in its first episode and his daughters in several, the series followed the decision of a New York couple to join two other couples in California. Uneasy in mood and style and with some awkwardness in the acting, the show failed to measure up to the generally highly literate ideals with which it was launched.

Another movie-based sitcom was *House Calls*, which starred Wayne Rogers (formerly Trapper John of *M*A*S*H*) and Lynn Redgrave, both of whom failed to bring to their rôles the panache of the movie originals (Walter Matthau and Glenda Jackson).

Similarly uneven in tone were two legal comedies. *The Associates* featured British veteran Wilfrid Hyde White as the head of a law firm in which he keeps a fatherly eye upon several whizz-kid lawyers. With former MTM and *Taxi* people involved on the production side the portents were good but the ratings were not. Also in legal land was *Foley Square*, which had the benefit of stronger writing and good performances from a cast headed by Margaret Colin.

Building a show around a grizzled white cop who has a sassy black housekeeper was an attempt to blend two tried sitcom forms but the result, *Gimme a Break*, starring Dolph Sweet and Nell Carter, proved less than was hoped for.

Then there were shows about a female taxi-driver who inherits a multi-million-dollar corporation (*One in a Million*), a waitress in a nightclub (*It's a Living*), and a lonely but game old man who goes to live with his college student grandson (*One of the Boys*). The latter starred Mickey Rooney and enjoyed a small measure of success but needed the injection of a new character after the one-joke format had worn thin. The new man was another old boy, played by Scatman

Crothers, who had also helped support the occasional hard times suffered by *Chico and the Man*.

Perfect Strangers is a curiously dated return to the old idea of a young man from some unspecified middle-European country, where people still ride in horse-drawn carts, who comes to America full of enthusiasm and no real idea of what modern life is like. Featuring Bronson Pinchot as Balki the immigrant and Mark Linn-Baker as Larry the cousin he inflicts himself upon, this particular single-joke idea had been fully exploited by the end of the first episode.

Fortunately, the two young actors had engaging personalities and began to demonstrate a flair for slapstick. Their well-timed comic routines helped maintain the show's good audience figures and go some way to compensate for its inevitable sentimentality.

Other 1980s shows like *Benson*, *Webster*, *Oh Madeline* and *The Golden Girls* have been touched upon earlier in this book, and while these enjoyed measures of success from good to sensational the kiss of death was quickly given to others.

When the TV version of *M*A*S*H* was first on the drawing-board, Elliott Gould, who was in the movie, was thought to be too big-time to approach for the series. By the mid-1980s attitudes towards TV had changed and Gould starred in *ER*, in which, playing a surgeon in a big-city hospital, he is hotly pursued by women. He's also having trouble with the wife he is trying to divorce but who has other ideas.

'What does she want from me? It can't be my blood. She knows I've had hepatitis.' He is also always broke:

'Do you know how embarrassing it is to have three wives and no car?'

Gould is Dad to a large, polyglot family in *Together We Stand*, one of many shows trailing Bill Cosby's bandwagon.

AfterMASH picked up the lives of three refugees from 4077 who were now back home in America. Harry Morgan, William Christopher and Jamie Farr were brought together for this show but audiences soon got tired of waiting for Hawkeye and Hotlips to appear and it fizzled away.

If the failure of *AfterMASH* was predictable, the failure of *Buffalo Bill* was considerably less easy to forecast. Well-written and performed, the show enjoyed critical approval and was much admired inside television, but the public, rallying for once to its old reputation for unpredictability, gave it the thumbs-down. Starring Dabney Coleman as Bill, a TV newsman in Buffalo, the show was similar in concept to *The Mary Tyler Moore Show*, which should have given it a boost but didn't. And Mary herself discovered in the 1980s that there's no accounting for taste. Her new show, *Mary*, failed too.

An unexpected success was *Cheers*, which set new standards surpassed only when *The Golden Girls* appeared.

Set in a Boston bar, *Cheers* centres upon the lives of the proprietor, Sam Malone (Ted Danson), and one of his waitresses, Diane Chambers (Shelley Long), and takes in other employees and a few of the regular customers.

Cheers is one of that growing number of shows which has a continuing storyline even though each episode is self-contained. Importantly, the characters are not cast in stone but are allowed to grow and develop and change. It is this last quality which makes *Cheers* so rewarding.

When the show began Sam Malone was a womanizing former ball-player and an alcoholic to boot. With a tough, wise-cracking waitress named Carla Tortelli (Rhea Pearlman) and a couple of barflies, Norm and Cliff (George Wendt and John Ratzenberger), the series could have managed a season before the joke wore thin. But in episode one Diane appears with her lover, who is leaving his wife to run off with her. By the end of the first episode the lover has gone back to his wife and Diane has taken a job as a waitress. Verbal sparks fly between Diane and Carla, because Diane is a tall, cool, blonde would-be intellectual while Carla is a short, streetwise Italian hardcase who gets pregnant whenever a man looks at her. Additionally, sexual attraction is sparking between Diane and Sam. From then onwards the series settled into a form that never fell into routine.

Sam's alcoholism was only one serious subject aired in the show: in addition, it

Bar staff and bar flies in Boston's favourite watering hole, Cheers *(George Wendt, John Ratzenberger, Ted Danson, Shelley Long).*

confronts the raising of Carla's 'semi-illegitimate' children; the homosexuality of an old friend of Sam's and the occasional suggestions that Cliff's inability to talk to women is a sign of similar inclination. Such topics, plus Diane's nervous breakdown when she can no longer cope with her attraction to Sam and Frasier Crane (Kelsey Grammer), a psychiatrist, all help give the show greater depth than most sitcoms. As producer James Burrows has observed, audiences are intrigued by such developments and want to know what happens.

Another regular character in the first series was assistant bartender Coach (Nicholas Colasanto), whose dumbness and eagerness to agree with everyone, even if it meant changing his position on a subject four times

in as many lines, was a constant delight. Sadly Colasanto died and was replaced by Woody Harrelson as young Woody Boyd, who proved to be similarly dumb.

Thanks to the decision by the producers to let the characters develop, the mutual attraction between Sam and Diane never becomes bogged down by the sentimentality that plagues most American comedy shows. After some sparring they eventually begin living together; later Diane goes off to Europe with Frasier, forcing Sam to reappraise exactly how he feels about her. On the brink of marrying Frasier, Diane changes her mind and goes to work as a cleaner in a convent as penance for her imagined sins, having already spent time in a sanatorium when she suffered her emotional collapse.

Sam's hormones want an early night in bed but Diane's are less eager (Shelley Long, Ted Danson).

When Sam finally decides to abandon his wayward lifestyle and asks Diane to marry him she turns him down, only to change her mind the next day – by which time Sam, whose outward confidence conceals a very tender ego, has withdrawn the offer.

This continual shifting of the balance between the central relationships allows writers and actors to give the show much more depth than might otherwise have been possible.

As Sam and Diane, Ted Danson and Shelley Long achieve a notable credibility in their off-going relationship. It is possible to believe that they really are attracted to one another and that the reasons each comes up with for avoiding total commitment are valid. Unlike the attempted development of characters in *Rhoda*, these work.

Ted Danson convincingly suggests the awkwardness of a man accustomed to reacting to his hormones rather than his emotions, while Shelley Long is equally successful in conveying the problems of a woman struggling between what her brain tells her and what her body wants to do.

Although the Sam-Diane relationship is of prime importance to the show it is not allowed to obscure the supporting characters, who each have their own moments in the front line. Coach had a serious affair with a woman; Frasier can't get over being jilted by Diane; Carla has regular but doomed attempts to form permanent relationships with men but her acid tongue usually gets in the way. The occasional reappearance of her ape-like ex-husband is another opportunity for some verbal fur to fly – but not always before she has allowed matters to progress to a point where pregnancy looms again.

Cliff, a postman, also has his day with those problems arising from his inability to relate to women, and by regularly putting his foot in his mouth in an attempt to air his knowledge, which is simultaneously encyclopaedic and wrong.

Norm's home life is afflicted by his antipathy to his wife Vera (who, wisely, never appears). He also has problems at work (he's an accountant) and, indeed, was fired early in the series; but he keeps bouncing back, even if the world is perpetually against him.

Norm's entry every week and his greeting of 'Hello, everybody' always draws the mass response of 'Norm!' as he makes his tubby way to his permanent seat at the end of the bar. For Norm, the best thing in life is the bar and his whole life revolves around it and his drinking.

The decision of Shelley Long to quit the series in 1987 has presented the writers with a problem, but as they include veterans of several other successful shows including *M*A*S*H, Taxi, Rhoda* and *The Mary Tyler Moore Show*, it is likely that they will rise to the challenge.

*

The significance of comedy on television in 1980s America was underlined when, in 1984, seven noted figures were inducted into the newly established Television Academy Hall of Fame. These first seven names included three from comedy: Milton Berle, Lucille Ball and Norman Lear.

Overall, however, the picture is less encouraging. There is more comedy on television today than ever before, yet any improvement in standards is illusory. The number of good shows created in the 1980s is not appreciably greater than in preceding decades but represents a very small percentage of the total output. TV comedy in the late 'eighties may seem to be better than it really is simply because the hits of the 1970s, the 1960s and even the 1950s are being regularly re-screened.

Of course, as time and television go on the struggle for originality becomes harder. Consider a scriptwriter, or even a team of them, trying to come up with a new family-based sitcom. They might try a tough, bullying wife who seeks to dominate her husband. No, it's been done: *The Larkins* and *George and Mildred.* Try turning it round and make the husband dominant. No, that's been done: *Till Death Us Do Part.*

Well, try changing the family structure and have a one-parent family with dad bringing up the kids: *Bachelor Father* (with Ian Carmichael), *Me and My Girl* (with Richard O'Sullivan) have covered that. Let mother bring up the children: *And Mother Makes*

Three; unmarried mum: *Miss Jones and Son* with Paula Wilcox. How about a foster father bringing up the kids with help from his butler, who stands in as a substitute mother? No, even that's been tried: *Family Affair* with Brian Keith and Sebastian Cabot. Suppose the kids bring up the parents, or at least attempt to indoctrinate them into the 'modern' world: *Bless This House* did this, with Sid James, Diana Coupland, Robin Stewart and Sally Geeson. As for father-and-son relationships, what can be said that hasn't already? We've had *Steptoe and Son, Home to Roost* and *Don't Wait Up.* The same comment applies to mother-and-son relationships: Thora Hird and Christopher Beeny explored this in *In Loving Memory*; Mollie Sugden and Christopher Blake in *That's My Boy* and Ronnie Corbett and Barbara Lott in *Sorry!* Brother and sister? Forget it, who can supersede Eric Sykes and Hattie Jacques in *Sykes* or Jimmy Jewel and Hylda Baker in *Nearest and Dearest*? Getting desperate now? Try a pair of non-gay men living together in slob-husband and fussy-wife rôles. No, even that's been done: Jack Klugman and Tony Randall in *The Odd Couple.* With even the Lucy-Ricky-Fred-Ethel situation mirrored (in reverse, so that the men are the zanies) in the cartoon comedy *The Flintstones*, it isn't surprising that the search goes on and on and on...

Unfortunately, not only is the struggle for originality usually lost but so also is the search for new and interesting ways to deal with old themes. As a result, the great mass of today's shows are unremittingly bland. This can be seen from the fact that sitcoms are now regarded as suitable pacifiers for passengers on some British airlines' short-haul flights. Like most comforts on offer in such circumstances — movies, music, food, the smiles of the stewardesses, the studiedly casual remarks of the captain — the shows chosen are predictably reassuring. There is no room here for *M*A*S*H* (blood), *Monty Python* (destruction) or *Steptoe and Son* (pessimism). Instead, stupefied passengers can lean back and allow the likes of *Home to Roost* and *That's My Boy* to take their minds off the fact that they could drop out of the sky like a stone at any moment.

The dominant strand of blandness is to some extent countered by the shock tactics of the 'alternative' comedians, but can anyone seriously believe that 30 years hence viewers will be watching re-runs of their shows with the same degree of pleasure that today's audiences find from watching Ernie Bilko or Tony Hancock?

As for those bland shows, can the British, who have given so much to TV comedy with their innovating series, learn something from America? That tradition, described earlier, of a single writer or two-handed team being responsible for an entire series, which if well received may be extended for several years, must invite staleness.

Already in Britain drama series are following the American pattern of using a pool of writers, and with considerable success. Comedy is just as much in need of the cross-fertilization of ideas such methods generate.

But where will those writers come from? Experienced old heads are needed, and so too are bright new minds. Unfortunately, the balance struck is often unsatisfactory. Some old heads also have reactionary minds; some of the bright young minds are wildly undisciplined.

It should not be beyond the capabilities of the BBC and the commercial network to collaborate with the independent programme-makers in establishing a system which pools and co-ordinates diverse talents.

Television comedy is a serious business and like all businesses it needs help and direction.

At the beginning of this book a question was asked: whatever became of television comedy? If the TV companies in Britain don't give the help which is so clearly needed, then very soon the answer may well be: it died.

But is there really no hope for the ailing patient? Fortunately, there is. The past forty years of TV comedy is notable for its ups and downs, the good frequently rubbing shoulders with the bad. If the late 1980s present a generally drab scene, illuminated only sporadically by bright spots, we can but reassure ourselves that, just as in past decades when all seemed lost, new shows and writers are surely just around the corner — ready to bring us more laughter in the years ahead.

APPENDIX

Certain fundamental differences have always existed between the way American TV is structured and the way British TV and its programme-makers operate, notwithstanding the recent growth of independent production companies, which are drawing the two countries closer together.

Once upon a time in America there was the DuMont network and recently Ted Turner's TBS and Rupert Murdoch's FBC have been set up, but for years there were just three major networks: ABC, CBS and NBC. These three networks generated much of the programming seen across the nation, especially during 'prime-time' (7.30 or 8 p.m. to 11 p.m. Eastern Standard Time).

Although allowed to own only five stations each, thanks to their location in main urban centres this 'restriction' actually gave the majors a captive audience of well over 50 million people. The local TV stations which dot every corner of the United States accept network shows in return for a cut of the network's advertising income. Additionally, and as a condition of the licence granted by the Federal Communications Commission, the local stations have 'local time', during which they are free to transmit their own programmes. As many local urban TV stations and most of those in rural areas have virtually no studio space beyond that required to house a local newsman or a continuity announcer, the reality is that when they are not screening networked shows they screen 'syndicated' programmes.

In broad terms, a syndicated programme is one originally screened by a network; the network later sells all existing episodes to a distributor who in turn leases them on to individual stations. Usually syndication occurs after a show has folded, although it is possible to syndicate simultaneously with first screening. Among the advantages of syndication enjoyed by the local station is that they can screen a show at any time they choose rather than that dictated by the networks, and they can

also edit them to take more commercials. Syndication is one of the reasons why the number of episodes of shows made for American TV greatly outnumbers those of their British counterparts. Syndication doesn't make much financial sense unless more than 100 episodes exist. At some 39 episodes per season in the earlier years, a three-year run was about the minimum; later, with fewer episodes the norm, it took longer to achieve 'syndicatabiliy'.

Early TV shows often sought sponsorship: for example, by a manufacturing company prepared to associate itself with a show throughout its run, which would therefore take all the advertising space available in the show's slot (and often benefited from having the show's star advertise the product during breaks). By the 1960s this practice began to loosen its hold as the networks took a firmer grip on the production of shows, which led to a greater dependency of the programme-makers on the goodwill of the network bosses. This in turn led to a wider spread of advertising during individual shows, with advertisers buying time in specific programmes.

As a result of this change the network started regarding its programmes in a different way. In order that its shows should attract the massive advertising revenue the network needed, shows had to 'guarantee' mass audiences. Great attention was therefore paid to the nature of the audience attracted to a particular show. There was no point in declaring large viewing figures if they were made up of the kind of person who would not (or could not afford to) buy the advertiser's products. The rise in the late 1970s of shows aimed at the teenage market demonstrates little more than a growing awareness of the spending power of this section of the community.

The power of the American networks in making programmes is no longer what it was. Considering what happened to, for example, Phil Silvers' show, this should give cause for thanks. But, as the giants, five now where once there were only three, jostle for places in the ratings, this might be an opportune moment to pause and wonder whether ABC, CBS, NBC, TBS or FBC will take the trouble to find and nurture another generation of American stars who will have the same future success that Lucille Ball and Phil Silvers had in the past.

BIBLIOGRAPHY

Andrews, Bart, *Lucy & Ricky & Fred & Ethel: the Story of I Love Lucy* (New York: E. P. Dutton, 1976)

Auty, Martyn, 'Keeping It in the Family', *Primetime,* vol. 1, no. 6/7, October/December 1983

Bennett, Tony, *et al* (eds.), *Popular Television and Film* (London: BFI, 1981)

Bier, Jesse, *The Rise and Fall of American Humor* (New York: Octagon, 1981)

Brambell, Wilfrid, *All Above Board* (London: W. H. Allen, 1976)

Chapman, Antony J., and Foot, Hugh C. (eds.), *It's a Funny Thing, Humour* (Oxford: Pergamon, 1977)

Cook, Jim (ed.), *Television Sitcom: BFI Dossier 17* (London: BFI, 1982)

Curry, Jack, 'The Cloning of "Cosby"', *American Film*, October 1986

Dark, Stephen, 'Two Cheers', *Primetime*, vol. 1, nos. 6 & 7, October/December 1983

Edmundson, Mark, 'Father Still Knows Best', *Channels of Communication*, vol. 6, no. 3, June 1986

Emery, Dick, *In Character: a Kind of Living Scrapbook* (London: Futura, 1974)

Feldman, Marty, 'Report on US Comedy', *Contrast: the Television Quarterly*, autumn 1962

Feuer, Jane; Kerr, Paul, and Vahimagi, Tise (eds.), *MTM 'Quality Television'* (London: BFI, 1984)

Fireman, Judy (ed.), *TV Book: the Ultimate Television Book* (New York: Workman, 1977)

Fussell, Paul, *Class* (London: Arrow, 1984)

Gray, Herman, 'Television and the new black man: black male images in prime-time situation comedy', *Media Culture and Society*, vol. 8, no. 2, April 1986

Greenfield, Jeff, *Television: the First 50 Years* (New York: Abrams, 1977)

Horowitz, Susan, 'Sitcom Domesticus: a Species Endangered by Social Change', *Channels of Communication*, vol. 4, no. 3, September/October 1984

Kalter, Susan, *The Complete Book of M*A*S*H* (New York: Abrams, 1984 and London: Columbus, 1984, reissued 1987)

Lear, Norman, 'The 1978 MacTaggart Lecture', *Edinburgh International Television Festival 1979: Official Programme*

Lennon, Peter, 'Sketched Out', *The Listener*, 11 September 1986

Lewis, Peter, *The Fifties* (London: Heinemann, 1978)

Lewis, Richard Warren, 'Cosby Takes Over', *TV Guide*, 4 October 1969

Lewis, Richard Warren, 'The Importance of Being Julia', *TV Guide*, 14 December 1968

MacDonald, J. Fred, *Blacks and White TV: Afro-Americans in Television Since 1948* (Chicago: Nelson-Hall, 1983)

Malone, Michael, '. . . and Gracie Begat Lucy Who Begat Laverne', *Channels of Communication*, vol. 1, no. 4, October/November 1981

Mara, Henry, 'Conversation with a Script Writer', *Contrast: the Television Quarterly*, autumn 1962

Midwinter, Eric, *Make 'Em Laugh* (London: Allen & Unwin, 1979)

Mitz, Rick, *The Great TV Sitcom Book* (New York: Perigee, 1983)

Morella, Joe and Epstein, Edward Z., *Lucy: the Bittersweet Life of Lucille Ball* (London: W. H. Allen, 1974)

Nathan, David, *The Laughtermakers: a Quest for Comedy* (London: Peter Owen, 1971)

Poole, Michael, 'Situations Vacant', *The Listener*, 18 October 1984

Redding, J. Saunders, 'The Negro Writer: Shadow and Substance', *Phylon*, winter, 1950

Rose, Brian G. (ed.), *TV Genres: a Handbook and Reference Guide* (Westport, Conn.: Greenwood Press, 1985)

Sherrin, Ned, 'Not and OTT – nice ideas, shame about the words', *The Listener*, 18 February 1982

Silvers, Phil, with Saffron, Robert, *The Man Who Was Bilko: the Autobiography of Phil Silvers* (London: W. H. Allen, 1974)

Sklar, Robert, *Prime-Time America: Life on and Behind the Television Screen* (New York: OUP, 1980)

Speight, Johnny, *Till Death Us Do Part* (London: Woburn Press, 1973)

Taylor, Laurie and Mullan, Bob, *Uninvited Guests: the Intimate Secrets of Television and Radio* (London: Chatto & Windus, 1986)

Took, Barry, *Laughter in the Air* (London: Robson, 1976)

Took, Barry, 'Whatever Happened to TV Comedy?', *The Listener*, 5 & 12 January 1984

Tynan, Kenneth, *Show People* (London: Virgin, 1981)

Wheen, Francis, *Television* (London: Century, 1985)

Wilmut, Roger, *From Fringe to Flying Circus: Celebrating a Unique Generation of Comedy 1960–1980* (London: Methuen, 1982)

In addition to the foregoing, reference has been made to various issues of the following magazines for background information, production details, cast lists, dates, etc., for various TV programmes: *Broadcast, Emmy, Film Comment, The Listener, Television Today, Televisual,* and, in particular, *Radio Times, TV Guide* and *TV Times.*

BBC Records have released numerous long-playing record albums of TV shows including REB 377, REB 405, REB 484, *Fawlty Towers*, REB 400, *Not the Nine O'Clock News*, REB 73, *Monty Python*, and REB 260, Tony Hancock in 'The Lift' and 'Twelve Angry Men'.

BBC Enterprises have issued numerous video cassette recordings of TV comedy shows including many of those featured in these pages.

ACKNOWLEDGEMENTS

The authors wish to express their gratitude to the comedian and TV expert A.J. Marriot for reading a draft of *Bring Me Laughter* and for his corrections and suggestions, which have greatly enhanced the text. Needless to say, however, all opinions expressed and any factual errors that might remain are the sole responsibility of the authors.

For permission to reproduce photographs, the authors and publishers would like to thank:

BBC, 60, 65, 66, 72, 74, 76, 79, 95, 96, 98, 100, 103, 124, 128 (top), 130, 146, 147, 149, 154, 158, 166, 167, 168, 170, 171

BBC/National Film Archive, 12, 13, 14, 64, 73, 112-13, 114, 128 (bottom), 129

BBC Hulton Picture Library, 52, 53, 56, 57

BBC Hulton Picture Library/The Bettmann Archive, 17, 19, 33, 45, 68, 80, 81, 87, 91, 93, 94, 104-5, 136, 137 (bottom), 161, 162, 175

Clifford Elson (Publicity) Ltd, 50, 51, 54, 55

Granada Television Ltd, 109

Granada Television Ltd/National Film Archive, 110-11

London Weekend Television Ltd/National Film Archive, 38, 77, 125, 126-7

National Broadcasting Company, Inc., 44, 47, 48, 138

National Film Archive, 22, 24, 25, 27, 28-9, 30, 82, 84, 89, 140, 141, 150, 174

New York Public Library, Schomberg Center for Research in Black Culture, 137 (top)

Thames Television/National Film Archive, 39, 41, 42, 157

Twentieth Century-Fox Film Corporation, 117, 119

Yorkshire Television Ltd, 75, 99.

Excerpts from *The Golden Girls* ©1986 Touchstone Pictures. Used by permission of copyright owner.

The authors and publishers would also like to thank the following people and organizations for further pictures and/or permission to quote from the scripts of shows: ABC TV, Alistair Beaton, CBS TV, Channel Four Television, John Cleese and Connie Booth, EMI, Ray Galton and Alan Simpson, Paramount Pictures Corporation, Johnny Speight, Hilton Tims, and Witt, Thomas and Harris.

Any pictures not accounted for in the above list are either the property of the authors or the publishers have been unable to trace a copyright holder. Apologies are offered in the event of any inadvertent omissions, and rectification will be made in subsequent editions of the book.

INDEX

Page references in italics refer to
illustrations.

Abbot, Russ 57
Abbott and Costello 40
Ackerman, Harry 23
Adams, Don 44, *45*
Addams, Charles 46
Addams Family, The 46
*Adventures of Ozzie and Harriet,
    The* 20, 60, 86, 162
*Adventures of Hiram Holliday,
    The* 18
After Hours 15, 74
AfterMASH 173
Agony 76, *77,* 101, 144
Alan, Ray 36, 57, 58, 143
Alas Smith and Jones 131
Albertson, Jack 78, *80*
Alda, Alan *117,* 118, *119,* 120,
    122, 135, 172
Alderton, John 37, *38*
Aldridge, Michael 73, 167
Alfred Marks Time 15
Alice 71, 94, *94,* 95
Alice Doesn't Live Here Anymore
    (1975) 94
Allen, Dave, 50, *50,* 52
Allen, Fred 26, 143
DaveAllen, Gracie 7, 16, *17,* 18,
    19, 143
Allen, Steve 132
Allen, Woody 18
All Gas and Gaiters 37
All in the Family 7, 32, 71, 90, 92,
    139, 141, 142, 146, *150,* 151
'Allo 'Allo! 115, 116, 133
Altman, Robert 108
American Graffiti (1973) 69
Amos 'n' Andy 16, 135, *136,* 137,
    139

Amsterdam, Morey 62, 135
And Mother Makes Five 67
And Mother Makes Three 67, 176
Andy Griffith Show, The 43
Any Which Way You Can (1980)
    102-5
Archie Bunker's Place 151
Arden, Eve 86, *87,* 88, 106
Are You Being Served? 54, 71,
    101
Armchair Theatre 10
Army Game, The 36, *109,* 110,
    111, *111*
Armstrong, Brian 35
Arnaz, Desi 21-3, *24, 25,* 32, 34,
    59, 78, 86
Arnaz, Desi Jr 32
Arnaz, Lucie 32, *33*
Arthur, Beatrice 92, *93,* 106
Ashley, Elizabeth 138
Askey, Arthur 10, 133, 153
Asner, Edward *89,* 90
Associates, The 172
Astin, John 46
Atkinson, Rowan 129, *130,* 131
At Last the 1948 Show 129
Audience with Jasper Carrott, An
    50
Auf Wiedersehen, Pet 165

Bachelor Father 176
Backus, Jim 46, 86
Baden-Semper, Nina 140
Bailey, Robin 167
Baio, Scott 70, 83
Baker, Hylda 177
Ball, Lucille 7, 20, 21-6, *22, 24, 25,*
    32, *33,* 34, 86, 88, 101, 160, 176,
    180
Banner, John 110
Barefoot in the Park 138

Barefoot in the Park (1967) 138
Barker, Ronnie 35, 73, *73,* 74, *74,*
    153, 167, *168,* 169
Barney Miller 43, 71, 80, *81*
Baron, Lynda 74
Barron, John 75
Barron, Keith 99, *99*
Bass, Alfie 36, *109,* 110, 111, *111*
Bassey, Shirley 42
Bateman, Jason 70
Bateman, Justine 70
Bates, Michael 73, 140
Baxter-Birney, Meredith 70
Beach, Ann 165
Beaton, Alistair 131
Beaton, Norman 140
Beatty, Warren 69
Beaumont, Hugh 69
Beavers, Louise 135
Beck, James *113,* 115
Beckinsale, Richard 73, *73,* 74,
    75, 95
Beeny, Christopher 16, 177
Before Your Very Eyes 10
Bel-Air Patrol 31
Bel Geddes, Barbara 16
Benchley, Robert 85
Bendix, William 162
Benjamin, Richard 47
Bennett, Alan 35, 123
Bennett, Hywel 169
Benny Hill Show, The 37, *39,* 144
Benny, Jack 7, 18, 108, 110, 133,
    135, 143
Benson 139, 173
Bentine, Michael 15
Berg, Gertrude 16
Berle, Milton 18, 24, 26, 27, 78,
    135, 176
Betty White Show, The 90
Beulah 135

Beverly Hillbillies, The 31, 43, 47, 63, 161, 162
Bewes, Rodney 35, *154*, 155
Bewitched 46
Beyond Our Ken 36
Beyond the Fringe (stage) 123, 133
Big Street, The (1942) 21
Bill Cosby Show, The 137, 139
Billingsley, Barbara 69
Bixby, Bill 45
Black Adder, The 131
Black Stuff, The 164
Blake, Christopher 177
Blake, Susie 102
Blankety Blank 53
Bleasdale, Alan 156, 164, 165
Bledsoe, Tempestt *140*, *141*
Bless This House 177
Bluthal, John 37
Bob Monkhouse Show, The 56
Bob's Full House 56
Bolam, James 35, *154*, 155
Bond-Owen, Nicholas 158
Bonet, Lisa *140*, *141*, 148
Booth, Anthony 148
Booth, Connie 76, 78
Booth, Shirley 47
Bootsie and Snudge 36, 58
Borgnine, Ernest 110
Bowles, Peter 160
Boyce, Max 49, 50
Boys from the Black Stuff 156, 164
Braben, Eddie 42
Brambell, Wilfrid 35, 63, *64*, *65*
Brando, Marlon 18
Bread 97
Brennan, Walter 20, 47, 160
Bresslaw, Bernard 110
Brice, Fanny 86, 135
Briers, Richard *158*, 159, 166, 167, *167*
Brisette, Tiffany 172
Brittain, R.S.M. 15
Britton, Tony 10, 165
Broadway Open House 60
Bron, Eleanor 35
Brooke, Henry 124
Brooke-Taylor, Tim 35, 125
Brooks, Mel 18, 44, 143
Brothers 101
Brothers-in-Law 159
Brown, Faith 57
Bruce, Lenny 7, 38, 132, 133
Bryan, Dora 123
Buffalo Bill 173
Buona Sera Mrs Campbell (1968) 31, 37
Burghoff, Gary 117, 120, 122
Burns, George 7, 16, *17*, 18, *19*, 39, 47, 143

Burstyn, Ellen 94
Butterflies 60, 67, 97, 171
Buttons, Red 47
Buzzi, Ruth *48*
Byington, Spring 102

Cabot, Sebastian 177
Caesar's Hour 18
Caesar, Sid 18, 44, 62, 120
Cadell, Simon 171
Caine, Marti 56
Callow, Simon 169
Cantor, Eddie 26, 135
Carey, Joyce 37
Car 54, Where Are You? 31, 32, 43, 44, *44*, 46, 80
Cargill, Patrick 37
Carmichael, Ian 176
Carne, Judy 48, 144
Carney, Art *161*, 162, *162*
Carroll, Diahann 101, 138, *138*
Carroll, Leo G. 20
Carrott, Jasper 49, 50
Carson, Frank 49
Carson, Johnny 62
Carter, Nell 172
Castle, Roy 53, *53*
Cavett, Dick 31
Chance in a Million 169
Chaplin, Charlie 38, 46, 143
Chapman, Graham 35, 125, 126, *129*
Chappell, Eric 75, 99
Charles in Charge 172
Charles, Maria *77*
Charters and Caldicott 167
Chayefsky, Paddy 10
Cheers 7, 102, 133, 173, 174, *174*, *175*, 176
Chesney, Diana 144
Chesney, Ronald 15
Chester, Charlie 36
Chico and the Man 69, 78, 80, *80*, 173
Childress, Alvin 135
Chitty, Erik 37
Christopher, William 120, 173
Christie, Audrey 144
Clarke, Roy 72, 74, 152
Clement, Dick 73, 155, 165
Cleese, John 35, 76-8, *79*, 125, 126, 129, 153
Cleveland, Carol *128*
Club Night 15
Coca, Imogene 18
Colasanto, Nicholas 174
Cole, George 164
Coleman, Dabney 173
Coleman, Gary 139
Colin, Margaret 172
Collins, Lewis 71

Colman, Ronald 20
Comedians, The 49
Comedy Playhouse 63
Comic Strip, The 133
Conaway, Jeff 82
Connolly, Billy 49, 50
Connor, Kenneth 15
Coogan, Jackie 46
Cook, Peter 35, 123
Cooke, Brian 156
Cooper, Tommy 39, 40
Cope, Kenneth 123, *124*
Copperfield, David 54
Corbett, Harry H. 35, 64, *65*
Corbett, Ronnie 35, 153, 165, 167, *168*, 169, 177
Correll, Charles 135
Cosby, Bill 137, *137*, 138, 140-42, *140*, *141*
Cosby Show, The 7, 140-42, *140*, *141*
Cossins, James 76
Coupland, Diana 177
Cover Girl (1944) 86
Cox, Wally 18
Craig, Wendy *60*, 67, 97
Crane, Bob 110
Crawford, Michael 72
Croft, David 101, 112, 115, 167, 170
Crosby, Bing 47
Crossman, Richard 124
Crothers, Scatman 173
Crowther, Leslie 53, 54, *54*
Cryer, Barry 132
Cuckoo Waltz, The 71
Culp, Robert 137, *137*, 142
Curry and Chips 140
Curtin, Jane 102, *103*

Dad's Army 7, 37, 112, *113*, 114, *114*, 115, 170
Dallas 16, 46
Damon, Cathryn 83
Dance, Girl, Dance (1940) 21, 32
Daniels, Bebe 15
Danson, Ted 173, *174*, *175*, 176
Danza, Tony 82
Date With the Angels, A 20
Davidson, Jim 55, *55*, 56
Davies, Richard 37
Davies, Windsor 101
Davis, Freddie 56
Davis, Joan 86
Davis, Sammy Jr 48
Dawber, Pam 83
Dawson, Les *52*, 53, 56
Debbie Reynolds Show, The 47
De Carlo, Yvonne 46, *46*
December Bride 20, 102, 105, 106
Dee, Sandra 47

De La Tour, Frances 74, *75*
Demarest, William 43
Dench, Judi 96, 166
Denning, Richard 21, 23
Dennis the Menace 20
De Vito, Danny 82, 83
De Witt, Joyce 146
Diamond, Selma 42
Dick Van Dyke Show, The 7, 26, 32, 43, 61, 62, 88, 135, 151
Diff'rent Strokes 70, 139
Diller, Phyllis 85
Dinsdale, Reece 165
Dodd, Ken 50, *51*
Don't Forget to Write 164
Don't Wait Up 165, 177
Do-Re-Mi (stage) 31
Doris Day Show, The 47
Douglas, Carlos 99
Drake, Charlie 36, 72
Driver, Harry 36, 140
Dunn, Clive *113*, 114
Dunne, Irene 16
Durante, Jimmy 18
Duty Free 97, 99, *99*
Dwyer, Leslie 171
Dynasty 47, 101, 138
Dyson, Noel 37

Eastwood, Clint 102
Ebsen, Buddy 161
Eddington, Paul 159, 165, 169, *170*
Eden, Barbara 46
Edmondson, Adrian 133
Edmundson, Mark 141
Edwards, Gus 26
Edwards, Jimmy 36, 37, 106
Ed Sullivan Show, The 144
Egan, Peter 166, *167*
Eisenhower, Dwight D. 24, 61
Elgar, Avril 157
Elphick, Michael 165
Elton, Ben 133
Emery! 167
Emery, Dick 15, 40, 167
Emney Enterprises 10
Emney, Fred 10
Empire Road 140
E. R. 173
Eshley, Norman 157
Esmonde, John 158
Estensen, Elizabeth 97
Evans, Norman 53, 153
Ever Decreasing Circles 166, 167, *167*
Everett, Kenny 131, 132

Fabrizi, Mario *111*
Fair Exchange 144
Fairly Secret Army 171

Fall and Rise of Reginald Perrin, The 75, 76, *76*, 145, 171
Family Affair 177
Family Fortunes 56
Family Ties 70
Fancy Pants (1950) 21
Farr, Jamie 120, 173
Farrell, Mike 118
Father, Dear Father 37
Father Knows Best 20, 61, 141
Fawlty Towers 7, 76-8, *79*
Faye, Herbie 28
Fearn, Sheila 158
Feldman, Marty 36, 39, 60, 62, 129, 132, 153
Feldon, Barbara 44
Fell, Norman 146
Field, Sally 47
Fields, W.C. 70, 85, 143
Filthy Rich and Catflap 133
Fine Romance, A 96, 166
Fireman, Judy 23
Flintstones, The 177
Flip Wilson Show, The 139
Flo 94
Fluck, Peter 125
Flying Nun, The 47
Foley Square 172
Fonda, Henry 21
Fonda, Jane 138
Ford, Paul 28
Forman, Sir Denis 15
Forsyth, Bruce 10, *54*, 55, 167
Forsyth, Brigit 156
Forsythe, John 47
Fosters, The 140
Four Seasons, The 172
Fowldes, Derek 169, *170*
Fowler, Harry *111*
Fox, Michael J. 70
Foxx, Redd 152
Foy, Eddie Jr 144
Francis, Jan 166, *166*
Frankenheimer, John 10
Franklyn, Bonnie 92
Fraser, Bill 36, *109*, 110, 111, *111*
Fraser, Liz 172
Frawley, William 23, 43
Freedland, Michael 133
Freeman, Mickey *29*
French, Dawn 133
Fresh Fields 63, 165
Frost, David 35, 123, *124*
Frost Report, The 35, 153
Funny Thing Happened on the Way to the Forum, A (stage, London) 39
Funny Thing Happened on the Way to the Forum, A (stage, New York) 32

Funny Thing Happened on the Way to the Forum, A (1966) 31

Gail, Maxwell 80, *81*
Galloway, Jack *98*
Galton, Ray 11, 12, 37, 63, 152
Garden, Graeme 35, 125
Garrison, David 70
Garwood, Patricia 165
Gaunt, William 165
Geeson, Judy 37, 177
Gelbart, Larry 18, 120, 122
General, The (1927) 108
Generation Game, The 55
George and Mildred 95, 145, 156-8, *157*, 176
George Burns and Gracie Allen Show, The 16, 18
Get Smart! 44, 45, *45*
Getty, Estelle 106
Gibson, Richard 116
Gidget 47
Gillespie, Robert 145
Gilliam, Terry 125, *129*
Gimme a Break 172
Girl with Something Extra, The 47
Girls on Top 56, 97, 133
Glass, Ron 80
Gleason, Jackie 161, *161*, 162, *162*
Glynis 47
Goddard, Liza 144
Godfather, The (1972) 80
Going My Way 47
Going Straight 74
Goldbergs, The 16, 60, 135
Golden Girls, The 7, 20, 84, 92, 105-7, 133, 135, 173
Golden Shot, The 56
Goldwyn, Sam 21
Gone with the Wind (1939) 135
Goodies, The 125, 129
Good Life, The 7, 97, 158-60, *158*
Good Times 139
Goodwin, Denis 56
Goon Show, The 15
Gordon, Gale 20, 32, 86, 101
Gordon, Ruth 102
Gosden, Freeman 135
Gosfield, Maurice 28, *29*, 31
Gould, Elliott 118, 173
Graduate, The (1967) 44
Grammer, Kelsey 174
Gray, Herman 139
Graziano, Rocky 27, 44
Green, Sid 42
Greene, Sir Hugh 125
Greene, Hughie 56
Grenfell, Joyce 123
Griffith, Andy 43
Griffiths, Leon 164

Griffiths, Richard *125*
Groh, David 90
Gross, Michael 70
Guillaume, Robert 83, 139
Guyler, Deryck 15
Gwynne, Fred 31, 43, 44, *44*, 46, *46*

Hackett, Buddy 27, 28
Hagman, Larry 46
Hale, Gareth 131
Hall, Willis 125
Halliwell, Leslie 151
Halls of Ivy 20
Hancock 12-14, *12, 13, 14*
Hancock's Half Hour 11
Hancock, Sheila 15, 16
Hancock, Tony 7, 11-14, *12-14*, 15, 20, 61, 133, 160, 177
Handley, Tommy 153
Happy Days 32, *68*, 69, 70, 71, 83, 163
Happy Ever After 166
Hard Day's Night, A (1964) 47
Harding, Mike 49, 50
Hardy, Oliver *see* Laurel and Hardy
Hare, Robertson 37
Harlem Detective 137
Harper, Valerie 90, *91*
Harrelson, Woody 174
Harris, Susan 83, 84, 102, 105
Hartman, Kim 116
Hartnell, William 110
Havers, Nigel 165
Hawn, Goldie 48, 95
Hawthorne, Nigel 169, *170*
Hawtrey, Charles 110
Hayes, Melvyn *100*, 101
Hayes, Patricia *12*
Haynes, Arthur 36
Hazel 47
He and She 47
Hearne, Richard 10
Heaven for Betsy 20
Hell's Bells 37
Helmond, Katherine 83, *84*
Hemsley, Sherman 139
Hendry, Ian 10
Henner, Marilu 82, *82*
Henry, Buck 44
Henry, Lenny 56, 57
Here's Lucy 32, *33*
Heston, Charlton 10
Hey, Landlord! 47
Hickman, Dwayne 69
Hi-de-Hi! 170, 171, *171*
High Button Shoes (stage) 26
Hiken, Gerald *29*
Hiken, Nat 26, 27, 43, 44
Hilary 56

Hill, Benny 37, 38, *39*
Hill Street Blues 44, 80, 164
Hilliard, Harriet *see* Nelson, Harriet
Hills, Dick 42
Hills, Julia 131
Hird, Thora 177
Hirsch, Judd 80, *82*, 83
Hodge, Patricia 96
Hoffman, Dustin 120
Hogan's Heroes 110
Holden, William 24
Holding the Fort 96
Holland, Diane 171
Holliday, Polly 94
Holloway, Stanley 47
Home, James 56
Home to Roost 165, 177
Honeymooners, The 20, 161, *161*, 162, *162*
Hooker, Richard 118
Hope, Bob 18, 21, 24, 56, 62, 143
Horne A'Plenty 36
Horne, Kenneth 36
House Calls 172
Howard, Barry 171
Howard, Ken 101
Howard, Ron *68*, 69, 70
Howells, Ursula 37
Howerd, Frankie 37-9
Howland, Beth 94
Howlett, Noel 37
Hudson, Rock 24
Hughes, Barnard 152
Hughes, Nerys *95*, 96
Hughes, Terry 106
Hume, Benita 20
Hunter, Tab 46
Hyde White, Wilfrid 144, 172

Idiot Weekly, Price 2d 15
Idle, Eric 35, 125, *129*
I Dream of Jeannie 46
I Love Lucy 20, 21-6, *22, 24, 25*, 32-4, 59, 60
I Married Joan 20, 86, 162
Imrie, Celia 102
Incredible Hulk, The 45
In Loving Memory 177
Inman, John 54, *54*, 71, 101
In Sickness and in Health 149, *149*
I Remember Mama (1948) 16
I Spy 137, *137*, 140, 142
It Ain't Half Hot, Mum 100, 140
It Takes a Worried Man 169
It's a Living 172
It's a Square World 15
It's Your Move 70

Jackson, Glenda 42, 172
Jacques, Hattie 15, 177

James, Jimmy 37, 53, 153
James, Polly *95*, 96
James, Sid 12-14, *14*, 177
Janssen, David 62
Jason, David *66*, 67, 74
Jay, Anthony 169
Jeffersons, The 71, 139
Jessell, George 26, 135
Jewel, Jimmy 177
Johns, Glynis 47
Johnson, Arte *48*
Jokers Wild 49
Jolson, Al 135
Jones, Carolyn 46
Jones, Peter 15, 16
Jones, Terry 35, 125, 126, *128*, *129*
Joyce, Yootha 95, *145*, 156, *157*
Julia 138, *138*, 139
Just Dennis see *Dennis the Menace*
Just Good Friends 166, *166*
Just William 144

Kahn, Madeline 144
Kanter, Hall 138
Kaplan, Gabriel 37
Karlin, Miriam 15, 16
Kate and Allie 102, *104*
Kaufman, Andy 82
Kavner, Julie 92
Kaye, Caren 70
Kaye, Danny 18, 143
Kaye, Gordon 115
Kearns, Joseph 20
Keaton, Buster 21, 108, 143
Keen, Diane 71
Keep It in the Family 144
Keith, Brian 177
Keith, Penelope *158*, 159, 160
Kelly, Gene 47
Kelly, Sam 116
Kendal, Felicity *96*, 97, *98*, *158*, 159
Kennedy, George 31
Kennedy, John F. 43, 124
Kernan, David *124*
Kerr, Bill 11
Kid, The (1921) 46
King, Martin Luther 43, 142
Kinnear, Roy 123
Klemperer, Werner 110
Klugman, Jack 177
Knight, Ted 90, 145
Knight-Pulliam, Keshia *140*
Kossoff, David 15
Kovacs, Ernie 18, 125

Ladd, Diane 94
La Frenais, Ian 73, 155, 165
Lancashire, Geoffrey 71

Landen, Dinsdale 144
Lane, Carla 96, 97
Larbey, Bob 158, 166
Lardner, Ring Jr 108
Larkins, The 15, 176
Last of the Summer Wine 72, *72*, 73
Last Picture Show, The (1971) 69
Laurel and Hardy 12, 37, 38, 40, 57, 143
Laurel, Stan *see* Laurel and Hardy
Laurie, John 114
Lavender, Ian *113*, 115
Laverne and Shirley 70, 163
Lavin, Linda 94, *94*
Law, John 153
Law, Roger 124
Leachman, Cloris 90
Lear, Norman 92, 101, 152, 176
Leave It to Beaver 20, 67
Leave It to Joan 86
Lembeck, Harvey 27, *29*
Le Mesurier, John 35, *113*, 114, *114*
Lemmon, Jack 20
Lester, Richard 47
Let There Be Love 165
Levant, Oscar 86
Levin, Bernard 124
Levis, Carroll 56
Lewis, Al 44, 46
Lewis, Emmanuel 139
Lewis, Jerry 34, 133
Lewis, Richard Warren 138
Life of Riley, The 20, 86, 162
Life with Elizabeth 20
Life with the Lyons 15, 165
Likely Lads, The 7, 37, 97, 155, 158, 165
Linden, Hal 80
Lindley, Audra 146
Linn-Baker, Mark 173
Linville, Larry *117*, 118, 121
Lipman, Maureen 76, *77*
Little, Rich 57
Liver Birds, The 95, 96, 97
Lloyd, Christopher 82, 83
Lloyd, Harold 37, 143
Lloyd, Jeremy 167
Long, Shelley 173, *174*, *175*, 176
Loring, Lynn 144
Lorne, Marion 46
Lott, Barbara 165, 177
Lou Grant 90
Love Thy Neighbour 140
Lovers, The 95
Lowe, Arthur 35, 112, *113*, *114*
Lubitsch, Ernst 108
Lucie Arnaz Show, The 144
Lucy Show, The 32

Lulu 37, 131
Lune, Ted *111*
Lynch, Joe 37
Lyndhurst, Nicholas *66*, *67*
Lynn, Jonathan 169
Lyon, Ben 15

MacDonald, J. Fred 137
Mackay, Fulton 73, *73*
Mackie, Philip 10
MacLeod, Gavin *89*, 90
MacMurray, Fred 43
Macy, Bill 92
Maddern, Victor 144
Madoc, Ruth 170, 171, *171*
Magician, The 45
Make Room for Daddy 20
Mama 16, 60, 135
Mama's Bank Account (K. Forbes) 16
Mama's Family 172
Man About the House 95, 145, *145*, 156
Mancini, Al *124*
Mandan, Robert 83, *84*
Manning, Bernard 49
Many Loves of Dobie Gillis, The 20, 67
Marie, Rose 26, 60
Marks, Alfred 15
Marner, Richard 116
Marriage Lines 159, 166
Marsden, Betty 36
Marsh, Reginald 157
Marshall, Penny 163
Martin, Dick 47, *47*, 48
Martin, Millicent 123, *124*
Marty 129
Marx, Arthur 94
Marx, Groucho 52, 85
Marx, Harpo 24
Mary 173
Mary Tyler Moore Show, The 7, 20, 32, 60, 71, 88-90, *89*, 92, 173, 176
M*A*S*H 7, 32, 71, 94, 95, 116, *117*, 118, *119*, 120-22, 135, 176, 177
M*A*S*H (1970) 108
Mathers, Jerry 69
Matthau, Walter 172
Matthews, Francis 164
Maude 32, 71, 92, 139, 142
Mayall, Rik 133
McClanahan, Rue 92, 105
McDaniel, Hattie 135
McGhee, Henry 36
McGrath, Rory 131
McHale's Navy 110
McKenzie, Julia 165
McKern, Leo 149, 164

Meadows, Audrey 161, *161*
Me and My Girl 176
Medwin, Michael 110
Melgar, Gabriel 80
Melville, Alan 123
Me Mammy 95
Merrill, Dina 31
Merriman, Eric 36
Merryfield, Buster *66*, *67*
Mervyn, William 37
Metcalfe, Burt 118
Midwinter, Eric 12, 36
Miller, Jonathan 35, 123
Miller, Max 155
Milligan, Spike 15, 108, 126, 132, 140
Minder 144, 164
Mission: Impossible 32
Miss Jones and Son 176
Mistress, The 97, *97*
Mitchell, Scoey 138
Mitchell, Warren 35, 92, *146*, *147*, 149, *149*
Mitz, Rick 46, 90, 94, 135
Mixed Blessings 140
Modley, Albert 153
Monkees, The 47
Monkhouse, Bob 56, *56*
Montague, Bruce 97, *127*
Montgomery, Elizabeth 46
Montgomery, Robert 46
Monty Python's Flying Circus 7, 125, 126, *128*, 129, *129*, 132, 144, 177
Moonlighting 164
Moore, Dudley 35, 123
Moore, Mary Tyler 61, 62, 88-90, *89*
Moore, Tim 135, *136*
Moorehead, Agnes 46
Morecambe and Wise Show, The 41, 42, *42*
Morecambe and Wise 7, 12, 37, 40, *41*, 42, *42*, 43, 133, 144
Morecambe, Eric 40, 42, 43
Morgan, Harry 106, 118, 122, 173
Mork and Mindy 45, 70, 83
Morris, Dave 15, 53, 153
Morse, Barry 125
Mortimer, John 164
Mortimer, Johnny 156
Morton, Gary 32
Mount, Peggy 15
Mr Ed 32, 46
Mr Peepers 18
Much Binding-in-the-Marsh 36
Muir, Frank 36, 37, 149
Mulligan, Richard 83, 144
Mulville, Jimmy 131
Munsters, The 43, 44, 45, 46, *46*
Murdoch, Richard 36

Murdoch, Rupert 179
Murphy, Brian 156, *157*
Muscle Market, The 164
Music Hall 10
Music, Lorenzo 92
My Favourite Husband 21
My Favourite Martian 45
My Three Sons 43
Mystery of Edwin Drood, The (stage) 43, 131

Nardino, Gary 101
Nathan, David 63
Nearest and Dearest 177
Nelson, David 61
Nelson, Harriet 60, 61
Nelson, Ozzie 59, 60, 61
Nelson, Ricky 61
Never Mind the Quality, Feel the Width 37
New Faces 56
New Gidget 47
Newley, Anthony 67
Newman, Nanette 165
New Phil Silvers Show, The 31
Nicholas, Paul 166, *166*
Nichols, Dandy *146*, 149, *149*
Nimmo, Derek 37
Nixon, Richard 26, 48
Nobbs, David 75
Noble, James 139
Nolan, Lloyd *138*
No Place Like Home 165
Norden, Denis 36, 37, 149
Norma Rae (1979) 47
North, Jay 20
Not in Front of the Children 67, 165
Not So Much a Programme, More a Way of Life 123
Not the Nine O'Clock News 129, *130*, 131, 132

O'Brien, Pat 46
O'Connor, Carroll *150*, 151
O'Connor, Des 56
Odd Couple, The 177
Odd Couple, The (1968) 177
Oddie, Bill 35, 125
Odunton, Muriel 140
O Happy Band 167
Oh Brother! 37
Oh Father! 37
O Madeline 144, 173
One Day at a Time 92, 94
O'Neill, Paddy 15
One in a Million 172
One of the Boys 172
Only Fools and Horses 66, 67, 160
On the Buses 71, 172

Open All Hours 74, *74*
Opportunity Knocks 54
O'Shea, Milo 95
O'Sullivan, Richard 145, *145*, 176
Our Man at St Marks 37
Our Man Higgins 47
Our Miss Brooks 20, 86, *87*, 88, 162
Over the Top 131, 132
Owen, Alun 10
Owen, Bill *72*, 73

Pace, Norman 131
Paddick, Hugh 36
Page, LaWanda 152
Palance, Jack 10
Palin, Michael 35, 125, 126, *128*, *129*
Paramor, Norrie 124
Palmer, Geoffrey 76, 97, *125*, 171
Patterson, Lorna 95
Paul Sand in Friends and Lovers 90
Pearce, Lennard *66*, 67
Penny, Sydney 47
Percival, Lance 123, *124*
Perfect Strangers 173
Perlman, Rhea 173
Perry, Jimmy 101, 112, 170
Pertwee, Bill 115
Peterson, Arthur *84*
Petticoat Junction 47
Phillips, Leslie 37
Phil Silvers Show: You'll Never Get Rich, The see *Sergeant Bilko*
Phyllis 90
Pig in the Middle 144
Pinchot, Bronson 173
Places in the Heart (1984) 47
Planer, Nigel 133
Platt, Edward 44
Play Your Cards Right 53
Please Sir! 37, *38*
Poitier, Sidney 37
Pollard, Michael J. 69
Pons, Beatrice 44
Pope, Philip 131
Porridge 7, 73, *73*, 74, 165
Powell, Sandy 57
Powell, Vince 140
Prentiss, Paula 47
Previn, André 42
Price Is Right, The 53, 54
Pride of the Family 20
Prinze, Freddie 78, 80, *80*
Private Benjamin (1980) 95
Private Benjamin 95
Private's Progress (1956) 111

Q5 126
Q6 126

Radford, Basil 167
Raeburn, Anna 76
Rag Trade, The 15
Randall, Tony 177
Randle, Frank 53, 153
Randolph, Joyce *161*
Rashad, Phylicia *140*, 142
Ratzenberger, John 173, *174*
Ray, Aldo 152
Ray, Ted 49, 153
Read, Al 11
Reagan, Nancy 139
Real McCoys, The 20, 160
Record Breakers, The 53
Redford, Robert 10, 138
Redgrave, Lynn 172
Reed, Paul 44
Reed, Tracy 138
Reggie 144
Regina, Paul 101
Reid, Beryl 123
Reid, Mike 49
Reiner, Carl 18, 151
Reiner, Rob 151
Reynolds, Gene 118, 122
Rhoda 71, 90, *91*, 92, 176
Rhys-Jones, Griff 129, *130*, 131
Richard Diamond 62
Richmond, Len 76
Ridley, Arnold *113*, 115
Rising Damp 7, 74, 75, *75*, 144, 167
Ritter, Jack 146
Rivers, Joan 85
Roach, Hal 37
Robbins, Michael 172
Robinson, Fred 15
Robinson, Hubbell 23, 26
Robinson, Sugar Ray 44
Robinson, Tony 131
Rockford Files, The 164
Rodgers, Anton 165
Rogers, Ted 54, *54*, 144
Rogers, Wayne *117*, 118, 172
Rogers, Will 43
Rolle, Esther 139
Room Service (1938) 32
Rooney, Mickey 47, 172
Roper, David 71
Ropers, The 145
Rose, Clarkson 11
Rosenthal, Jack 36, 95
Ross, Joe E. 31, 43, *44*
Rossiter, Leonard 74, 75, *75*, *76*, 167
Rosten, Leo 134
Round the Horne 36
Routledge, Patricia 102
Rowan and Martin's Laugh-In 47, *47*, 48, *48*
Rowan, Dan 47, *47*

Rumpole of the Bailey 164
Running Wild 40
Rushton, William 35, 123, *124*
Ryan, Irene 161

Sachs, Andrew 76, 78
Sahl, Mort 132
St James, Susan 102, *103*
Sales, Freddie 144
Sallis, Peter 73
Sanderson, Joan 37, 77
Sanford 152
Sanford and Son 67, 152
Sanford Arms, The 152
Saturday Gang 131
Saturday Live 133
Saunders, Jennifer 133
Saville, Philip 10, 164
Sayle, Alexei 131
Scales, Prunella 78, 159
Schwartz, Lew 96
Scott, Terry 165
Secombe, Harry 15, 108
Sedgwick, Eddie 21
Sellers, Peter 15, 108, 149
Sergeant Bilko 7, 20, 21, 26-31,
   27, *29*, *30*, 34, 43, 44
Serling, Rod 10
Seven Faces of Jim 37
Shane, Paul 170, *171*
Shelley 169
Sherrin, Ned 123
Sid Caesar Invites You 18
Sierra, Gregory 80, *81*
Silvers, Phil 18, 20, 21, 26-32, *27*,
   29, *30*, 34, 37, 63, 78, 133, 135,
   179, 180
Simon, George T. 61
Simon, Neil 18
Simpson, Alan 11, 12, 38, 63, 152
Sinclair, Edward 115
Sinden, Donald 37
Six More Faces of Jim 37
Skelton, Red 18, 24
Slinger's Day 55, 167
Small Wonder 172
Smethurst, Jack 140
Smith, Cecil 23
Smith, Mel 129, *130*, 131
Soap 71, 83, *84*, 101, 139
Some Mothers Do Have 'Em 72
Somers, Suzanne 146
Soo, Jack 80, *81*
Sorrowful Jones (1949) 21
Sorry! 165, 177
Sorvino, Paul 152
Speight, Johnny 35, 140, 146, 148,
   152
Spitting Image 123, 125
Stacey, Neil 99, *99*
Staefel, Sheila 36

Staff, Kathy *72*
Stalag 17 (stage) 110
Stapleton, Jean *150*, 151
Starr, Freddie 57
Star Trek 32
Stephenson, Pamela 129, *130*,
   131
Steptoe and Son 7, 11, 37, 63-7,
   64, *65*, 152, 160, 177
Stevens, George 16
Stevenson, McLean 118, 120
Stewart, Robin 177
Stiers, David Ogden 118
Stone, Cynthia 20
Stone Pillow (1985) 32
Strange World of Gurney Slade,
   The 67
Streisand, Barbra 86
Stritch, Elaine 46
Struthers, Sally 151
Stubbs, Una 148
Sugden, Mollie 71, 177
Sullivan, John 152, 160, 166
Sunday Night at the London
   Palladium 10, 53
Sunday Night Theatre 10
Sutherland, Donald 118
Sweet, Dolph 172
Swit, Loretta *117*, 118, 120, 122
Sybil 47
Sykes 15, 177
Sykes, Eric 15, 108, 140, 177

Take It From Here 36
Tandoori Nights 140
Tarrant, Chris 131
Taxi 71, 80, 82, *82*, 83, 95, 176
Tayback, Vic 94
Taylor, Gwen 99, *99*
Taylor, Myra 96
Temple, John G. 71
Terry and June 165
Terry-Thomas 144
Texaco Star Theatre 18
That Girl 88
That's My Boy 177
That Was the Week That Was 7,
   37, 123-5, *124*, 129, 131, 150
That Wonderful Guy 20
Thaw, John 165
Thomas, Danny 20, 88
Thomas, Marlo 88
Thomsett, Sally 145, *145*
Thorne, Angela 165
Thornton, Frank *13*
Three of a Kind 56
Three Little Words 58
Three's Company 145
3-2-1 54
Three Up, Two Down 165
Throb! 172

Thurber, James 85
Tilbury, Peter 169
Till Death Us Do Part 7, 37, 63, 92,
   140, 146, *146*, *147*, 148-50, 160,
   176
Tinker, Grant 88
To Be Or Not To Be (1942) 108,
   110
Together We Stand 173
Tomlin, Lily 48
Tonight Show, The 58
Too Close For Comfort 145
Took, Barry 36, 39, 56
Tootsie (1982) 120
Top Banana (stage) 26, 62
Topper 20
Torch Song Trilogy (stage) 106
To Sir with Love (1967) 37
To the Manor Born 160
Tracy, Lee 152
Travolta, John 37
Trinder, Tommy 10, 133, 144
Tripper's Day 167
Tucker, Sophie 26
Turner, Ted 179
Two Ronnies, The 35, *168*, 169

Ullman, Tracey 56
Up Pompeii 39
Up the Elephant and Round the
   Castle 56

Vance, Vivian 23, 32
Van Druten, John 16
Van Dyke, Dick 31, 61, 62, 160
Van Gyseghem, Joanna 99, *99*,
   144
Varney, Reg 15, 16, 71, 172
Vaughan, Norman 10
Victoria Wood – As Seen On TV
   102, *103*
Vigoda, Abe 80, *81*

Walker, Nancy 90
Walker, Rudolph 140
Wall, Max 133
Walston, Ray 45
Walters, Julie 102, *103*
Waltons, The 16
Waring, Richard 67
Warner, Malcolm-Jamal *140*,
   141, 142
Warr, Jean 99
Warrington, Don 74, *75*
Waterhouse, Keith 125
Waterman, Dennis 144, 164
Waters, Ethel 135
Watford, Gwen 164
Wattis, Richard 15
Wayne, John 24, 48
Wayne, Naunton 167

Wendt, George 173, *174*
Webster 70, 139, 140, 173
Welcome Back, Kotter 37
Weld, Tuesday 69
Wesley 67
Whack-O! 37
Whatever Happened to the Likely Lads? *154*, 155, 156, 165, 171
Wheeler and Woolsley 40
White, Betty 20, 90, 92, 105
Whitelaw, Billie 10
Whitfield, June 165
Who Dares Wins 131
Whoops Apocalypse! 125, *125*, *127*
Widmark, Richard 24
Wilcox, Paula 95, 145, *145*, 177
Wildcat (stage) 32
Wilde, Brian 73
Williams, Anson *68*

Williams, Charlie 49
Williams, Cindy 163
Williams, Frank 115
Williams, Kate 140
Williams, Kenneth 36
Williams, Liberty *94*
Williams, Michael 166
Williams, Robin 83
Williams, Spencer Jr 135, *136*
Wills, Sy 86
Wilson, Demond 152
Wilton, Penelope 166
Wilton, Robb 53, 112, 153
Winkler, Henry *68*, 69, 70
Wisdom, Norman 10
Wise, Ernie 7, 40, *41*, 42, *42*, 43, 131
Wolfe, Ronald 15
Wood, Natalie 20
Wood, Victoria 102, *103*

Worker, The 36
World According to Smith and Jones, The 131
Worth, Harry 57, 167
Wray, Fay 20
Wyatt, Jane 61

Yarwood, Mike 55, *55*, 57, *57*
Yates, Pauline 75
Yes, Minister 169, 170, *170*
Yes, Prime Minister 169
Yothers, Tina 70
You Again 165
You Bet Your Life 52
You'll Never Get Rich see *Sergeant Bilko*
Young, Alan 46
Young, Robert 61
Young Ones, The 133
Your Show of Shows 18